MznLnx

Missing Links Exam Preps

Exam Prep for

Microeconomics

Samuelson, Nordhaus, 18th Edition

The MznLnx Exam Prep is your link from the texbook and lecture to your exams.
The MznLnx Exam Preps are unauthorized and comprehensive reviews of your textbooks.

All material provided by MznLnx and Rico Publications (c) 2010
Textbook publishers and textbook authors do not particpate in or contribute to these reviews.

MznLnx

Rico Publications

Exam Prep for Microeconomics
18th Edition
Samuelson, Nordhaus

Publisher: Raymond Houge
Assistant Editor: Michael Rouger
Text and Cover Designer: Lisa Buckner
Marketing Manager: Sara Swagger
Project Manager, Editorial Production: Jerry Emerson
Art Director: Vernon Lowerui

Product Manager: Dave Mason
Editorial Assitant: Rachel Guzmanji
Pedagogy: Debra Long
Cover Image: Jim Reed/Getty Images
Text and Cover Printer: City Printing, Inc.
Compositor: Media Mix, Inc.

(c) 2010 Rico Publications
ALL RIGHTS RESERVED. No part of this work
covered by the copyright may be reproduced or
used in any form or by an means--graphic, electronic,
or mechanical, including photocopying, recording,
taping, Web distribution, information storage, and
retrieval systems, or in any other manner--without the
written permission of the publisher.

Printed in the United States
ISBN:

For more information about our products, contact us at:
Dave.Mason@RicoPublications.com

For permission to use material from this text or
product, submit a request online to:
Dave.Mason@RicoPublications.com

Contents

CHAPTER 1
The Fundamentals of Economics — 1

CHAPTER 2
Markets and Government in a Modern Economy — 11

CHAPTER 3
Basic Elements of Supply and Demand — 33

CHAPTER 4
Applications of Supply and Demand — 39

CHAPTER 5
Demand and Consumer Behavior — 50

CHAPTER 6
Production and Business Organization — 60

CHAPTER 7
Analysis of Costs — 71

CHAPTER 8
Analysis of Perfectly Competitive Markets — 84

CHAPTER 9
Imperfect Competition and Monopoly — 96

CHAPTER 10
Oligopoly and Monopolistic Competition — 109

CHAPTER 11
Uncertainty and Game Theory — 126

CHAPTER 12
How Markets Determine Incomes — 137

CHAPTER 13
The Labor Market — 151

CHAPTER 14
Land and Capital — 164

CHAPTER 15
Comparative Advantage and Protectionism — 185

CHAPTER 16
Government Taxation and Expenditure — 202

CHAPTER 17
Promoting More Efficient Markets — 222

CHAPTER 18
Protecting the Environment — 235

CHAPTER 19
Efficiency vs. Equality: The Big Tradeoff — 246

ANSWER KEY — 261

TO THE STUDENT

COMPREHENSIVE

The *MznLnx* Exam Prep series is designed to help you pass your exams. Editors at MznLnx review your textbooks and then prepare these practice exams to help you master the textbook material. Unlike study guides, workbooks, and practice tests provided by the texbook publisher and textbook authors, *MznLnx* gives you **all** of the material in each chapter in exam form, not just samples, so you can be sure to nail your exam.

MECHANICAL

The MznLnx Exam Prep series creates exams that will help you learn the subject matter as well as test you on your understanding. Each question is designed to help you master the concept. Just working through the exams, you gain an understanding of the subject--its a simple mechanical process that produces success.

INTEGRATED STUDY GUIDE AND REVIEW

MznLnx is not just a set of exams designed to test you, its also a comprehensive review of the subject content. Each exam question is also a review of the concept, making sure that you will get the answer correct without having to go to other sources of material. You learn as you go! Its the easiest way to pass an exam.

HUMOR

Studying can be tedious and dry. MznLnx's instructional design includes moderate humor within the exam questions on occassion, to break the tedium and revitalize the brain

Chapter 1. The Fundamentals of Economics 1

1. The _____ is a heterodox school of economics that emphasizes the spontaneous organizing power of the price mechanism. It holds that the complexity of subjective human choices makes mathematical modelling of the evolving market extremely difficult and advocates a laissez faire approach to the economy. _____ economists advocate the enforcement of voluntary contractual agreements between economic agents, but otherwise the smallest imposition of coercive force on commercial transactions.

   a. ACCRA Cost of Living Index
   b. Austrian School
   c. Economic calculation problem
   d. ACEA agreement

2. _____s is the social science that studies the production, distribution, and consumption of goods and services. The term _____s comes from the Ancient Greek οἰκονομῐ́α from οἶκος (oikos, 'house') + νόμος (nomos, 'custom' or 'law'), hence 'rules of the house(hold)'. Current _____ models developed out of the broader field of political economy in the late 19th century, owing to a desire to use an empirical approach more akin to the physical sciences.

   a. Inflation
   b. Energy economics
   c. Opportunity cost
   d. Economic

3. A _____ is an object whose consumption increases the utility of the consumer, for which the quantity demanded exceeds the quantity supplied at zero price. _____s are usually modeled as having diminishing marginal utility. The first individual purchase has high utility; the second has less.

   a. Good
   b. Pie method
   c. Merit good
   d. Composite good

4. _____ was a survey conducted by the U.S. Department of Justice to gauge the prevalence of alcohol and illegal drug use among prior arrestees. It was a reformulation of the prior Drug Use Forecasting (DUF) program, focused on five drugs in particular: cocaine, marijuana, methamphetamine, opiates, and PCP.

Participants were randomly selected from arrest records in major metropolitan areas; because no personally identifying information is taken from each record chosen, the resulting data can be correlated to arrest rates, but not to the total population of persons charged.

   a. ACCRA Cost of Living Index
   b. Arrestee Drug Abuse Monitoring
   c. AD-IA Model
   d. ACEA agreement

5. _____ was a Scottish moral philosopher and a pioneer of political economy. One of the key figures of the Scottish Enlightenment, Smith is the author of The Theory of Moral Sentiments and An Inquiry into the Nature and Causes of the Wealth of Nations. The latter, usually abbreviated as The Wealth of Nations, is considered his magnum opus and the first modern work of economics.

   a. Adam Smith
   b. Adolf Hitler
   c. Alan Greenspan
   d. Adolph Fischer

6. _____s is concerned with the tasks of developing and applying quantitative or statistical methods to the study and elucidation of economic principles. _____s combines economic theory with statistics to analyze and test economic relationships. Theoretical _____s considers questions about the statistical properties of estimators and tests, while applied _____s is concerned with the application of _____ methods to assess economic theories.

   a. Experimental economics
   b. Evolutionary economics
   c. Economic
   d. Econometric

Chapter 1. The Fundamentals of Economics

7. The _____ was written by the English economist John Maynard Keynes. The book, generally considered to be his magnum opus, is largely credited with creating the terminology and shape of modern macroeconomics. Published in February 1936 it sought to bring about a revolution, commonly referred to as the 'Keynesian Revolution', in the way economists thought - especially in relation to the proposition that a market economy tends naturally to restore itself to full employment after temporary shocks.

   a. Human Action
   b. The General Theory of Employment, Interest and Money
   c. Black Book of Communism
   d. General Theory of Employment, Interest and Money

8. The _____ was a worldwide economic downturn starting in most places in 1929 and ending at different times in the 1930s or early 1940s for different countries. It was the largest and most important economic depression in the 20th century, and is used in the 21st century as an example of how far the world's economy can fall. The _____ originated in the United States; historians most often use as a starting date the stock market crash on October 29, 1929, known as Black Tuesday.

   a. Jarrow March
   b. British Empire Economic Conference
   c. Wall Street Crash of 1929
   d. Great Depression

9. _____ is a fee paid on borrowed assets. It is the price paid for the use of borrowed money , or, money earned by deposited funds . Assets that are sometimes lent with _____ include money, shares, consumer goods through hire purchase, major assets such as aircraft, and even entire factories in finance lease arrangements.

   a. Interest
   b. Asset protection
   c. Insolvency
   d. Internal debt

10. _____, 1st Baron Keynes was a renowned economist from Britain whose many ideas on economic and political theories as well as on many governments' monetary policies influenced America. He advocated a government that played an active role in the lives of people regarding business, economy, etc. In this role, the government would use fiscal measures to reduce the consequences of recessions, economic depressions and booms.

    a. Adolph Fischer
    b. John Maynard Keynes
    c. Adam Smith
    d. Adolf Hitler

11. _____ is a branch of economics that deals with the performance, structure, and behavior of a national or regional economy as a whole. Along with microeconomics, _____ is one of the two most general fields in economics. It is the study of the behavior and decision-making of entire economies.

    a. Nominal value
    b. Tobit model
    c. New Trade Theory
    d. Macroeconomics

12. A _____ is an economy based on the division of labor in which the prices of goods and services are determined in a free price system set by supply and demand. This is often contrasted with a planned economy, in which a central government determines the price of goods and services using a fixed price system. Market economies are contrasted with mixed economy where the price system is not entirely free but under some government control that is not extensive enough to constitute a planned economy.

    a. Nutritional Economics
    b. Market economy
    c. Network Economy
    d. Commons-based peer production

13. _____ is a branch of economics that studies how individuals, households and firms and some states make decisions to allocate limited resources, typically in markets where goods or services are being bought and sold. _____ examines how these decisions and behaviours affect the supply and demand for goods and services, which determines prices; and how prices, in turn, determine the supply and demand of goods and services.

Whereas macroeconomics involves the 'sum total of economic activity, dealing with the issues of growth, inflation and unemployment, and with national economic policies relating to these issues' and the effects of government actions on them.

  a. Countercyclical
  c. Recession
  b. New Keynesian economics
  d. Microeconomics

14. An Inquiry into the Nature and Causes of the _____ is the magnum opus of the Scottish economist Adam Smith. It is a clearly written account of economics at the dawn of the Industrial Revolution, as well as a rhetorical piece written for the generally educated individual of the 18th century - advocating a free market economy as more productive and more beneficial to society.

The work is credited as a watershed in history and economics due to its comprehensive, largely accurate characterization of economic mechanisms that survive in modern economics; and also for its effective use of rhetorical technique, including structuring the work to contrast real world examples of free and fettered markets.

  a. The Rise and Fall of the Great Powers
  c. The Bell Curve
  b. Black Book of Communism
  d. Wealth of Nations

15. _____ is the development of economic wealth of countries or regions for the well-being of their inhabitants. It is the process by which a nation improves the economic, political, and social well being of its people. From a policy perspective, _____ can be defined as efforts that seek to improve the economic well-being and quality of life for a community by creating and/or retaining jobs and supporting or growing incomes and the tax base.
  a. Economic development
  c. Economic methodology
  b. Experimental economics
  d. Inflation

16. A _____ arises when one infers that something is true of the whole from the fact that it is true of some part of the whole (or even of every proper part.) For example: 'This fragment of metal cannot be broken with a hammer, therefore the machine of which it is a part cannot be broken with a hammer.' This is clearly fallacious, because many machines can be broken into their constituent parts without any of those parts being breakable.

This fallacy is often confused with the fallacy of hasty generalization, in which an unwarranted inference is made from a statement about a sample to a statement about the population from which it is drawn.

  a. 1921 recession
  c. 100-year flood
  b. 130-30 fund
  d. Fallacy of composition

17. To _____ is to impose a financial charge or other levy upon a taxpayer by a state or the functional equivalent of a state.

Chapter 1. The Fundamentals of Economics

_____es are also imposed by many subnational entities. _____es consist of direct _____ or indirect _____, and may be paid in money or as its labour equivalent (often but not always unpaid.)

a. 130-30 fund
b. 1921 recession
c. 100-year flood
d. Tax

18. A _____ is a reduction in taxes. Economic stimulus via _____s, along with interest rate intervention and deficit spending, are one of the central tenets of Keynesian economics.

The immediate effects of a _____ are, generally, a decrease in the real income of the government and an increase in the real income of those whose tax rate has been lowered.

a. Popiwek
b. Direct taxes
c. Withholding tax
d. Tax cut

19. _____ is a term used to describe how different aspects between economies are integrated. The basics of this theory were written by the Hungarian Economist Béla Balassa in the 1960s. As _____ increases, the barriers of trade between markets diminishes.

a. Inward investment
b. Import
c. Import license
d. Economic integration

20. The _____, sometimes called the fundamental _____, is one of the fundamental economic theories in the operation of any economy. It asserts that there is scarcity, that the finite resources available are insufficient to satisfy all human wants. The problem then becomes how to determine what is to be produced and how the factors of production (such as capital and labour) are to be allocated.

a. Eclectic paradigm
b. Endogenous growth theory
c. Economic nationalism
d. Economic problem

21. In economics, _____ is how a natione;s total economy is distributed among its population. ._____ has always been a central concern of economic theory and economic policy. Classical economists such as Adam Smith, Thomas Malthus and David Ricardo were mainly concerned with factor _____, that is, the distribution of income between the main factors of production, land, labour and capital.

a. Income distribution
b. Equipment trust certificate
c. Eco commerce
d. Authorised capital

22. _____ is the branch of economics that incorporates value judgments (that is, normative judgements) about what the economy ought to be like or what particular policy actions ought to be recommended to achieve a desirable goal. _____ looks at the desirability of certain aspects of the economy. It underlies expressions of support for particular economic policies.

a. Broad money
b. Nanoeconomics
c. Normative economics
d. Double bottom line

23. _____ is the branch of economics that concerns the description and explanation of economic phenomena (Wong, 1987, p. 920.) It focuses on facts and cause-and-effect relationships and includes the development and testing of economics theories.

a. 130-30 fund
b. Regulatory economics
c. 100-year flood
d. Positive economics

24. In economics, the term _____ of income or _____ refers to a simple economic model which describes the reciprocal circulation of income between producers and consumers. In the _____ model, the inter-dependent entities of producer and consumer are referred to as 'firms' and 'households' respectively and provide each other with factors in order to facilitate the flow of income. Firms provide consumers with goods and services in exchange for consumer expenditure and 'factors of production' from households.
   a. 1921 recession
   b. 100-year flood
   c. 130-30 fund
   d. Circular flow

25. A _____ or directed economy is an economic system in which the government or workers' councils manages the economy. It is an economic system in which the central government makes all decisions on the production and consumption of goods and services. Its most extensive form is referred to as a _____, centrally planned economy, or command and control economy.
   a. Nutritional Economics
   b. Command economy
   c. Transition economy
   d. Subsistence economy

26. An _____ or Å"conomic system is a system that involves the production, distribution and consumption of goods and services between the entities in a particular society. It is the method used by society to produce and distribute goods and services. The _____ is composed of people and institutions, including their relationships to productive resources, such as through the convention of property.
   a. Intention economy
   b. Information economy
   c. Indicative planning
   d. Economic system

27. _____ is a term used to describe a policy of allowing events to take their own course. The term is a French phrase literally meaning 'let do'. It is a doctrine that states that government generally should not intervene in the marketplace.
   a. Communization
   b. Theory of Productive Forces
   c. Laissez-faire
   d. Heroic capitalism

28. _____ is used to assign the available resources in an economic way. It is part of resource management.

In strategic planning, is a plan for using available resources, for example human resources, especially in the near term, to achieve goals for the future.

   a. 1921 recession
   b. 130-30 fund
   c. 100-year flood
   d. Resource allocation

29. _____ is an economic system in which wealth, and the means of producing wealth, are privately owned. Through _____, the land, labor, and capital are owned, operated, and traded for the purpose of generating profits, without force or fraud, by private individuals either singly or jointly, and investments, distribution, income, production, pricing and supply of goods, commodities and services are determined by voluntary private decision in a market economy. A distinguishing feature of _____ is that each person owns his or her own labor and therefore is allowed to sell the use of it to employers.
   a. Socialism for the rich and capitalism for the poor
   b. Capitalism
   c. Late capitalism
   d. Creative capitalism

Chapter 1. The Fundamentals of Economics

30. A _____ is any systematic process enabling many market players to bid and ask: helping bidders and sellers interact and make deals. It is not just the price mechanism but the entire system of regulation, qualification, credentials, reputations and clearing that surrounds that mechanism and makes it operate in a social context.

Because a _____ relies on the assumption that players are constantly involved and unequally enabled, a _____ is distinguished specifically from a voting system where candidates seek the support of voters on a less regular basis.

- a. Competitive equilibrium
- b. Price mechanism
- c. Contestable market
- d. Market system

31. In law and economics, the _____, describes the economic efficiency of an economic allocation or outcome in the presence of externalities. The theorem states that when trade in an externality is possible and there are no transaction costs, bargaining will lead to an efficient outcome regardless of the initial allocation of property rights. In practice, obstacles to bargaining or poorly defined property rights can prevent Coasian bargaining.

- a. Coase theorem
- b. Prior appropriation water rights
- c. Means test
- d. General Mining Act of 1872

32. In economics, _____ are the resources employed to produce goods and services. They facilitate production but do not become part of the product (as with raw materials) or significantly transformed by the production process (as with fuel used to power machinery.) To 19th century economists, the _____ were land (natural resources, gifts from nature), labor (the ability to work), and capital goods (human-made tools and equipment.)

- a. Long-run
- b. Product Pipeline
- c. Factors of production
- d. Hicks-neutral technical change

33. _____ is the term denoting either an entrance or changes which are inserted into a system and which activate/modify a process. It is an abstract concept, used in the modeling, system(s) design and system(s) exploitation. It is usually connected with other terms, e.g., _____ field, _____ variable, _____ parameter, _____ value, _____ signal, _____ device and _____ file.

- a. ACEA agreement
- b. Input
- c. ACCRA Cost of Living Index
- d. AD-IA Model

34. _____s (economically referred to as land or raw materials) occur naturally within environments that exist relatively undisturbed by mankind, in a natural form. A _____'s is often characterized by amounts of biodiversity existent in various ecosystems.

Mining, petroleum extraction, fishing, hunting, and forestry are generally considered natural-resource industries.

- a. 1921 recession
- b. 130-30 fund
- c. Natural resource
- d. 100-year flood

35. In microeconomics, _____ is quite simply the conversion of inputs into outputs. It is an economic process that uses resources to create a good or service that is suitable for exchange. This can include manufacturing, storing, shipping, and packaging.

Chapter 1. The Fundamentals of Economics 7

    a. Solved   b. Red Guards
    c. MET   d. Production

36. _____ is the increase in the amount of the goods and services produced by an economy over time. It is conventionally measured as the percent rate of increase in real gross domestic product, or real GDP. Growth is usually calculated in real terms, i.e. inflation-adjusted terms, in order to net out the effect of inflation on the price of the goods and services produced.
    a. ACCRA Cost of Living Index   b. ACEA agreement
    c. AD-IA Model   d. Economic growth

37. In economics, a _____ is a good that is non-rivaled and non-excludable. This means, respectively, that consumption of the good by one individual does not reduce availability of the good for consumption by others; and that no one can be effectively excluded from using the good. In the real world, there may be no such thing as an absolutely non-rivaled and non-excludable good; but economists think that some goods approximate the concept closely enough for the analysis to be economically useful.
    a. Demand-pull theory   b. Neoclassical synthesis
    c. Happiness economics   d. Public good

38. _____ is a common concept in economics, and gives rise to derived concepts such as consumer debt. Generally _____ is defined by opposition to production. But the precise definition can vary because different schools of economists define production quite differently.
    a. Cash or share options   b. Foreclosure data providers
    c. Consumption   d. Federal Reserve Bank Notes

39. In economics, economic output is divided into physical goods and intangible services. Consumption of _____ is assumed to produce utility. It is often used when referring to a _____ Tax.
    a. Private good   b. Composite good
    c. Manufactured goods   d. Goods and services

40. A _____ is defined in economics as a good that exhibits these properties:

- Excludable - it is reasonably possible to prevent a class of consumers (e.g. those who have not paid for it) from consuming the good.
- Rivalrous - consumptions by one consumer prevents simultaneous consumption by other consumers. _____s satisfies an individual want while public good satisfies a collective want of the society.

A _____ is the opposite of a public good, as they are almost exclusively made for profit.

An example of the _____ is bread: bread eaten by a given person cannot be consumed by another (rivalry), and it is easy for a baker to refuse to trade a loaf (excludable

    a. Pie method   b. Demerit good
    c. Positional goods   d. Private good

41. In economics and especially in the theory of competition, _____ are obstacles in the path of a firm that make it difficult to enter a given market.

Chapter 1. The Fundamentals of Economics

_____ are the source of a firm's pricing power - the ability of a firm to raise prices without losing all its customers.

The term refers to hindrances that an individual may face while trying to gain entrance into a profession or trade.

   a. Social dumping
   c. Group boycott

   b. Limit price
   d. Barriers to entry

42. _____ is a situation in which the limited resources of a firm are allocated in accordance with the wishes of consumers. An allocatively efficient economy produces an 'optimal mix' of commodities. A firm is allocatively efficient when its price is equal to its marginal costs (that is, P = MC) in a perfect market.
   a. Economic efficiency
   c. Allocative efficiency

   b. ACCRA Cost of Living Index
   d. ACEA agreement

43. _____ or economic opportunity loss is the value of the next best alternative foregone as the result of making a decision. _____ analysis is an important part of a company's decision-making processes but is not treated as an actual cost in any financial statement. The next best thing that a person can engage in is referred to as the _____ of doing the best thing and ignoring the next best thing to be done.
   a. Industrial organization
   c. Economic

   b. Economic ideology
   d. Opportunity cost

44. _____ occurs when the economy is operating at its production possibility frontier (PPF.) This takes place when production of one good is achieved at the lowest cost possible, given the production of the other good(s.) Equivalently, it is when the highest possible output of one good is produced, given the production level of the other good(s.)
   a. Productive efficiency
   c. Preclusive purchasing

   b. Free contract
   d. Discretionary spending

45. A _____ is a situation that involves losing one quality or aspect of something in return for gaining another quality or aspect. It implies a decision to be made with full comprehension of both the upside and downside of a particular choice.

In economics the term is expressed as opportunity cost, referring the most preferred alternative given up.

   a. Whitemail
   c. Nonmarket

   b. Friedman-Savage utility function
   d. Trade-off

46. The term _____ refers to economy-wide fluctuations in production or economic activity over several months or years. These fluctuations occur around a long-term growth trend, and typically involve shifts over time between periods of relatively rapid economic growth (expansion or boom), and periods of relative stagnation or decline (contraction or recession.)

These fluctuations are often measured using the growth rate of real gross domestic product.

   a. Nominal value
   c. Consumer theory

   b. Tobit model
   d. Business cycle

Chapter 1. The Fundamentals of Economics

47. _____ Theory (or _____ Theory) is a class of macroeconomic models in which business cycle fluctuations to a large extent can be accounted for by real (in contrast to nominal) shocks. (The four primary economic fluctuations are secular (trend), business cycle, seasonal, and random.) Unlike other leading theories of the business cycle, it sees recessions and periods of economic growth as the efficient response to exogenous changes in the real economic environment.
   a. SIMIC
   b. Balanced-growth equilibrium
   c. Real business cycle
   d. Monetary policy reaction function

48. In economics, a _____ is a general slowdown in economic activity over a sustained period of time, or a business cycle contraction. During _____s, many macroeconomic indicators vary in a similar way. Production as measured by Gross Domestic Product (GDP), employment, investment spending, capacity utilization, household incomes and business profits all fall during _____s.
   a. Monetary economics
   b. Treasury View
   c. Recession
   d. Leading indicators

49. _____ in political thought refers to economic theories of social organization advocating collective ownership and administration of the means of production and distribution of goods, and a society characterized by equality for all individuals, with an egalitarian method of compensation. Modern _____ originated in the late 19th-century intellectual and working class political movement that criticized the effects of industrialization and private ownership on society. Karl Marx posited that _____ would be achieved via class struggle and a proletarian revolution after a transitional stage from capitalism called the dictatorship of the proletariat.
   a. Socialism
   b. Adolf Hitler
   c. Adam Smith
   d. Adolph Fischer

50. An inverse or negative relationship is a mathematical relationship in which one variable, say y, decreases as another, say x, increases. For a linear (straight-line) relation, this can be expressed as y = a-bx, where -b is a constant value less than zero and a is a constant. For example, there is an _____ between education and unemployment -- that is, as education increases, the rate of unemployment decreases.
   a. Inverse relationship
   b. AD-IA Model
   c. ACEA agreement
   d. ACCRA Cost of Living Index

51. In mathematics, a _____ system is a system which is not linear, that is, a system which does not satisfy the superposition principle, or whose output is not proportional to its input. Less technically, a _____ system is any problem where the variable(s) to be solved for cannot be written as a linear combination of independent components. A nonhomogeneous system, which is linear apart from the presence of a function of the independent variables, is _____ according to a strict definition, but such systems are usually studied alongside linear systems, because they can be transformed to a linear system of multiple variables.
   a. Nonlinear
   b. Nonlinear system
   c. 130-30 fund
   d. 100-year flood

52. In economics, the _____ is a single mathematical function used to express consumer spending. It was developed by John Maynard Keynes and detailed most famously in his book The General Theory of Employment, Interest, and Money. The function is used to calculate the amount of total consumption in an economy.
   a. Liquidity preference
   b. DAD-SAS model
   c. Consumption function
   d. Procyclical

Chapter 1. The Fundamentals of Economics

53. The _____ or gross domestic income (GDI), a basic measure of an economy's economic performance, is the market value of all final goods and services produced within the borders of a nation in a year. _____ can be defined in three ways, all of which are conceptually identical. First, it is equal to the total expenditures for all final goods and services produced within the country in a stipulated period of time (usually a 365-day year.)
   a. Gross Domestic Product
   b. Countercyclical
   c. Monopolistic competition
   d. Market structure

54. In economics, _____ is the ratio of the percent change in one variable to the percent change in another variable. It is a tool for measuring the responsiveness of a function to changes in parameters in a relative way. Commonly analyzed are _____ of substitution, price and wealth.
   a. ACCRA Cost of Living Index
   b. ACEA agreement
   c. Elasticity of demand
   d. Elasticity

55. A _____ is an expression that compares quantities relative to each other. The most common examples involve two quantities, but any number of quantities can be compared. _____s are represented mathematically by separating each quantity with a colon, for example the _____ 2:3, which is read as the _____ 'two to three'.
   a. 130-30 fund
   b. Ratio
   c. 100-year flood
   d. Y-intercept

56. _____ is an economic model based on price, utility and quantity in a market. It predicts that in a competitive market, price will function to equalize the quantity demanded by consumers, and the quantity supplied by producers, resulting in an economic equilibrium of price and quantity. The model incorporates other factors changing equilibrium as a shift of demand and/or supply.
   a. Deferred gratification
   b. Joint demand
   c. Supply and demand
   d. Rational addiction

57. Economics:

   - _____, the desire to own something and the ability to pay for it
   - _____ curve, a graphic representation of a _____ schedule
   - _____ deposit, the money in checking accounts
   - _____ pull theory, the theory that inflation occurs when _____ for goods and services exceeds existing supplies
   - _____ schedule, a table that lists the quantity of a good a person will buy it each different price
   - _____ side economics, the school of economics at believes government spending and tax cuts open economy by raising _____

   a. Production
   b. McKesson ' Robbins scandal
   c. Demand
   d. Variability

Chapter 2. Markets and Government in a Modern Economy

1. _____ was a survey conducted by the U.S. Department of Justice to gauge the prevalence of alcohol and illegal drug use among prior arrestees. It was a reformulation of the prior Drug Use Forecasting (DUF) program, focused on five drugs in particular: cocaine, marijuana, methamphetamine, opiates, and PCP.

   Participants were randomly selected from arrest records in major metropolitan areas; because no personally identifying information is taken from each record chosen, the resulting data can be correlated to arrest rates, but not to the total population of persons charged.

   a. Arrestee Drug Abuse Monitoring
   b. AD-IA Model
   c. ACCRA Cost of Living Index
   d. ACEA agreement

2. _____ is an economic system in which wealth, and the means of producing wealth, are privately owned. Through _____, the land, labor, and capital are owned, operated, and traded for the purpose of generating profits, without force or fraud, by private individuals either singly or jointly, and investments, distribution, income, production, pricing and supply of goods, commodities and services are determined by voluntary private decision in a market economy. A distinguishing feature of _____ is that each person owns his or her own labor and therefore is allowed to sell the use of it to employers.

   a. Creative capitalism
   b. Late capitalism
   c. Socialism for the rich and capitalism for the poor
   d. Capitalism

3. A _____ or directed economy is an economic system in which the government or workers' councils manages the economy. It is an economic system in which the central government makes all decisions on the production and consumption of goods and services. Its most extensive form is referred to as a _____, centrally planned economy, or command and control economy.

   a. Transition economy
   b. Subsistence economy
   c. Nutritional Economics
   d. Command economy

4. _____s is the social science that studies the production, distribution, and consumption of goods and services. The term _____s comes from the Ancient Greek οἰκονομία from οἶκος (oikos, 'house') + νόμος (nomos, 'custom' or 'law'), hence 'rules of the house(hold)'. Current _____ models developed out of the broader field of political economy in the late 19th century, owing to a desire to use an empirical approach more akin to the physical sciences.

   a. Energy economics
   b. Economic
   c. Inflation
   d. Opportunity cost

5. An _____ or Ä"conomic system is a system that involves the production, distribution and consumption of goods and services between the entities in a particular society. It is the method used by society to produce and distribute goods and services. The _____ is composed of people and institutions, including their relationships to productive resources, such as through the convention of property.

   a. Indicative planning
   b. Intention economy
   c. Economic system
   d. Information economy

6. _____ is a term used to describe a policy of allowing events to take their own course. The term is a French phrase literally meaning 'let do'. It is a doctrine that states that government generally should not intervene in the marketplace.

   a. Theory of Productive Forces
   b. Communization
   c. Heroic capitalism
   d. Laissez-faire

7. A _____ is an economy based on the division of labor in which the prices of goods and services are determined in a free price system set by supply and demand. This is often contrasted with a planned economy, in which a central government determines the price of goods and services using a fixed price system. Market economies are contrasted with mixed economy where the price system is not entirely free but under some government control that is not extensive enough to constitute a planned economy.

- a. Commons-based peer production
- b. Nutritional Economics
- c. Network Economy
- d. Market economy

8. _____ is a term from economics referring to the use of money exchanged by buyers and sellers with an open and understood system of value and time trade offs to produce the best distribution of goods and services. The use of the _____ does not imply a free market: there can be captive or controlled markets which seek to use supply and demand, or some other form of charging for scarcity, both in social situations and in engineering.

The _____ assumes perfect competition and is regulated by demand and supply.

- a. Two-sided markets
- b. Partial equilibrium
- c. Product-Market Growth Matrix
- d. Market mechanism

9. _____ is the incidence or process of transferring ownership of a business, enterprise, agency or public service from the public sector (government) to the private sector (business.) In a broader sense, _____ refers to transfer of any government function to the private sector including governmental functions like revenue collection and law enforcement.

The term '_____' also has been used to describe two unrelated transactions.

- a. Privatization
- b. Compound empowerment
- c. Performance reports
- d. Ricardian equivalence

10. _____ was a Scottish moral philosopher and a pioneer of political economy. One of the key figures of the Scottish Enlightenment, Smith is the author of The Theory of Moral Sentiments and An Inquiry into the Nature and Causes of the Wealth of Nations. The latter, usually abbreviated as The Wealth of Nations, is considered his magnum opus and the first modern work of economics.

- a. Alan Greenspan
- b. Adam Smith
- c. Adolf Hitler
- d. Adolph Fischer

11. An Inquiry into the Nature and Causes of the _____ is the magnum opus of the Scottish economist Adam Smith. It is a clearly written account of economics at the dawn of the Industrial Revolution, as well as a rhetorical piece written for the generally educated individual of the 18th century - advocating a free market economy as more productive and more beneficial to society.

The work is credited as a watershed in history and economics due to its comprehensive, largely accurate characterization of economic mechanisms that survive in modern economics; and also for its effective use of rhetorical technique, including structuring the work to contrast real world examples of free and fettered markets.

- a. The Rise and Fall of the Great Powers
- b. The Bell Curve
- c. Black Book of Communism
- d. Wealth of Nations

Chapter 2. Markets and Government in a Modern Economy   13

12. There are two main interpretations of the idea of a _____:

   - A model in which the state assumes primary responsibility for the welfare of its citizens. This responsibility in theory ought to be comprehensive, because all aspects of welfare are considered and universally applied to citizens as a 'right'. _____ can also mean the creation of a 'social safety net' of minimum standards of varying forms of welfare. Here is found some confusion between a '_____' and a 'welfare society' in common debate about the definition of the term.
   - The provision of welfare in society. In many '_____s', especially in continental Europe, welfare is not actually provided by the state, but by a combination of independent, voluntary, mutualist and government services. The functional provider of benefits and services may be a central or state government, a state-sponsored company or agency, a private corporation, a charity or another form of non-profit organization. However, this phenomenon has been more appropriately termed a 'welfare society,' and the term 'welfare system' has been used to describe the range of _____ and welfare society mixes that are found.

The English term '_____' is believed by Asa Briggs to have been coined by Archbishop William Temple during the Second World War, contrasting wartime Britain with the 'warfare state' of Nazi Germany. Friedrich Hayek contends that the term derived from the older German word Wohlfahrtsstaat, which itself was used by nineteenth century historians to describe a variant of the ideal of Polizeistaat . It was fully developed by the German academic Sozialpolitiker--'socialists of the chair'--from 1870 and first implemented through Bismarck's 'state socialism'. Bismarck's policies have also been seen as the creation of a _____.

   a. 1921 recession
   b. Welfare state
   c. 100-year flood
   d. 130-30 fund

13. _____ has several particular meanings:

   - in mathematics
     - _____ function
     - Euler _____
     - _____
     - _____ subgroup
     - method of _____s (partial differential equations)
   - in physics and engineering
     - any _____ curve that shows the relationship between certain input- and output parameters, e.g.
     - an I-V or current-voltage _____ is the current in a circuit as a function of the applied voltage
     - Receiver-Operator _____
   - in fiction
     - in Dungeons ' Dragons, _____ is another name for ability score

   a. Technocracy
   b. Russian financial crisis
   c. Demand
   d. Characteristic

14. A _____ is an economic system that incorporates a mixture of private and government ownership or control, or a mixture of capitalism and socialism.

Chapter 2. Markets and Government in a Modern Economy

There is not one single definition for a _____, but relevant aspects include: a degree of private economic freedom (including privately owned industry) intermingled with centralized economic planning and government regulation (which may include regulation of the market for environmental concerns and social welfare, or state ownership and management of some of the means of production for national or social objectives.)

For some states, there is not a consensus on whether they are capitalist, socialist, or mixed economies.

  a. Mixed economy
  b. Dual economy
  c. Hunter-gatherer
  d. Planned liberalism

15. The _____ , established in 1848, is the world's oldest futures and options exchange. More than 50 different options and futures contracts are traded by over 3,600 _____ members through open outcry and eTrading. Volumes at the exchange in 2003 were a record breaking 454 million contracts.
  a. 130-30 fund
  b. 100-year flood
  c. New York Mercantile Exchange
  d. Chicago Board of Trade

16. _____s are a type of administrative division, in some countries managed by a local government. They vary greatly in size, spanning entire regions or counties, several municipalities, or subdivisions of municipalities.

In Austria, a _____ or Bezirk is an administrative division normally encompassing several municipalities, roughly equivalent to the Landkreis in Germany.

  a. 1921 recession
  b. 100-year flood
  c. 130-30 fund
  d. District

17. A _____ is the space, actual or metaphorical, in which a market operates. The term is also used in a trademark law context to denote the actual consumer environment, ie. the 'real world' in which products and services are provided and consumed.
  a. Marketplace
  b. 100-year flood
  c. 1921 recession
  d. 130-30 fund

18. The _____ is the world's largest physical commodity futures exchange, located in New York City. Its two principal divisions are the _____ and Commodity Exchange, Inc (COMEX) which were once separate but are now merged. The parent company of the _____, Inc., New York Mercantile ExchangeX Holdings, Inc.
  a. Commodity Exchange
  b. 130-30 fund
  c. New York Mercantile Exchange
  d. 100-year flood

19. A _____ is any systematic process enabling many market players to bid and ask: helping bidders and sellers interact and make deals. It is not just the price mechanism but the entire system of regulation, qualification, credentials, reputations and clearing that surrounds that mechanism and makes it operate in a social context.

Because a _____ relies on the assumption that players are constantly involved and unequally enabled, a _____ is distinguished specifically from a voting system where candidates seek the support of voters on a less regular basis.

a. Competitive equilibrium
c. Market system
b. Contestable market
d. Price mechanism

20. _____ is a broad label that refers to any individuals or households that use goods and services generated within the economy. The concept of a _____ is used in different contexts, so that the usage and significance of the term may vary.

Typically when business people and economists talk of _____s they are talking about person as _____, an aggregated commodity item with little individuality other than that expressed in the buy/not-buy decision.

a. 100-year flood
c. 1921 recession
b. 130-30 fund
d. Consumer

21. _____ are final goods specifically intended for the mass market. For instance, _____ do not include investment assets, like precious antiques, even though these antiques are final goods.

Manufactured goods are goods that have been processed by way of machinery.

a. G-20 Leaders Summit on Financial Markets and the World Economy
c. Fiscal stimulus plans
b. Bulgarian-American trade
d. Consumer goods

22. The _____, sometimes called the fundamental _____, is one of the fundamental economic theories in the operation of any economy. It asserts that there is scarcity, that the finite resources available are insufficient to satisfy all human wants. The problem then becomes how to determine what is to be produced and how the factors of production (such as capital and labour) are to be allocated.

a. Eclectic paradigm
c. Economic nationalism
b. Economic problem
d. Endogenous growth theory

23. In economics, _____ are the resources employed to produce goods and services. They facilitate production but do not become part of the product (as with raw materials) or significantly transformed by the production process (as with fuel used to power machinery.) To 19th century economists, the _____ were land (natural resources, gifts from nature), labor (the ability to work), and capital goods (human-made tools and equipment.)

a. Hicks-neutral technical change
c. Product Pipeline
b. Long-run
d. Factors of production

24. _____ theory is a branch of theoretical economics. It seeks to explain the behavior of supply, demand and prices in a whole economy with several or many markets. It is often assumed that agents are price takers and in that setting two common notions of equilibrium exist: Walrasian (or competitive) equilibrium, and its generalization; a price equilibrium with transfers.

a. General equilibrium
c. New Keynesian economics
b. Rational choice theory
d. Human capital

Chapter 2. Markets and Government in a Modern Economy

25. In economics, economic equilibrium is simply a state of the world where economic forces are balanced and in the absence of external influences the (equilibrium) values of economic variables will not change. It is the point at which quantity demanded and quantity supplied are equal. _____, for example, refers to a condition where a market price is established through competition such that the amount of goods or services sought by buyers is equal to the amount of goods or services produced by sellers.
- a. Regulated market
- b. Product-Market Growth Matrix
- c. Marketization
- d. Market equilibrium

26. _____ describes a deliberate attempt to interfere with the free and fair operation of the market and create artificial, false or misleading appearances with respect to the price of a security, commodity or currency. _____ is prohibited under Section 9(a)(2) of the Securities Exchange Act of 1934, and in Australia under Section s 1041A of the Corporations Act 2001. The Act defines _____ as transactions which create an artificial price or maintain an artificial price for a tradable security.
- a. Managerial economics
- b. Market manipulation
- c. Legal monopoly
- d. Net domestic product

27. _____ is an economic concept with commonplace familiarity. It is the price that a good or service is offered at, or will fetch, in the marketplace. It is of interest mainly in the study of microeconomics.
- a. Noisy market hypothesis
- b. Paper trading
- c. Market anomaly
- d. Market price

28. _____ in economics and business is the result of an exchange and from that trade we assign a numerical monetary value to a good, service or asset. If Alice trades Bob 4 apples for an orange, the _____ of an orange is 4 apples. Inversely, the _____ of an apple is 1/4 oranges.
- a. Price book
- b. Premium pricing
- c. Price war
- d. Price

29. A _____ is message sent to consumers and producers in the form of a price charged for a commodity; this is seen as indicating a signal for producers to increase supplies and/or consumers to reduce demand.

For example, in a free price system, rising prices may indicate a shortage of supply, increase in demand, or a rise in input costs. Regardless of the underlying reason--and without the consumer needing to know the cause--the price increase communicates the notion that consumer demand (at this new, higher price) should recede or that supplies should increase.

- a. Market demand schedule
- b. Threshold population
- c. Mohring effect
- d. Price signal

30. In economics, _____ is the process by which a firm determines the price and output level that returns the greatest profit. There are several approaches to this problem. The total revenue--total cost method relies on the fact that profit equals revenue minus cost, and the marginal revenue--marginal cost method is based on the fact that total profit in a perfectly competitive market reaches its maximum point where marginal revenue equals marginal cost.
- a. Profit margin
- b. Profit maximization
- c. 100-year flood
- d. Normal profit

Chapter 2. Markets and Government in a Modern Economy

31. _____ is an economic model based on price, utility and quantity in a market. It predicts that in a competitive market, price will function to equalize the quantity demanded by consumers, and the quantity supplied by producers, resulting in an economic equilibrium of price and quantity. The model incorporates other factors changing equilibrium as a shift of demand and/or supply.
   a. Joint demand
   b. Rational addiction
   c. Deferred gratification
   d. Supply and demand

32. Competition law, known in the United States as _____ law, has three main elements:

   - prohibiting agreements or practices that restrict free trading and competition between business entities. This includes in particular the repression of cartels.
   - banning abusive behaviour by a firm dominating a market, or anti-competitive practices that tend to lead to such a dominant position. Practices controlled in this way may include predatory pricing, tying, price gouging, refusal to deal, and many others.
   - supervising the mergers and acquisitions of large corporations, including some joint ventures. Transactions that are considered to threaten the competitive process can be prohibited altogether, or approved subject to 'remedies' such as an obligation to divest part of the merged business or to offer licences or access to facilities to enable other businesses to continue competing.

   The substance and practice of competition law varies from jurisdiction to jurisdiction. Protecting the interests of consumers (consumer welfare) and ensuring that entrepreneurs have an opportunity to compete in the market economy are often treated as important objectives. Competition law is closely connected with law on deregulation of access to markets, state aids and subsidies, the privatisation of state owned assets and the establishment of independent sector regulators. In recent decades, competition law has been viewed as a way to provide better public services.

   a. Anti-Inflation Act
   b. United Kingdom competition law
   c. Intellectual property law
   d. Antitrust

33. In economics, the term _____ of income or _____ refers to a simple economic model which describes the reciprocal circulation of income between producers and consumers. In the _____ model, the inter-dependent entities of producer and consumer are referred to as 'firms' and 'households' respectively and provide each other with factors in order to facilitate the flow of income. Firms provide consumers with goods and services in exchange for consumer expenditure and 'factors of production' from households.
   a. 130-30 fund
   b. 100-year flood
   c. 1921 recession
   d. Circular flow

Chapter 2. Markets and Government in a Modern Economy

34. Economics:

- _____, the desire to own something and the ability to pay for it
- _____ curve, a graphic representation of a _____ schedule
- _____ deposit, the money in checking accounts
- _____ pull theory, the theory that inflation occurs when _____ for goods and services exceeds existing supplies
- _____ schedule, a table that lists the quantity of a good a person will buy it each different price
- _____ side economics, the school of economics at believes government spending and tax cuts open economy by raising _____

a. McKesson ' Robbins scandal
b. Production
c. Variability
d. Demand

35. A _____ is an object whose consumption increases the utility of the consumer, for which the quantity demanded exceeds the quantity supplied at zero price. _____s are usually modeled as having diminishing marginal utility. The first individual purchase has high utility; the second has less.

a. Merit good
b. Composite good
c. Pie method
d. Good

36. In microeconomics, _____ is quite simply the conversion of inputs into outputs. It is an economic process that uses resources to create a good or service that is suitable for exchange. This can include manufacturing, storing, shipping, and packaging.

a. MET
b. Solved
c. Red Guards
d. Production

37. The _____ consists of a number of economic theories which describe the nature of the firm, company including its existence, its behaviour, and its relationship with the market.

In simplified terms, the _____ aims to answer these questions:

1. Existence - why do firms emerge, why are not all transactions in the economy mediated over the market?
2. Boundaries - why the boundary between firms and the market is located exactly there? Which transactions are performed internally and which are negotiated on the market?
3. Organization - why are firms structured in such specific way? What is the interplay of formal and informal relationships?

Despite looking simple, these questions are not answered by the established economic theory, which usually views firms as given, and treats them as black boxes without any internal structure.

The First World War period saw a change of emphasis in economic theory away from industry-level analysis which mainly included analysing markets to analysis at the level of the firm, as it became increasingly clear that perfect competition was no longer an adequate model of how firms behaved. Economic theory till then had focussed on trying to understand markets alone and there had been little study on understanding why firms or organisations exist.

Chapter 2. Markets and Government in a Modern Economy

a. Technology gap
c. Theory of the firm
b. Khazzoom-Brookes postulate
d. Policy Ineffectiveness Proposition

38. _____ are the prices that the factors of production of a finished item attract.

There has been some economic debate as to what determines these prices. Classical and Marxist economists argued that the _____ decided the value of a product and so value was intrinsic within the product.

a. Factor prices
c. Productivity model
b. Marginal product of labor
d. Marginal product

39. In economics, _____ is how a natione;s total economy is distributed among its population. ._____ has always been a central concern of economic theory and economic policy. Classical economists such as Adam Smith, Thomas Malthus and David Ricardo were mainly concerned with factor _____, that is, the distribution of income between the main factors of production, land, labour and capital.

a. Eco commerce
c. Authorised capital
b. Income distribution
d. Equipment trust certificate

40. A variety of measures of _____ and output are used in economics to estimate total economic activity in a country or region, including gross domestic product (GDP), gross national product (GNP), and net _____

There are three main ways of calculating these numbers; the output approach, the income approach and the expenditure approach. In theory, the three must yield the same, because total expenditures on goods and services must equal the total income paid to the producers (Gnational income), and that must also equal the total value of the output of goods and services (GNP.)

a. Volume index
c. Gross world product
b. GNI per capita
d. National income

41. A _____ represents the combinations of goods and services that a consumer can purchase given current prices and his income. Consumer theory uses the concepts of a _____ and a preference map to analyze consumer choices. Both concepts have a ready graphical representation in the two-good case.

a. Joint demand
c. Budget constraint
b. Revealed preference
d. Quality bias

42. In economics, the _____ is the term economists use to describe the self-regulating nature of the marketplace. The _____ is a metaphor coined by the economist Adam Smith in The Wealth of Nations.

Adam Smith mentions the metaphor in Book IV of The Wealth of Nations, arguing that people in any society will certainly employ their capital in foreign trading only if the profits available by that method far exceed those available locally, and that in such a case it is better for society as a whole if they so did.

a. ACEA agreement
c. Invisible hand
b. ACCRA Cost of Living Index
d. AD-IA Model

43. _____ is a mechanism that allows people easily to buy and sell products. Services are often included in the scope of the term. _____ regulation is an economic term that describes restrictions in the market.
   a. Market dominance
   b. Product market
   c. Fixed exchange rate system
   d. Financialization

44. In economics, an _____ or spillover of an economic transaction is an impact on a party that is not directly involved in the transaction. In such a case, prices do not reflect the full costs or benefits in production or consumption of a product or service. A positive impact is called an external benefit, while a negative impact is called an external cost.
   a. Existence value
   b. Environmental tariff
   c. Environmental impact assessment
   d. Externality

45. _____ is a situation in which the limited resources of a firm are allocated in accordance with the wishes of consumers. An allocatively efficient economy produces an 'optimal mix' of commodities. A firm is allocatively efficient when its price is equal to its marginal costs (that is, P = MC) in a perfect market.
   a. Economic efficiency
   b. ACCRA Cost of Living Index
   c. Allocative efficiency
   d. ACEA agreement

46. In law and economics, the _____, describes the economic efficiency of an economic allocation or outcome in the presence of externalities. The theorem states that when trade in an externality is possible and there are no transaction costs, bargaining will lead to an efficient outcome regardless of the initial allocation of property rights. In practice, obstacles to bargaining or poorly defined property rights can prevent Coasian bargaining.
   a. General Mining Act of 1872
   b. Prior appropriation water rights
   c. Coase theorem
   d. Means test

47. _____ is the increase in the amount of the goods and services produced by an economy over time. It is conventionally measured as the percent rate of increase in real gross domestic product, or real GDP. Growth is usually calculated in real terms, i.e. inflation-adjusted terms, in order to net out the effect of inflation on the price of the goods and services produced.
   a. Economic growth
   b. ACCRA Cost of Living Index
   c. AD-IA Model
   d. ACEA agreement

48. The _____ was a period in the late 18th and early 19th centuries when major changes in agriculture, manufacturing, mining, and transportation had a profound effect on the socioeconomic and cultural conditions in Britain. The changes subsequently spread throughout Europe, North America, and eventually the world. The onset of the _____ marked a major turning point in human society; almost every aspect of daily life was eventually influenced in some way.
   a. Adolph Fischer
   b. Adam Smith
   c. Adolf Hitler
   d. Industrial Revolution

49. In economics, a _____ exists when the production or use of goods and services by the market is not efficient. That is, there exists another outcome where all involved can be made better off. _____s can be viewed as scenarios where individuals' pursuit of pure self-interest leads to results that are not efficient - that can be improved upon from the societal point-of-view.
   a. Fixed exchange rate
   b. Market failure
   c. General equilibrium
   d. Financial economics

Chapter 2. Markets and Government in a Modern Economy

50. In economics, a _____ exists when a specific individual or enterprise has sufficient control over a particular product or service to determine significantly the terms on which other individuals shall have access to it. Monopolies are thus characterized by a lack of economic competition for the good or service that they provide and a lack of viable substitute goods. The verb 'monopolize' refers to the process by which a firm gains persistently greater market share than what is expected under perfect competition.
    a. 1921 recession
    b. 130-30 fund
    c. 100-year flood
    d. Monopoly

51. In neoclassical economics and microeconomics, _____ describes the perfect being a market in which there are many small firms, all producing homogeneous goods. In the short term, such markets are productively inefficient as output will not occur where mc is equal to ac, but allocatively efficient, as output under _____ will always occur where mc is equal to mr, and therefore where mc equals ar. However, in the long term, such markets are both allocatively and productively efficient.
    a. Co-operative economics
    b. Perfect competition
    c. Law of supply
    d. General equilibrium

52. _____ is exchange of capital, goods, and services across international borders or territories. In most countries, it represents a significant share of gross domestic product (GDP.) While _____ has been present throughout much of history, its economic, social, and political importance has been on the rise in recent centuries.
    a. Intra-industry trade
    b. Import license
    c. Incoterms
    d. International trade

53. _____ is a term used to describe how different aspects between economies are integrated. The basics of this theory were written by the Hungarian Economist Béla Balassa in the 1960s. As _____ increases, the barriers of trade between markets diminishes.
    a. Economic integration
    b. Inward investment
    c. Import license
    d. Import

54. In economics, a _____ is a mechanism that allows people to easily buy and sell (trade) financial securities (such as stocks and bonds), commodities (such as precious metals or agricultural goods), and other fungible items of value at low transaction costs and at prices that reflect the efficient-market hypothesis.

    _____s have evolved significantly over several hundred years and are undergoing constant innovation to improve liquidity.

    Both general markets (where many commodities are traded) and specialized markets (where only one commodity is traded) exist.

    a. Convertible arbitrage
    b. Financial market
    c. Market anomaly
    d. Noise trader

55. _____ in its literal sense is the process of transformation of local or regional phenomena into global ones. It can be described as a process by which the people of the world are unified into a single society and function together.

    This process is a combination of economic, technological, sociocultural and political forces.

a. Globally Integrated Enterprise
b. Helsinki Process on Globalisation and Democracy
c. Global Cosmopolitanism
d. Globalization

56. In economics, economic output is divided into physical goods and intangible services. Consumption of _____ is assumed to produce utility. It is often used when referring to a _____ Tax.
   a. Goods and services
   b. Composite good
   c. Private good
   d. Manufactured goods

57. _____ is subcontracting a process, such as product design or manufacturing, to a third-party company. The decision to outsource is often made in the interest of lowering cost or making better use of time and energy costs, redirecting or conserving energy directed at the competencies of a particular business, or to make more efficient use of land, labor, capital, (information) technology and resources. _____ became part of the business lexicon during the 1980s.
   a. Averch-Johnson effect
   b. Outsourcing
   c. Electronic business
   d. Additional Funds Needed

58. _____ is the economic policy of restraining trade between states, through methods such as tariffs on imported goods, restrictive quotas, and a variety of other restrictive government regulations designed to discourage imports, and prevent foreign take-over of local markets and companies. This policy is closely aligned with anti-globalization, and contrasts with free trade, where government barriers to trade are kept to a minimum. The term is mostly used in the context of economics, where _____ refers to policies or doctrines which 'protect' businesses and workers within a country by restricting or regulating trade with foreign nations.
   a. Digital economy
   b. Knowledge economy
   c. Google economy
   d. Protectionism

59. In economics a _____ is an entity that owes a debt to someone else. The entity may be an individual, a firm, a government, a company or other legal person. The counterparty is called a creditor.
   a. Decision process tool
   b. Senior stretch loan
   c. Duration gap
   d. Debtor

60. The term financial crisis is applied broadly to a variety of situations in which some financial institutions or assets suddenly lose a large part of their value. In the 19th and early 20th centuries, many _____ were associated with banking panics, and many recessions coincided with these panics. Other situations that are often called _____ include stock market crashes and the bursting of other financial bubbles, currency crises, and sovereign defaults.
   a. Microeconomics
   b. General equilibrium
   c. Financial crises
   d. Georgism

61. In economics, _____ is inflation that is very high or 'out of control', a condition in which prices increase rapidly as a currency loses its value. Definitions used by the media vary from a cumulative inflation rate over three years approaching 100% to 'inflation exceeding 50% a month.' In informal usage the term is often applied to much lower rates. As a rule of thumb, normal inflation is reported per year, but _____ is often reported for much shorter intervals, often per month.
   a. 100-year flood
   b. 1921 recession
   c. Hyperinflation
   d. 130-30 fund

62. In economics, _____ is a rise in the general level of prices of goods and services in an economy over a period of time. When the general price level rises, each unit of currency buys fewer goods and services; consequently, _____ is also a decline in the real value of money--a loss of purchasing power in the medium of exchange which is also the monetary unit of account in the economy. A chief measure of general price-level _____ is the general _____ rate, which is the percentage change in a general price index (normally the Consumer Price Index) over time.

a. Economic
b. Inflation
c. Energy economics
d. Opportunity cost

63. In economics, _____ is the total amount of money available in an economy at a particular point in time. There are several ways to define 'money', but standard measures usually include currency in circulation and demand deposits.

_____ data are recorded and published, usually by the government or the central bank of the country.

a. Neutrality of money
b. Money supply
c. Veil of money
d. Velocity of money

64. The _____ is the market for securities, where companies and governments can raise longterm funds. It is a market in which money is lent for periods longer than a year. The _____ includes the stock market and the bond market.

a. Multi-family office
b. Financial instrument
c. Performance attribution
d. Capital Market

65. The term _____ is applied broadly to a variety of situations in which some financial institutions or assets suddenly lose a large part of their value. In the 19th and early 20th centuries, many financial crises were associated with banking panics, and many recessions coincided with these panics. Other situations that are often called financial crises include stock market crashes and the bursting of other financial bubbles, currency crises, and sovereign defaults.

a. Macroeconomics
b. Market failure
c. Co-operative economics
d. Financial crisis

66. _____ is a type of trade policy that allows traders to act and transact without interference from government. Thus, the policy permits trading partners mutual gains from trade, with goods and services produced according to the theory of comparative advantage.

Under a _____ policy, prices are a reflection of true supply and demand, and are the sole determinant of resource allocation.

a. Free trade
b. 100-year flood
c. 130-30 fund
d. 1921 recession

67. A _____ is the exclusive authority to determine how a resource is used, whether that resource is owned by government or by individuals. All economic goods have a _____s attribute. This attribute has three broad components

1. The right to use the good
2. The right to earn income from the good
3. The right to transfer the good to others

The concept of _____s as used by economists and legal scholars are related but distinct. The distinction is largely seen in the economists' focus on the ability of an individual or collective to control the use of the good.

   a. Post-sale restraint
   b. High-reeve
   c. Property right
   d. Holder in due course

68. In economics and especially in the theory of competition, _____ are obstacles in the path of a firm that make it difficult to enter a given market.

_____ are the source of a firm's pricing power - the ability of a firm to raise prices without losing all its customers.

The term refers to hindrances that an individual may face while trying to gain entrance into a profession or trade.

   a. Limit price
   b. Group boycott
   c. Social dumping
   d. Barriers to entry

69. _____ is a common concept in economics, and gives rise to derived concepts such as consumer debt. Generally _____ is defined by opposition to production. But the precise definition can vary because different schools of economists define production quite differently.

   a. Cash or share options
   b. Foreclosure data providers
   c. Federal Reserve Bank Notes
   d. Consumption

70. In economic theory, _____ is the competitive situation in any market where the conditions necessary for perfect competition are not satisfied. It is a market structure that does not meet the conditions of perfect competition.

Forms of _____ include:

- Monopoly, in which there is only one seller of a good.
- Oligopoly, in which there is a small number of sellers.
- Monopolistic competition, in which there are many sellers producing highly differentiated goods.
- Monopsony, in which there is only one buyer of a good.
- Oligopsony, in which there is a small number of buyers.

There may also be _____ in markets due to buyers or sellers lacking information about prices and the goods being traded.

There may also be _____ due to a time lag in a market.

   a. AD-IA Model
   b. Imperfect competition
   c. ACCRA Cost of Living Index
   d. ACEA agreement

71. _____ is used to assign the available resources in an economic way. It is part of resource management.

Chapter 2. Markets and Government in a Modern Economy

In strategic planning, is a plan for using available resources, for example human resources, especially in the near term, to achieve goals for the future.

a. 130-30 fund
b. 100-year flood
c. 1921 recession
d. Resource allocation

72. _____ is the concept or idea of fairness in economics, particularly as to taxation or welfare economics.

In welfare economics, _____ may be distinguished from economic efficiency in overall evaluation of social welfare. Although '_____' has broader uses, it may be posed as a counterpart to economic inequality in yielding a 'good' distribution of welfare.

a. ACCRA Cost of Living Index
b. ACEA agreement
c. AD-IA Model
d. Equity

73. In calculus, a function f defined on a subset of the real numbers with real values is called _____, if for all x and y such that x >≤ y one has f(x) >≤ f(y), so f preserves the order. In layman's terms, the sign of the slope is always positive (the curve tending upwards) or zero (i.e., non-decreasing, or asymptotic, or depicted as a horizontal, flat line) Likewise, a function is called monotonically decreasing (non-increasing) if, whenever x >≤ y, then f(x) >≥ f(y), so it reverses the order.

a. 1921 recession
b. 100-year flood
c. Monotonic
d. 130-30 fund

74. In economics, a _____ occurs when, due to the economies of scale of a particular industry, the maximum efficiency of production and distribution is realized through a single supplier.

Natural monopolies arise where the largest supplier in an industry, often the first supplier in a market, has an overwhelming cost advantage over other actual or potential competitors. This tends to be the case in industries where capital costs predominate, creating economies of scale which are large in relation to the size of the market, and hence high barriers to entry; examples include water services and electricity.

a. Privatizing profits and socializing losses
b. Collective goods
c. Common-pool resource
d. Natural monopoly

75. Many _____ are related to the environmental consequences of production and use

- Systemic risk describes the risks to the overall economy arising from the risks which the banking system takes. That the private costs of banking failure may be smaller than the social costs justifies banking regulations, although regulations could create a moral hazard.

- Anthropogenic climate change is attributed to greenhouse gas emissions from burning oil, gas, and coal. Global warming has been ranked as the #1 externality of all economic activity, in the magnitude of potential harms and yet remains unmitigated.

a. Green certificate
b. Total Economic Value
c. White certificates
d. Negative externalities

76. Examples of _____ include:

- A beekeeper keeps the bees for their honey. A side effect or externality associated with his activity is the pollination of surrounding crops by the bees. The value generated by the pollination may be more important than the value of the harvested honey.

- An individual planting an attractive garden in front of his house may provide benefits to others living in the area, and even financial benefits in the form of increased property values for all property owners.

- An individual buying a product that is interconnected in a network (e.g., a video cellphone) will increase the usefulness of such phones to other people who have a video cellphone. When each new user of a product increases the value of the same product owned by others, the phenomenon is called a network externality or a network effect. Network externalities often have 'tipping points' where, suddenly, the product reaches general acceptance and near-universal usage, a phenomenon which can be seen in the near universal take-up of cellphones in some Scandinavian countries.

- Knowledge spillover of inventions and information - once an invention (or most other forms of practical information) is discovered or made more easily accessible, others benefit by exploiting the invention or information. Copyright and intellectual property law are mechanisms to allow the inventor or creator to benefit from a temporary, state-protected monopoly in return for 'sharing' the information through publication or other means.

a. Positive externalities
b. Total Economic Value
c. Weighted average cost of carbon
d. Negative externalities

77. _____s are externalities of economic activity or processes upon those who are not directly involved in it. Odours from a rendering plant are negative _____s upon its neighbours; the beauty of a homeowner's flower garden is a positive _____ upon neighbours.

In the same way, the economic benefits of increased trade are the _____s anticipated in the formation of multilateral alliances of many of the regional nation states: e.g. SARC (South Asian Regional Cooperation), ASpillover effectAN (Association of South East Asian Nations)

In reference to psychology, the _____ is when other people's emotions affect the emotions of those around them.

a. Business sector
b. Cobb-Douglas
c. Public good
d. Spillover effect

78. In economics, a _____ is a good that is non-rivaled and non-excludable. This means, respectively, that consumption of the good by one individual does not reduce availability of the good for consumption by others; and that no one can be effectively excluded from using the good. In the real world, there may be no such thing as an absolutely non-rivaled and non-excludable good; but economists think that some goods approximate the concept closely enough for the analysis to be economically useful.

a. Happiness economics
b. Neoclassical synthesis
c. Demand-pull theory
d. Public good

79. The _____ is a measure of statistical dispersion, commonly used as a measure of inequality of income distribution or inequality of wealth distribution. It is defined as a ratio with values between 0 and 1: A low _____ indicates more equal income or wealth distribution, while a high _____ indicates more unequal distribution. 0 corresponds to perfect equality (everyone having exactly the same income) and 1 corresponds to perfect inequality (where one person has all the income, while everyone else has zero income.)

a. Suits index
b. Compensating variation
c. Leapfrogging
d. Gini coefficient

80. _____ is the prospect that a party insulated from risk may behave differently from the way it would behave if it were fully exposed to the risk. In insurance, _____ that occurs without conscious or malicious action is called morale hazard.

_____ is related to information asymmetry, a situation in which one party in a transaction has more information than another.

a. Moral hazard
b. 1921 recession
c. 100-year flood
d. 130-30 fund

81. In mathematics, a _____ is a constant multiplicative factor of a certain object. For example, in the expression $9x^2$, the _____ of x^2 is 9.

The object can be such things as a variable, a vector, a function, etc.

a. 130-30 fund
b. 1921 recession
c. 100-year flood
d. Coefficient

82. In mathematics, an _____ is a statement about the relative size or order of two objects, or about whether they are the same or not

- The notation a < b means that a is less than b.
- The notation a > b means that a is greater than b.
- The notation a ≠ b means that a is not equal to b, but does not say that one is greater than the other or even that they can be compared in size.

In each statement above, a is not equal to b. These relations are known as strict inequalities. The notation a < b may also be read as 'a is strictly less than b'.

a. AD-IA Model
b. ACEA agreement
c. ACCRA Cost of Living Index
d. Inequality

83. To _____ is to impose a financial charge or other levy upon a taxpayer by a state or the functional equivalent of a state.

_____es are also imposed by many subnational entities. _____es consist of direct _____ or indirect _____, and may be paid in money or as its labour equivalent (often but not always unpaid.)

a. 1921 recession
c. 100-year flood
b. 130-30 fund
d. Tax

84. To tax is to impose a financial charge or other levy upon a taxpayer by a state or the functional equivalent of a state.

_____ are also imposed by many subnational entities. _____ consist of direct tax or indirect tax, and may be paid in money or as its labour equivalent (often but not always unpaid.)

a. 1921 recession
c. 100-year flood
b. Taxes
d. 130-30 fund

85. The term _____ refers to economy-wide fluctuations in production or economic activity over several months or years. These fluctuations occur around a long-term growth trend, and typically involve shifts over time between periods of relatively rapid economic growth (expansion or boom), and periods of relative stagnation or decline (contraction or recession.)

These fluctuations are often measured using the growth rate of real gross domestic product.

a. Tobit model
c. Nominal value
b. Business cycle
d. Consumer theory

86. _____ is a term that refers both to:

- a formal discipline used to help appraise, or assess, the case for a project or proposal, which itself is a process known as project appraisal; and
- an informal approach to making decisions of any kind.

Under both definitions the process involves, whether explicitly or implicitly, weighing the total expected costs against the total expected benefits of one or more actions in order to choose the best or most profitable option. The formal process is often referred to as either CBA (_____) or BCost-benefit analysis

A hallmark of CBA is that all benefits and all costs are expressed in money terms, and are adjusted for the time value of money, so that all flows of benefits and flows of project costs over time (which tend to occur at different points in time) are expressed on a common basis in terms of their e;present value.e; Closely related, but slightly different, formal techniques include Cost-effectiveness analysis, Economic impact analysis, Fiscal impact analysis and Social Return on Investment(SROI) analysis. The latter builds upon the logic of _____, but differs in that it is explicitly designed to inform the practical decision-making of enterprise managers and investors focused on optimising their social and environmental impacts.

a. Decision theory
b. 130-30 fund
c. 100-year flood
d. Cost-benefit analysis

87. _____ refers to an absence of excessive fluctuations in the macroeconomy. An economy with fairly constant output growth and low and stable inflation would be considered economically stable. An economy with frequent large recessions, a pronounced business cycle, very high or variable inflation, or frequent financial crises would be considered economically unstable.

a. Income effect
b. Export subsidy
c. Economic stability
d. Export-led growth

88. The term _____ refers to government debt, expenditures and revenues, or to finance (particularly financial revenue) in general.

- _____ deficit is the budget deficit of federal or local government
- _____ policy is the discretionary spending of governments. Contrasts with monetary policy.
- _____ year and _____ quarter are reporting periods for firms and other agencies.

a. Drawdown
b. Procter ' Gamble
c. Bucket shop
d. Fiscal

89. In economics, _____ is the use of government spending and revenue collection to influence the economy.

_____ can be contrasted with the other main type of economic policy, monetary policy, which attempts to stabilize the economy by controlling interest rates and the supply of money. The two main instruments of _____ are government spending and taxation.

a. 100-year flood
b. Fiscalism
c. Sustainable investment rule
d. Fiscal policy

90. In economics, _____ is the transfer of income, wealth or property from some individuals to others.

One premise of _____ is that money should be distributed to benefit the poorer members of society, and that the rich have an obligation to assist the poor, thus creating a more financially egalitarian society. Another argument is that the rich exploit the poor or otherwise gain unfair benefits.

a. Redistribution
b. 130-30 fund
c. 100-year flood
d. 1921 recession

91. _____, 1st Baron Keynes was a renowned economist from Britain whose many ideas on economic and political theories as well as on many governments' monetary policies influenced America. He advocated a government that played an active role in the lives of people regarding business, economy, etc. In this role, the government would use fiscal measures to reduce the consequences of recessions, economic depressions and booms.

a. Adolf Hitler
b. Adolph Fischer
c. John Maynard Keynes
d. Adam Smith

92. _____ and Keynesian Theory) is a macroeconomic theory based on the ideas of 20th-century British economist John Maynard Keynes. _____ argues that private sector decisions sometimes lead to inefficient macroeconomic outcomes and therefore advocates active policy responses by the public sector, including monetary policy actions by the central bank and fiscal policy actions by the government to stabilize output over the business cycle.

The theories forming the basis of _____ were first presented in The General Theory of Employment, Interest and Money, published in 1936.

a. Keynesian economics
b. Rational choice theory
c. Market failure
d. Deflation

93. The _____ was a fundamental reworking of economic theory concerning the factors determining employment levels in the overall economy. The revolution was set against the orthodox classical economic framework, which based on Say's Law argued that unless special conditions prevailed the free market would naturally establish full employment equilibrium with no need for government intervention. Employers will be able to make a profit by employing all available workers as long as workers drop their wages below the value of the total output they are able to produce - and classical economics assumed that in a free market workers would be willing to lower their wage demands accordingly, because they are rational agents who would rather work for less than face unemployment.

a. Military Keynesianism
b. Speculative demand
c. Neo-Keynesian economics
d. Keynesian revolution

94. _____ is the process by which the government, central bank (ii) availability of money, and (iii) cost of money or rate of interest, in order to attain a set of objectives oriented towards the growth and stability of the economy. Monetary theory provides insight into how to craft optimal _____.

_____ is referred to as either being an expansionary policy where an expansionary policy increases the total supply of money in the economy, and a contractionary policy decreases the total money supply.

a. Monetary policy
b. 1921 recession
c. 130-30 fund
d. 100-year flood

95. A _____ is a tax by which the tax rate increases as the taxable amount increases. 'Progressive' describes a distribution effect on income or expenditure, referring to the way the rate progresses from low to high, where the average tax rate is less than the marginal tax rate. It can be applied to individual taxes or to a tax system as a whole; a year, multi-year, or lifetime.

a. Proportional tax
b. Progressive tax
c. 130-30 fund
d. 100-year flood

96. In economics, a _____ is a general slowdown in economic activity over a sustained period of time, or a business cycle contraction. During _____s, many macroeconomic indicators vary in a similar way. Production as measured by Gross Domestic Product (GDP), employment, investment spending, capacity utilization, household incomes and business profits all fall during _____s.

Chapter 2. Markets and Government in a Modern Economy 31

a. Recession
b. Treasury View
c. Leading indicators
d. Monetary economics

97. In economics, a _____ is a redistribution of income in the market system. These payments are considered to be nonexhaustive because they do not directly absorb resources or create output. Examples of certain _____s include welfare (financial aid), social security, and government subsidies for certain businesses (firms.)
   a. 130-30 fund
   b. 100-year flood
   c. 1921 recession
   d. Transfer payment

98. The term surplus is used in economics for several related quantities. The _____ is the amount that consumers benefit by being able to purchase a product for a price that is less than they would be willing to pay. The producer surplus is the amount that producers benefit by selling at a market price mechanism that is higher than they would be willing to sell for.
   a. Necessity good
   b. Microeconomic reform
   c. Consumer surplus
   d. Marginal rate of technical substitution

99. A _____ is the transfer of wealth from one party (such as a person or company) to another. A _____ is usually made in exchange for the provision of goods, services or both, or to fulfill a legal obligation.

The simplest and oldest form of _____ is barter, the exchange of one good or service for another.

   a. Payment
   b. Soft count
   c. Going concern
   d. Social gravity

100. _____ in economics refers to metrics and measures of output from production processes, per unit of input. Labor _____, for example, is typically measured as a ratio of output per labor-hour, an input. _____ may be conceived of as a metrics of the technical or engineering efficiency of production.
   a. Piece work
   b. Production-possibility frontier
   c. Fordism
   d. Productivity

101. _____ was an American economist, statistician and public intellectual, and a recipient of the Nobel Memorial Prize in Economic Sciences. He is best known among scholars for his theoretical and empirical research, especially consumption analysis, monetary history and theory, and for his demonstration of the complexity of stabilization policy. A global public followed his restatement of a political philosophy that insisted on minimizing the role of government in favor of the private sector.
   a. Adolf Hitler
   b. Adam Smith
   c. Adolph Fischer
   d. Milton Friedman

102. _____ is the public sector analogy to market failure and occurs when a government intervention causes a more inefficient allocation of goods and resources than would occur without that intervention. Likewise, the government's failure to intervene in a market failure that would result in a socially preferable mix of output is referred to as passive _____ (Weimer and Vining, 2004.) Just as with market failures, there are many different kinds of _____s that describe corresponding distortions.
   a. Government-granted monopoly
   b. Privatizing profits and socializing losses
   c. Natural monopoly
   d. Government failure

Chapter 2. Markets and Government in a Modern Economy

103. _____ is the socio-economic status of unfree peasants under feudalism, and specifically relates to Manorialism. It was a condition of bondage or modified slavery which developed primarily during the High Middle Ages in Europe. _____ was the enforced labour of serfs on the fields of landowners, in return for protection and the right to work on their leased fields.
   a. Metayage
   b. Serfdom
   c. Rural tenancy
   d. Landwirtschaftliche Produktionsgenossenschaft

104. _____ in political thought refers to economic theories of social organization advocating collective ownership and administration of the means of production and distribution of goods, and a society characterized by equality for all individuals, with an egalitarian method of compensation. Modern _____ originated in the late 19th-century intellectual and working class political movement that criticized the effects of industrialization and private ownership on society. Karl Marx posited that _____ would be achieved via class struggle and a proletarian revolution after a transitional stage from capitalism called the dictatorship of the proletariat.
   a. Socialism
   b. Adolph Fischer
   c. Adolf Hitler
   d. Adam Smith

Chapter 3. Basic Elements of Supply and Demand　　　　33

1. _____ is a broad label that refers to any individuals or households that use goods and services generated within the economy. The concept of a _____ is used in different contexts, so that the usage and significance of the term may vary.

Typically when business people and economists talk of _____s they are talking about person as _____, an aggregated commodity item with little individuality other than that expressed in the buy/not-buy decision.

- a. 130-30 fund
- b. 1921 recession
- c. 100-year flood
- d. Consumer

2. A _____ is an object whose consumption increases the utility of the consumer, for which the quantity demanded exceeds the quantity supplied at zero price. _____s are usually modeled as having diminishing marginal utility. The first individual purchase has high utility; the second has less.
- a. Composite good
- b. Merit good
- c. Good
- d. Pie method

3. In economics, economic output is divided into physical goods and intangible services. Consumption of _____ is assumed to produce utility. It is often used when referring to a _____ Tax.
- a. Private good
- b. Manufactured goods
- c. Composite good
- d. Goods and services

4. _____ is an economic concept with commonplace familiarity. It is the price that a good or service is offered at, or will fetch, in the marketplace. It is of interest mainly in the study of microeconomics.
- a. Market price
- b. Market anomaly
- c. Paper trading
- d. Noisy market hypothesis

5. _____ in economics and business is the result of an exchange and from that trade we assign a numerical monetary value to a good, service or asset. If Alice trades Bob 4 apples for an orange, the _____ of an orange is 4 apples. Inversely, the _____ of an apple is 1/4 oranges.
- a. Premium pricing
- b. Price war
- c. Price book
- d. Price

6. _____ is defined as the measure of responsiveness in the quantity demanded for a commodity as a result of change in price of the same commodity. It is a measure of how consumers react to a change in price. In other words, it is percentage change in quantity demanded as per the percentage change in price of the same commodity.
- a. 1921 recession
- b. 130-30 fund
- c. 100-year flood
- d. Price elasticity of demand

7. In economics, the _____ is defined as a numerical measure of the responsiveness of the quantity supplied of product (A) to a change in price of product (A) alone. It is the measure of the way quantity supplied reacts to a change in price.

For example, if, in response to a 10% rise in the price of a good, the quantity supplied increases by 20%, the _____ would be 20%/10% = 2.

Chapter 3. Basic Elements of Supply and Demand

    a. Passive income
    b. Demand shaping
    c. Hedonimetry
    d. Price elasticity of supply

8. A _____ or market-based mechanism is any of a wide variety of ways to match up buyers and sellers.

An example of a _____ uses announced bid and ask prices. Generally speaking, when two parties wish to engage in a trade, the purchaser will announce a price he is willing to pay (the bid price) and seller will announce a price he is willing to accept (the ask price.)

    a. Horizontal market
    b. Price mechanism
    c. Marketization
    d. Market equilibrium

9. _____ is an economic model based on price, utility and quantity in a market. It predicts that in a competitive market, price will function to equalize the quantity demanded by consumers, and the quantity supplied by producers, resulting in an economic equilibrium of price and quantity. The model incorporates other factors changing equilibrium as a shift of demand and/or supply.

    a. Supply and demand
    b. Rational addiction
    c. Joint demand
    d. Deferred gratification

10. Competition law, known in the United States as _____ law, has three main elements:

- prohibiting agreements or practices that restrict free trading and competition between business entities. This includes in particular the repression of cartels.
- banning abusive behaviour by a firm dominating a market, or anti-competitive practices that tend to lead to such a dominant position. Practices controlled in this way may include predatory pricing, tying, price gouging, refusal to deal, and many others.
- supervising the mergers and acquisitions of large corporations, including some joint ventures. Transactions that are considered to threaten the competitive process can be prohibited altogether, or approved subject to 'remedies' such as an obligation to divest part of the merged business or to offer licences or access to facilities to enable other businesses to continue competing.

The substance and practice of competition law varies from jurisdiction to jurisdiction. Protecting the interests of consumers (consumer welfare) and ensuring that entrepreneurs have an opportunity to compete in the market economy are often treated as important objectives. Competition law is closely connected with law on deregulation of access to markets, state aids and subsidies, the privatisation of state owned assets and the establishment of independent sector regulators. In recent decades, competition law has been viewed as a way to provide better public services.

    a. Intellectual property law
    b. United Kingdom competition law
    c. Anti-Inflation Act
    d. Antitrust

11. In economics, _____ is equal to total cost divided by the number of goods produced (the output quantity, Q.) It is also equal to the sum of average variable costs (total variable costs divided by Q) plus average fixed costs (total fixed costs divided by Q.) _____s may be dependent on the time period considered (increasing production may be expensive or impossible in the short term, for example.)

Chapter 3. Basic Elements of Supply and Demand

a. Average variable cost
b. Average fixed cost
c. Average cost
d. Explicit cost

12. In economics, the term _____ of income or _____ refers to a simple economic model which describes the reciprocal circulation of income between producers and consumers. In the _____ model, the inter-dependent entities of producer and consumer are referred to as 'firms' and 'households' respectively and provide each other with factors in order to facilitate the flow of income. Firms provide consumers with goods and services in exchange for consumer expenditure and 'factors of production' from households.
   a. 130-30 fund
   b. 1921 recession
   c. 100-year flood
   d. Circular flow

13. Economics:

- _____, the desire to own something and the ability to pay for it
- _____ curve, a graphic representation of a _____ schedule
- _____ deposit, the money in checking accounts
- _____ pull theory, the theory that inflation occurs when _____ for goods and services exceeds existing supplies
- _____ schedule, a table that lists the quantity of a good a person will buy it each different price
- _____ side economics, the school of economics at believes government spending and tax cuts open economy by raising _____

   a. McKesson ' Robbins scandal
   b. Production
   c. Variability
   d. Demand

14. In economics, _____ is the ratio of the percent change in one variable to the percent change in another variable. It is a tool for measuring the responsiveness of a function to changes in parameters in a relative way. Commonly analyzed are _____ of substitution, price and wealth.
   a. ACCRA Cost of Living Index
   b. Elasticity of demand
   c. Elasticity
   d. ACEA agreement

15. Price _____ is defined as the measure of responsiveness in the quantity demanded for a commodity as a result of change in price of the same commodity. It is a measure of how consumers react to a change in price. In other words, it is percentage change in quantity demanded by the percentage change in price of the same commodity.
   a. ACEA agreement
   b. Elasticity
   c. Elasticity of demand
   d. ACCRA Cost of Living Index

16. In microeconomics, _____ is quite simply the conversion of inputs into outputs. It is an economic process that uses resources to create a good or service that is suitable for exchange. This can include manufacturing, storing, shipping, and packaging.
   a. Solved
   b. Red Guards
   c. MET
   d. Production

17. _____ is a concept with somewhat disparate meanings in several fields. It also has a common meaning which has a loose connection with some of those more definite meanings.

Casually, it is typically used to denote a lack of order, or purpose, or cause.

a. 1921 recession
b. 130-30 fund
c. 100-year flood
d. Randomness

18. In economics, the _____ can be defined as the graph depicting the relationship between the price of a certain commodity, and the amount of it that consumers are willing and able to purchase at that given price. It is a graphic representation of a demand schedule. The _____ for all consumers together follows from the _____ of every individual consumer: the individual demands at each price are added together.

a. Kuznets curve
b. Cost curve
c. Wage curve
d. Demand curve

19. In economics, a _____ is a table that lists the quantity of a good a person will buy it each different price See Demand curve.

a. Federal Reserve districts
b. Rational irrationality
c. Demand schedule
d. Free contract

20. Necessary _____s:

If x is a necessary _____ of y, then the presence of y necessarily implies the presence of x. The presence of x, however, does not imply that y will occur.

Sufficient _____s:

If x is a sufficient _____ of y, then the presence of x necessarily implies the presence of y.

a. Philosophy of economics
b. Political philosophy
c. Cause
d. Materialism

21. In economics, the _____ is the change in consumption resulting from a change in real income.

Another important item that can change is the money income of the consumer. The _____ is the phenomenon observed through changes in purchasing power.

a. Equilibrium wage
b. Inflation hedge
c. Income effect
d. Export subsidy

22. In economics, _____ refers to how the marginal contribution of a factor of production usually decreases as more of the factor is used. According to this relationship, in a production system with fixed and variable inputs, beyond some point, each additional unit of the variable input yields smaller and smaller increases in output. Conversely, producing one more unit of output costs more and more in variable inputs.

a. Patent troll
b. Derivatives law
c. Community property
d. Diminishing returns

Chapter 3. Basic Elements of Supply and Demand 37

23. _____ is the term denoting either an entrance or changes which are inserted into a system and which activate/modify a process. It is an abstract concept, used in the modeling, system(s) design and system(s) exploitation. It is usually connected with other terms, e.g., _____ field, _____ variable, _____ parameter, _____ value, _____ signal, _____ device and _____ file.
   a. Input
   b. ACCRA Cost of Living Index
   c. AD-IA Model
   d. ACEA agreement

24. In algebra, a _____ is a function depending on n that associates a scalar, det(A), to an n×n square matrix A. The fundamental geometric meaning of a _____ is a scale factor for measure when A is regarded as a linear transformation. _____s are important both in calculus, where they enter the substitution rule for several variables, and in multilinear algebra.

For a fixed nonnegative integer n, there is a unique _____ function for the n×n matrices over any commutative ring R. In particular, this function exists when R is the field of real or complex numbers.

   a. 1921 recession
   b. 100-year flood
   c. Determinant
   d. 130-30 fund

25. _____ theory is a branch of theoretical economics. It seeks to explain the behavior of supply, demand and prices in a whole economy with several or many markets. It is often assumed that agents are price takers and in that setting two common notions of equilibrium exist: Walrasian (or competitive) equilibrium, and its generalization; a price equilibrium with transfers.
   a. Rational choice theory
   b. General equilibrium
   c. Human capital
   d. New Keynesian economics

26. In economics, economic equilibrium is simply a state of the world where economic forces are balanced and in the absence of external influences the (equilibrium) values of economic variables will not change. It is the point at which quantity demanded and quantity supplied are equal. _____, for example, refers to a condition where a market price is established through competition such that the amount of goods or services sought by buyers is equal to the amount of goods or services produced by sellers.
   a. Regulated market
   b. Product-Market Growth Matrix
   c. Marketization
   d. Market equilibrium

27. The _____ is a heterodox school of economics that emphasizes the spontaneous organizing power of the price mechanism. It holds that the complexity of subjective human choices makes mathematical modelling of the evolving market extremely difficult and advocates a laissez faire approach to the economy. _____ economists advocate the enforcement of voluntary contractual agreements between economic agents, but otherwise the smallest imposition of coercive force on commercial transactions.
   a. ACEA agreement
   b. Economic calculation problem
   c. ACCRA Cost of Living Index
   d. Austrian School

28. _____ to the arrival of new individuals into a habitat or population. It is a biological concept and is important in population ecology, differentiated from emigration and migration.

_____ is a modern phenomenon.

a. ACEA agreement
b. AD-IA Model
c. ACCRA Cost of Living Index
d. Immigration

29. _____ is a term in economics, where demand for one good or service occurs as a result of demand for another. This may occur as the former is a part of production of the second. For example, demand for coal leads to _____ for mining, as coal must be mined for coal to be consumed.
   a. Leontief production function
   b. Derived demand
   c. Days Sales Outstanding
   d. Rate risk

30. _____ is a term from economics referring to the use of money exchanged by buyers and sellers with an open and understood system of value and time trade offs to produce the best distribution of goods and services. The use of the _____ does not imply a free market: there can be captive or controlled markets which seek to use supply and demand, or some other form of charging for scarcity, both in social situations and in engineering.

The _____ assumes perfect competition and is regulated by demand and supply.

   a. Partial equilibrium
   b. Market mechanism
   c. Two-sided markets
   d. Product-Market Growth Matrix

31. _____ is the controlled distribution of resources and scarce goods or services. _____ controls the size of the ration, one's allotted portion of the resources being distributed on a particular day or at a particular time.

In economics, it is often common to use the word '_____' to refer to one of the roles that prices play in markets, while _____ is called 'non-price _____.' Using prices to ration means that those with the most money (or other assets) and who want a product the most are first to receive it.

   a. Rationing
   b. 100-year flood
   c. 130-30 fund
   d. 1921 recession

32. _____s is the social science that studies the production, distribution, and consumption of goods and services. The term _____s comes from the Ancient Greek oá¼°κονομῖα from oá¼¶κος (oikos, 'house') + νÏŒμος (nomos, 'custom' or 'law'), hence 'rules of the house(hold)'. Current _____ models developed out of the broader field of political economy in the late 19th century, owing to a desire to use an empirical approach more akin to the physical sciences.
   a. Economic
   b. Inflation
   c. Energy economics
   d. Opportunity cost

33. The _____, sometimes called the fundamental _____, is one of the fundamental economic theories in the operation of any economy. It asserts that there is scarcity, that the finite resources available are insufficient to satisfy all human wants. The problem then becomes how to determine what is to be produced and how the factors of production (such as capital and labour) are to be allocated.
   a. Eclectic paradigm
   b. Economic problem
   c. Economic nationalism
   d. Endogenous growth theory

Chapter 4. Applications of Supply and Demand

1. _____ is a branch of economics that studies how individuals, households and firms and some states make decisions to allocate limited resources, typically in markets where goods or services are being bought and sold. _____ examines how these decisions and behaviours affect the supply and demand for goods and services, which determines prices; and how prices, in turn , determine the supply and demand of goods and services.

Whereas macroeconomics involves the 'sum total of economic activity, dealing with the issues of growth, inflation and unemployment, and with national economic policies relating to these issues' and the effects of government actions on them.

- a. Countercyclical
- b. Microeconomics
- c. Recession
- d. New Keynesian economics

2. _____ in economics and business is the result of an exchange and from that trade we assign a numerical monetary value to a good, service or asset. If Alice trades Bob 4 apples for an orange, the _____ of an orange is 4 apples. Inversely, the _____ of an apple is 1/4 oranges.
- a. Price book
- b. Price war
- c. Premium pricing
- d. Price

3. _____ is a mechanism that allows people easily to buy and sell products. Services are often included in the scope of the term. _____ regulation is an economic term that describes restrictions in the market.
- a. Financialization
- b. Fixed exchange rate system
- c. Product market
- d. Market dominance

4. _____ is an economic model based on price, utility and quantity in a market. It predicts that in a competitive market, price will function to equalize the quantity demanded by consumers, and the quantity supplied by producers, resulting in an economic equilibrium of price and quantity. The model incorporates other factors changing equilibrium as a shift of demand and/or supply.
- a. Deferred gratification
- b. Joint demand
- c. Rational addiction
- d. Supply and demand

5. Economics:

- _____,the desire to own something and the ability to pay for it
- _____ curve,a graphic representation of a _____ schedule
- _____ deposit, the money in checking accounts
- _____ pull theory,the theory that inflation occurs when _____ for goods and services exceeds existing supplies
- _____ schedule,a table that lists the quantity of a good a person will buy it each different price
- _____ side economics,the school of economics at believes government spending and tax cuts open economy by raising _____

- a. Variability
- b. Production
- c. McKesson ' Robbins scandal
- d. Demand

Chapter 4. Applications of Supply and Demand

6. In economics, _____ is the ratio of the percent change in one variable to the percent change in another variable. It is a tool for measuring the responsiveness of a function to changes in parameters in a relative way. Commonly analyzed are _____ of substitution, price and wealth.
   a. Elasticity of demand
   b. ACCRA Cost of Living Index
   c. Elasticity
   d. ACEA agreement

7. In mathematics, a _____ is a constant multiplicative factor of a certain object. For example, in the expression $9x^2$, the _____ of x^2 is 9.

The object can be such things as a variable, a vector, a function, etc.

   a. 130-30 fund
   b. 1921 recession
   c. 100-year flood
   d. Coefficient

8. _____ is a broad label that refers to any individuals or households that use goods and services generated within the economy. The concept of a _____ is used in different contexts, so that the usage and significance of the term may vary.

Typically when business people and economists talk of _____s they are talking about person as _____, an aggregated commodity item with little individuality other than that expressed in the buy/not-buy decision.

   a. 130-30 fund
   b. 100-year flood
   c. Consumer
   d. 1921 recession

9. A _____ is an object whose consumption increases the utility of the consumer, for which the quantity demanded exceeds the quantity supplied at zero price. _____s are usually modeled as having diminishing marginal utility. The first individual purchase has high utility; the second has less.
   a. Composite good
   b. Merit good
   c. Pie method
   d. Good

10. In economics, economic output is divided into physical goods and intangible services. Consumption of _____ is assumed to produce utility. It is often used when referring to a _____ Tax.
    a. Private good
    b. Goods and services
    c. Manufactured goods
    d. Composite good

11. In economics, _____ describes demand that is not very sensitive to a change in price.
    a. Inelastic
    b. Inflation hedge
    c. Effective unemployment rate
    d. Export-led growth

12. _____ is defined as the measure of responsiveness in the quantity demanded for a commodity as a result of change in price of the same commodity. It is a measure of how consumers react to a change in price. In other words, it is percentage change in quantity demanded as per the percentage change in price of the same commodity.
    a. 1921 recession
    b. 130-30 fund
    c. 100-year flood
    d. Price elasticity of demand

Chapter 4. Applications of Supply and Demand

13. Necessary _____ s:

If x is a necessary _____ of y, then the presence of y necessarily implies the presence of x. The presence of x, however, does not imply that y will occur.

Sufficient _____ s:

If x is a sufficient _____ of y, then the presence of x necessarily implies the presence of y.

- a. Cause
- c. Materialism
- b. Political philosophy
- d. Philosophy of economics

14. Price _____ is defined as the measure of responsiveness in the quantity demanded for a commodity as a result of change in price of the same commodity. It is a measure of how consumers react to a change in price. In other words, it is percentage change in quantity demanded by the percentage change in price of the same commodity.
- a. ACCRA Cost of Living Index
- c. Elasticity
- b. ACEA agreement
- d. Elasticity of demand

15. _____ is an economic concept with commonplace familiarity. It is the price that a good or service is offered at, or will fetch, in the marketplace. It is of interest mainly in the study of microeconomics.
- a. Noisy market hypothesis
- c. Paper trading
- b. Market price
- d. Market anomaly

16. Competition law, known in the United States as _____ law, has three main elements:

- prohibiting agreements or practices that restrict free trading and competition between business entities. This includes in particular the repression of cartels.
- banning abusive behaviour by a firm dominating a market, or anti-competitive practices that tend to lead to such a dominant position. Practices controlled in this way may include predatory pricing, tying, price gouging, refusal to deal, and many others.
- supervising the mergers and acquisitions of large corporations, including some joint ventures. Transactions that are considered to threaten the competitive process can be prohibited altogether, or approved subject to 'remedies' such as an obligation to divest part of the merged business or to offer licences or access to facilities to enable other businesses to continue competing.

The substance and practice of competition law varies from jurisdiction to jurisdiction. Protecting the interests of consumers (consumer welfare) and ensuring that entrepreneurs have an opportunity to compete in the market economy are often treated as important objectives. Competition law is closely connected with law on deregulation of access to markets, state aids and subsidies, the privatisation of state owned assets and the establishment of independent sector regulators. In recent decades, competition law has been viewed as a way to provide better public services.

- a. Intellectual property law
- c. Antitrust
- b. Anti-Inflation Act
- d. United Kingdom competition law

17. In economics, the _____ can be defined as the graph depicting the relationship between the price of a certain commodity, and the amount of it that consumers are willing and able to purchase at that given price. It is a graphic representation of a demand schedule. The _____ for all consumers together follows from the _____ of every individual consumer: the individual demands at each price are added together.
   a. Demand curve
   b. Kuznets curve
   c. Wage curve
   d. Cost curve

18. _____ is a fee paid on borrowed assets. It is the price paid for the use of borrowed money, or, money earned by deposited funds. Assets that are sometimes lent with _____ include money, shares, consumer goods through hire purchase, major assets such as aircraft, and even entire factories in finance lease arrangements.
   a. Asset protection
   b. Internal debt
   c. Insolvency
   d. Interest

Chapter 4. Applications of Supply and Demand   **43**

19. A _____ is:

   - Rewrite _____, in generative grammar and computer science
   - Standardization, a formal and widely-accepted statement, fact, definition, or qualification
   - Operation, a determinate _____ for performing a mathematical operation and obtaining a certain result (Mathematics, Logic)
     - Unary operation
     - Binary operation
   - _____ of inference, a function from sets of formulae to formulae (Mathematics, Logic)
   - _____ of thumb, principle with broad application that is not intended to be strictly accurate or reliable for every situation. Also often simply referred to as a _____
   - Moral, an atomic element of a moral code for guiding choices in human behavior
   - Heuristic, a quantized '_____' which shows a tendency or probability for successful function
   - A regulation, as in sports
   - A Production _____, as in computer science
   - Procedural law, a _____ set governing the application of laws to cases
     - A law, which may informally be called a '_____'
     - A court ruling, a decision by a court
   - In the U.S. Government, a regulation mandated by Congress, but written or expanded upon by the Executive Branch.
   - Norm (sociology), an informal but widely accepted _____, concept, truth, definition, or qualification (social norms, legal norms, coding norms)
   - Norm (philosophy), a kind of sentence or a reason to act, feel or believe
   - 'Rulership' is the concept of governance by a government:
     - Military _____, governance by a military body
     - Monastic _____, a collection of precepts that guides the life of monks or nuns in a religious order where the superior holds the place of Christ
   - Slide _____

   - '_____,' a song by Ayumi Hamasaki
   - '_____,' a song by rapper Nas
   - '_____s,' an album by the band The Whitest Boy Alive
   - _____s: Pyaar Ka Superhit Formula, a 2003 Bollywood film
   - ruler, an instrument for measuring lengths
   - _____, a component of an astrolabe, circumferator or similar instrument
   - The _____s, a bestselling self-help book
   - _____ Project (Run Up-to-date Linux Everywhere), a project that aims to use up-to-date Linux software on old PCs
   - _____ engine, a software system that helps managing business _____s
   - Ja _____, a hip hop artist
     - R.U.L.E., a 2005 greatest hits album by rapper Ja _____
   - '_____s,' a KMFDM song

   a. Rule   b. Procter ' Gamble
   c. Demand   d. Technocracy

20. _____ is the total money received from the sale of any given quantity of output.

The _____ is calculated by taking the price of the sale times the quantity sold, i.e.

_____ = price X quantity.

- a. Small numbers game
- b. Total revenue
- c. Ceteris paribus
- d. Market development funds

21. _____ exists when sales of identical goods or services are transacted at different prices from the same provider. In a theoretical market with perfect information, no transaction costs or prohibition on secondary exchange (or re-selling) to prevent arbitrage, _____ can only be a feature of monopoly and oligopoly markets, where market power can be exercised. Otherwise, the moment the seller tries to sell the same good at different prices, the buyer at the lower price can arbitrage by selling to the consumer buying at the higher price but with a tiny discount.
- a. Lerner Index
- b. Loss leader
- c. Price discrimination
- d. Transfer pricing

22. The _____ is the apparent contradiction that although water is on the whole more useful, in terms of survival, than diamonds, diamonds command a higher price in the market. The economist Adam Smith is often considered to be the classic presenter of this paradox. Nicolaus Copernicus, John Locke, John Law and others had previously tried to explain the disparity.
- a. St. Petersburg paradox
- b. 100-year flood
- c. 130-30 fund
- d. Paradox of value

23. In law and economics, the _____, describes the economic efficiency of an economic allocation or outcome in the presence of externalities. The theorem states that when trade in an externality is possible and there are no transaction costs, bargaining will lead to an efficient outcome regardless of the initial allocation of property rights. In practice, obstacles to bargaining or poorly defined property rights can prevent Coasian bargaining.
- a. Coase theorem
- b. General Mining Act of 1872
- c. Prior appropriation water rights
- d. Means test

24. In economics, the _____ is defined as a numerical measure of the responsiveness of the quantity supplied of product (A) to a change in price of product (A) alone. It is the measure of the way quantity supplied reacts to a change in price.

For example, if, in response to a 10% rise in the price of a good, the quantity supplied increases by 20%, the _____ would be 20%/10% = 2.

- a. Hedonimetry
- b. Demand shaping
- c. Passive income
- d. Price elasticity of supply

25. To _____ is to impose a financial charge or other levy upon a taxpayer by a state or the functional equivalent of a state.

Chapter 4. Applications of Supply and Demand   45

_____es are also imposed by many subnational entities. _____es consist of direct _____ or indirect _____, and may be paid in money or as its labour equivalent (often but not always unpaid.)

   a. 100-year flood   b. 130-30 fund
   c. 1921 recession   d. Tax

26. To tax is to impose a financial charge or other levy upon a taxpayer by a state or the functional equivalent of a state.

_____ are also imposed by many subnational entities. _____ consist of direct tax or indirect tax, and may be paid in money or as its labour equivalent (often but not always unpaid.)

   a. 1921 recession   b. 130-30 fund
   c. 100-year flood   d. Taxes

27. In economics, _____ are the resources employed to produce goods and services. They facilitate production but do not become part of the product (as with raw materials) or significantly transformed by the production process (as with fuel used to power machinery.) To 19th century economists, the _____ were land (natural resources, gifts from nature), labor (the ability to work), and capital goods (human-made tools and equipment.)
   a. Hicks-neutral technical change   b. Factors of production
   c. Product Pipeline   d. Long-run

28. In microeconomics, _____ is quite simply the conversion of inputs into outputs. It is an economic process that uses resources to create a good or service that is suitable for exchange. This can include manufacturing, storing, shipping, and packaging.
   a. Solved   b. MET
   c. Red Guards   d. Production

29. A _____ is a measure of the average price of consumer goods and services purchased by households. A _____ measures a price change for a constant market basket of goods and services from one period to the next within the same area (city, region, or nation.) It is a price index determined by measuring the price of a standard group of goods meant to represent the typical market basket of a typical urban consumer.
   a. CPI   b. Cost-of-living index
   c. Lipstick index   d. Consumer price index

30. _____s is the social science that studies the production, distribution, and consumption of goods and services. The term _____s comes from the Ancient Greek oá¼°κονομῑα from oá¼¶κος (oikos, 'house') + vÏŒμος (nomos, 'custom' or 'law'), hence 'rules of the house(hold)'. Current _____ models developed out of the broader field of political economy in the late 19th century, owing to a desire to use an empirical approach more akin to the physical sciences.
   a. Economic   b. Energy economics
   c. Inflation   d. Opportunity cost

31. In economic models, the _____ time frame assumes no fixed factors of production. Firms can enter or leave the marketplace, and the cost (and availability) of land, labor, raw materials, and capital goods can be assumed to vary. In contrast, in the short-run time frame, certain factors are assumed to be fixed, because there is not sufficient time for them to change.

a. Long-run
b. Productivity world
c. Price/performance ratio
d. Diseconomies of scale

32. _____ is the shortage of common things such as food, clothing, shelter and safe drinking water, all of which determine the quality of life. It may also include the lack of access to opportunities such as education and employment which aid the escape from _____ and/or allow one to enjoy the respect of fellow citizens. According to Mollie Orshansky who developed the _____ measurements used by the U.S. government, 'to be poor is to be deprived of those goods and services and pleasures which others around us take for granted.' Ongoing debates over causes, effects and best ways to measure _____, directly influence the design and implementation of _____-reduction programs and are therefore relevant to the fields of public administration and international development.
a. Poverty map
b. Liberal welfare reforms
c. Growth Elasticity of Poverty
d. Poverty

33. A _____ is a normalized average (typically a weighted average) of prices for a given class of goods or services in a given region, during a given interval of time. It is a statistic designed to help to compare how these prices, taken as a whole, differ between time periods or geographical locations.

Price indices have several potential uses.

a. Price index
b. Two-part tariff
c. Product sabotage
d. Transactional Net Margin Method

34. The _____ is the labour pool in employment. It is generally used to describe those working for a single company or industry, but can also apply to a geographic region like a city, country, state, etc. The term generally excludes the employers or management, and implies those involved in manual labour.
a. Collective bargaining
b. Grenelle agreements
c. Departmentalization
d. Workforce

35. In economics, tax incidence is the analysis of the effect of a particular tax on the distribution of economic welfare. Tax incidence is said to 'fall' upon the group that, at the end of the day, bears the burden of the tax. The key concept is that the tax incidence or _____ does not depend on where the revenue is collected, but on the price elasticity of demand and price elasticity of supply.
a. 130-30 fund
b. 1921 recession
c. 100-year flood
d. Tax burden

36. In economics, an _____ or spillover of an economic transaction is an impact on a party that is not directly involved in the transaction. In such a case, prices do not reflect the full costs or benefits in production or consumption of a product or service. A positive impact is called an external benefit, while a negative impact is called an external cost.
a. Environmental tariff
b. Existence value
c. Environmental impact assessment
d. Externality

37. _____ was a survey conducted by the U.S. Department of Justice to gauge the prevalence of alcohol and illegal drug use among prior arrestees. It was a reformulation of the prior Drug Use Forecasting (DUF) program, focused on five drugs in particular: cocaine, marijuana, methamphetamine, opiates, and PCP.

Chapter 4. Applications of Supply and Demand   47

Participants were randomly selected from arrest records in major metropolitan areas; because no personally identifying information is taken from each record chosen, the resulting data can be correlated to arrest rates, but not to the total population of persons charged.

- a. ACEA agreement
- b. AD-IA Model
- c. ACCRA Cost of Living Index
- d. Arrestee Drug Abuse Monitoring

38. _____ and Keynesian Theory) is a macroeconomic theory based on the ideas of 20th-century British economist John Maynard Keynes. _____ argues that private sector decisions sometimes lead to inefficient macroeconomic outcomes and therefore advocates active policy responses by the public sector, including monetary policy actions by the central bank and fiscal policy actions by the government to stabilize output over the business cycle.

The theories forming the basis of _____ were first presented in The General Theory of Employment, Interest and Money, published in 1936.

- a. Deflation
- b. Market failure
- c. Rational choice theory
- d. Keynesian economics

39. A _____ is the lowest hourly, daily or monthly wage that employers may legally pay to employees or workers. Equivalently, it is the lowest wage at which workers may sell their labor. Although _____ laws are in effect in a great many jurisdictions, there are differences of opinion about the benefits and drawbacks of a _____.

- a. Permanent war economy
- b. Marginal propensity to consume
- c. Microfoundations
- d. Minimum wage

40. A _____ is a government- or group-imposed limit on how low a price can be charged for a product. In order for a _____ to be effective, it must be greater than the equilibrium price. An ineffective _____, below equilibrium price.

A _____ can be set below the free-market equilibrium price.

- a. Flat rate
- b. Two-part tariff
- c. Price markdown
- d. Price floor

41. Economic _____ is defined as an excess distribution to any factor in a production process above that which is required to induce the factor into the process or any excess above that which is necessary to keep the factor in its current use..

Classical Factor _____ is primarily concerned with the fee paid for the use of fixed (e.g. natural) resources. The classical definition is expressed as any excess payment above that required to induce or provide for production.

- a. Rent
- b. 1921 recession
- c. 130-30 fund
- d. 100-year flood

42. _____ refers to laws or ordinances that set price controls on the renting of residential housing. It functions as a price ceiling.

48 *Chapter 4. Applications of Supply and Demand*

_____ exists in approximately 40 countries around the world.

   a. 100-year flood
   c. National Housing Conference
   b. Rent control
   d. Tenant rights

43. _____ was a Scottish moral philosopher and a pioneer of political economy. One of the key figures of the Scottish Enlightenment, Smith is the author of The Theory of Moral Sentiments and An Inquiry into the Nature and Causes of the Wealth of Nations. The latter, usually abbreviated as The Wealth of Nations, is considered his magnum opus and the first modern work of economics.

   a. Adolf Hitler
   c. Adam Smith
   b. Alan Greenspan
   d. Adolph Fischer

44. In economics, the people in the _____ are the suppliers of labor. The _____ is all the nonmilitary people who are employed or unemployed. In 2005, the worldwide _____ was over 3 billion people.

   a. Departmentalization
   c. Grenelle agreements
   b. Distributed workforce
   d. Labor force

45. A variety of measures of _____ and output are used in economics to estimate total economic activity in a country or region, including gross domestic product (GDP), gross national product (GNP), and net _____

There are three main ways of calculating these numbers; the output approach, the income approach and the expenditure approach. In theory, the three must yield the same, because total expenditures on goods and services must equal the total income paid to the producers (Gnational income), and that must also equal the total value of the output of goods and services (GNP.)

   a. Volume index
   c. National income
   b. Gross world product
   d. GNI per capita

46. A _____ is a government imposed limit on how high a price can be charged on a product. For a _____ to be effective, it must differ from the free market price. In the graph at right, the supply and demand curves intersect to determine the free-market quantity and price.

   a. Product sabotage
   c. Fire sale
   b. Pricing
   d. Price ceiling

47. A _____ represents the combinations of goods and services that a consumer can purchase given current prices and his income. Consumer theory uses the concepts of a _____ and a preference map to analyze consumer choices. Both concepts have a ready graphical representation in the two-good case.

   a. Budget constraint
   c. Joint demand
   b. Quality bias
   d. Revealed preference

48. _____ is the controlled distribution of resources and scarce goods or services. _____ controls the size of the ration, one's allotted portion of the resources being distributed on a particular day or at a particular time.

In economics, it is often common to use the word '_____' to refer to one of the roles that prices play in markets, while _____ is called 'non-price _____.' Using prices to ration means that those with the most money (or other assets) and who want a product the most are first to receive it.

a. 100-year flood
b. 130-30 fund
c. 1921 recession
d. Rationing

49. The underground economy or _____ is a market where all commerce is conducted without regard to taxation, law or regulations of trade. The term is also often known as the underdog, shadow economy, black economy, parallel economy or phantom trades.

In modern societies the underground economy covers a vast array of activities.

a. Protectionism
b. Market economy
c. Social market economy
d. Black market

Chapter 5. Demand and Consumer Behavior

1. _____ is a broad label that refers to any individuals or households that use goods and services generated within the economy. The concept of a _____ is used in different contexts, so that the usage and significance of the term may vary.

   Typically when business people and economists talk of _____s they are talking about person as _____, an aggregated commodity item with little individuality other than that expressed in the buy/not-buy decision.

   a. 100-year flood
   b. Consumer
   c. 1921 recession
   d. 130-30 fund

2. _____ is the study of when, why, how, where and what people do or do not buy products. It blends elements from psychology, sociology, social psychology, anthropology and economics. It attempts to understand the buyer decision making process, both individually and in groups.

   a. Situational theory of publics
   b. Consumption smoothing
   c. Shopping Neutral
   d. Consumer behavior

3. Economics:

   - _____, the desire to own something and the ability to pay for it
   - _____ curve, a graphic representation of a _____ schedule
   - _____ deposit, the money in checking accounts
   - _____ pull theory, the theory that inflation occurs when _____ for goods and services exceeds existing supplies
   - _____ schedule, a table that lists the quantity of a good a person will buy it each different price
   - _____ side economics, the school of economics at believes government spending and tax cuts open economy by raising _____

   a. Variability
   b. McKesson ' Robbins scandal
   c. Production
   d. Demand

4. In economics, the _____ can be defined as the graph depicting the relationship between the price of a certain commodity, and the amount of it that consumers are willing and able to purchase at that given price. It is a graphic representation of a demand schedule. The _____ for all consumers together follows from the _____ of every individual consumer: the individual demands at each price are added together.

   a. Wage curve
   b. Cost curve
   c. Kuznets curve
   d. Demand curve

5. In economics, the _____ of a good or of a service is the utility of the specific use to which an agent would put a given increase in that good or service, or of the specific use that would be abandoned in response to a given decrease. In other words, _____ is the utility of the marginal use -- which, on the assumption of economic rationality, would be the least urgent use of the good or service, from the best feasible combination of actions in which its use is included. Under the mainstream assumptions, the _____ of a good or service is the posited quantified change in utility obtained by increasing or by decreasing use of that good or service.

Chapter 5. Demand and Consumer Behavior

a. 1921 recession
b. 130-30 fund
c. 100-year flood
d. Marginal utility

6. _____ in economics and business is the result of an exchange and from that trade we assign a numerical monetary value to a good, service or asset. If Alice trades Bob 4 apples for an orange, the _____ of an orange is 4 apples. Inversely, the _____ of an apple is 1/4 oranges.
   a. Price war
   b. Premium pricing
   c. Price
   d. Price book

7. _____ is defined as the measure of responsiveness in the quantity demanded for a commodity as a result of change in price of the same commodity. It is a measure of how consumers react to a change in price. In other words, it is percentage change in quantity demanded as per the percentage change in price of the same commodity.
   a. 130-30 fund
   b. 1921 recession
   c. Price elasticity of demand
   d. 100-year flood

8. _____ is an economic model based on price, utility and quantity in a market. It predicts that in a competitive market, price will function to equalize the quantity demanded by consumers, and the quantity supplied by producers, resulting in an economic equilibrium of price and quantity. The model incorporates other factors changing equilibrium as a shift of demand and/or supply.
   a. Rational addiction
   b. Deferred gratification
   c. Joint demand
   d. Supply and demand

9. In economics, _____ is a measure of the relative satisfaction from consumption of various goods and services. Given this measure, one may speak meaningfully of increasing or decreasing _____, and thereby explain economic behavior in terms of attempts to increase one's _____. For illustrative purposes, changes in _____ are sometimes expressed in units called utils.
   a. Utility function
   b. Utility
   c. Expected utility hypothesis
   d. Ordinal utility

10. In economics, _____ is the ratio of the percent change in one variable to the percent change in another variable. It is a tool for measuring the responsiveness of a function to changes in parameters in a relative way. Commonly analyzed are _____ of substitution, price and wealth.
    a. ACCRA Cost of Living Index
    b. ACEA agreement
    c. Elasticity of demand
    d. Elasticity

11. Price _____ is defined as the measure of responsiveness in the quantity demanded for a commodity as a result of change in price of the same commodity. It is a measure of how consumers react to a change in price. In other words, it is percentage change in quantity demanded by the percentage change in price of the same commodity.
    a. ACEA agreement
    b. ACCRA Cost of Living Index
    c. Elasticity
    d. Elasticity of demand

12. _____ is a way of expressing knowledge or belief that an event will occur or has occurred. In mathematics the concept has been given an exact meaning in _____ theory, that is used extensively in such areas of study as mathematics, statistics, finance, gambling, science, and philosophy to draw conclusions about the likelihood of potential events and the underlying mechanics of complex systems.

The word _____ does not have a consistent direct definition.

a. 130-30 fund
b. Probability
c. 1921 recession
d. 100-year flood

13. _____ was a survey conducted by the U.S. Department of Justice to gauge the prevalence of alcohol and illegal drug use among prior arrestees. It was a reformulation of the prior Drug Use Forecasting (DUF) program, focused on five drugs in particular: cocaine, marijuana, methamphetamine, opiates, and PCP.

Participants were randomly selected from arrest records in major metropolitan areas; because no personally identifying information is taken from each record chosen, the resulting data can be correlated to arrest rates, but not to the total population of persons charged.

a. AD-IA Model
b. ACEA agreement
c. Arrestee Drug Abuse Monitoring
d. ACCRA Cost of Living Index

14. In economics, _____ is a theory of utility under which the utility (roughly, satisfaction) gained from a particular good or service can be measured and that the magnitude of the measurement is meaningful. Under _____ theory, the util is a unit of measurement much like the metre or second. A util has a fixed size, making comparisons based on ratios of utils possible.

a. 100-year flood
b. 130-30 fund
c. Cardinal utility
d. Weakly additive

15. _____ is a common concept in economics, and gives rise to derived concepts such as consumer debt. Generally _____ is defined by opposition to production. But the precise definition can vary because different schools of economists define production quite differently.

a. Foreclosure data providers
b. Cash or share options
c. Consumption
d. Federal Reserve Bank Notes

16. _____ theory states that while the utility of a particular good and service cannot be measured using an objective scale, a consumer is capable of ranking different alternatives available. Goods are often considered in 'bundles' or 'baskets'. For example, does individual A prefer 3 apples and 2 oranges or 3 oranges and 2 apples? When a large number of baskets of goods are compared, the preferences of the individual can be seen.

a. Utility function
b. Expected utility hypothesis
c. Ordinal utility
d. Utility

17. _____ can be generally defined as the course of action or inaction taken by governmental entities with regard to a particular issue or set of issues. Other scholars define it as a system of 'courses of action, regulatory measures, laws, and funding priorities concerning a given topic promulgated by a governmental entity or its representatives.' _____ is commonly embodied 'in constitutions, legislative acts, and judicial decisions.'

In the United States, this concept refers not only to the end result of policies, but more broadly to the decision-making and analysis of governmental decisions. _____ is also considered an academic discipline, as it is studied by professors and students at _____ schools of major universities throughout the country.

Chapter 5. Demand and Consumer Behavior 53

   a. 130-30 fund
   c. 100-year flood
   b. 1921 recession
   d. Public policy

18. _____ was a Scottish moral philosopher and a pioneer of political economy. One of the key figures of the Scottish Enlightenment, Smith is the author of The Theory of Moral Sentiments and An Inquiry into the Nature and Causes of the Wealth of Nations. The latter, usually abbreviated as The Wealth of Nations, is considered his magnum opus and the first modern work of economics.
   a. Adam Smith
   c. Alan Greenspan
   b. Adolf Hitler
   d. Adolph Fischer

19. A variety of measures of _____ and output are used in economics to estimate total economic activity in a country or region, including gross domestic product (GDP), gross national product (GNP), and net _____

There are three main ways of calculating these numbers; the output approach, the income approach and the expenditure approach. In theory, the three must yield the same, because total expenditures on goods and services must equal the total income paid to the producers (Gnational income), and that must also equal the total value of the output of goods and services (GNP.)

   a. GNI per capita
   c. National income
   b. Gross world product
   d. Volume index

20. A _____ represents the combinations of goods and services that a consumer can purchase given current prices and his income. Consumer theory uses the concepts of a _____ and a preference map to analyze consumer choices. Both concepts have a ready graphical representation in the two-good case.
   a. Quality bias
   c. Joint demand
   b. Revealed preference
   d. Budget constraint

21. The _____ is a heterodox school of economics that emphasizes the spontaneous organizing power of the price mechanism. It holds that the complexity of subjective human choices makes mathematical modelling of the evolving market extremely difficult and advocates a laissez faire approach to the economy. _____ economists advocate the enforcement of voluntary contractual agreements between economic agents, but otherwise the smallest imposition of coercive force on commercial transactions.
   a. ACCRA Cost of Living Index
   c. Economic calculation problem
   b. ACEA agreement
   d. Austrian School

22. _____ and behavioral finance are closely related fields that have evolved to be a separate branch of economic and financial analysis which applies scientific research on human and social, cognitive and emotional factors to better understand economic decisions by consumers, borrowers, investors, and how they affect market prices, returns and the allocation of resources.

The field is primarily concerned with the bounds of rationality (selfishness, self-control) of economic agents. Behavioral models typically integrate insights from psychology with neo-classical economic theory.

   a. Neoclassical economics
   c. Mainstream economics
   b. Georgism
   d. Behavioral economics

Chapter 5. Demand and Consumer Behavior

23. A _____ is an object whose consumption increases the utility of the consumer, for which the quantity demanded exceeds the quantity supplied at zero price. _____s are usually modeled as having diminishing marginal utility. The first individual purchase has high utility; the second has less.
    a. Composite good
    b. Good
    c. Merit good
    d. Pie method

24. In economics, economic output is divided into physical goods and intangible services. Consumption of _____ is assumed to produce utility. It is often used when referring to a _____ Tax.
    a. Manufactured goods
    b. Private good
    c. Composite good
    d. Goods and services

25. In microeconomic theory, an _____ is a graph showing different bundles of goods, each measured as to quantity, between which a consumer is indifferent. That is, at each point on the curve, the consumer has no preference for one bundle over another. In other words, they are all equally preferred.
    a. Engel curve
    b. Expenditure minimization problem
    c. Indifference curve
    d. Indifference map

26. _____ is an economic concept with commonplace familiarity. It is the price that a good or service is offered at, or will fetch, in the marketplace. It is of interest mainly in the study of microeconomics.
    a. Market anomaly
    b. Paper trading
    c. Noisy market hypothesis
    d. Market price

27. Competition law, known in the United States as _____ law, has three main elements:

    - prohibiting agreements or practices that restrict free trading and competition between business entities. This includes in particular the repression of cartels.
    - banning abusive behaviour by a firm dominating a market, or anti-competitive practices that tend to lead to such a dominant position. Practices controlled in this way may include predatory pricing, tying, price gouging, refusal to deal, and many others.
    - supervising the mergers and acquisitions of large corporations, including some joint ventures. Transactions that are considered to threaten the competitive process can be prohibited altogether, or approved subject to 'remedies' such as an obligation to divest part of the merged business or to offer licences or access to facilities to enable other businesses to continue competing.

    The substance and practice of competition law varies from jurisdiction to jurisdiction. Protecting the interests of consumers (consumer welfare) and ensuring that entrepreneurs have an opportunity to compete in the market economy are often treated as important objectives. Competition law is closely connected with law on deregulation of access to markets, state aids and subsidies, the privatisation of state owned assets and the establishment of independent sector regulators. In recent decades, competition law has been viewed as a way to provide better public services.

    a. Intellectual property law
    b. Anti-Inflation Act
    c. Antitrust
    d. United Kingdom competition law

Chapter 5. Demand and Consumer Behavior

28. _____s is the social science that studies the production, distribution, and consumption of goods and services. The term _____s comes from the Ancient Greek οá¼°κονομῖα from οá¼¶κος (oikos, 'house') + vΐŒμος (nomos, 'custom' or 'law'), hence 'rules of the house(hold)'. Current _____ models developed out of the broader field of political economy in the late 19th century, owing to a desire to use an empirical approach more akin to the physical sciences.
    a. Economic
    b. Inflation
    c. Energy economics
    d. Opportunity cost

29. The _____ or cash market is a commodities or securities market in which goods are sold for cash and delivered immediately. Contracts bought and sold on these markets are immediately effective. _____s can operate wherever the infrastructure exists to conduct the transaction.
    a. Currency band
    b. Triangular arbitrage
    c. Foreign exchange trading
    d. Spot market

30. In economics, the _____ is the change in consumption resulting from a change in real income.

    Another important item that can change is the money income of the consumer. The _____ is the phenomenon observed through changes in purchasing power.

    a. Inflation hedge
    b. Equilibrium wage
    c. Income effect
    d. Export subsidy

31. In economics, the _____ of demand measures the responsiveness of the demand of a good to the change in the income of the people demanding the good. It is calculated as the ratio of the percent change in demand to the percent change in income. For example, if, in response to a 10% increase in income, the demand of a good increased by 20%, the _____ of demand would be 20%/10% = 2.
    a. ACCRA Cost of Living Index
    b. ACEA agreement
    c. AD-IA Model
    d. Income elasticity

32. _____ is the income of individuals or nations after adjusting for inflation. It is calculated by subtracting inflation from the nominal income. Real variables, such as _____, real GDP, and real interest rate are variables that are measured in physical units, while nominal variables such as nominal income, nominal GDP, and nominal interest rate are measured in monetary units.
    a. Family income
    b. Windfall gain
    c. Net national income
    d. Real income

33. Necessary _____s:

If x is a necessary _____ of y, then the presence of y necessarily implies the presence of x. The presence of x, however, does not imply that y will occur.

Sufficient _____s:

If x is a sufficient _____ of y, then the presence of x necessarily implies the presence of y.

a. Political philosophy
b. Cause
c. Philosophy of economics
d. Materialism

34. In economics, an _____ or spillover of an economic transaction is an impact on a party that is not directly involved in the transaction. In such a case, prices do not reflect the full costs or benefits in production or consumption of a product or service. A positive impact is called an external benefit, while a negative impact is called an external cost.
    a. Environmental tariff
    b. Environmental impact assessment
    c. Existence value
    d. Externality

35. In consumer theory, an _____ is a good that decreases in demand when consumer income rises, unlike normal goods, for which the opposite is observed. It is a good that consumers demand increases when their income increases. Inferiority, in this sense, is an observable fact relating to affordability rather than a statement about the quality of the good.
    a. Information good
    b. Inferior good
    c. Export-oriented
    d. Independent goods

36. _____ are those things that are neither used with, nor instead of, the item of interest. Their use is independent of the use of the good being considered. A person's demand of nails is independent of his or her demand for bread.
    a. Export-oriented
    b. Information good
    c. Inferior good
    d. Independent goods

37. In economics, a _____ is a good or service whose consumption is considered unhealthy, degrading, or otherwise socially undesirable due to the perceived negative effects on the consumers themselves. It is over-consumed if left to market forces. Examples of _____s include tobacco, alcoholic beverages, recreational drugs, gambling, junk food and prostitution.
    a. Durable good
    b. Search good
    c. Credence good
    d. Demerit good

38. The concept of a _____ introduced in economics introduced by Richard Musgrave (1957, 1959) is a commodity which is judged that an individual or society should have on the basis of some concept of need, rather than ability and willingness to pay. The term is, perhaps, less often used today than it was in the 1960s to 1980s but the concept still lies behind many economic actions by governments which are not performed specifically for financial reasons or by supporting incomes (eg via tax rebates.) Examples include the provision of food stamps to support nutrition, the delivery of health services to improve quality of life and reduce morbidity, subsidized housing and arguably education.
    a. Final good
    b. Positional goods
    c. Private good
    d. Merit good

39. _____ is a voluntary transfer of resources from one country to another, given at least partly with the objective of benefiting the recipient country. It may have other functions as well: it may be given as a signal of diplomatic approval, or to strengthen a military ally, to reward a government for behaviour desired by the donor, to extend the donor's cultural influence, to provide infrastructure needed by the donor for resource extraction from the recipient country, or to gain other kinds of commercial access. Humanitarianism and altruism are, nevertheless, significant motivations for the giving of _____.
    a. AID
    b. ACCRA Cost of Living Index
    c. AD-IA Model
    d. ACEA agreement

Chapter 5. Demand and Consumer Behavior

40. The _____ is the apparent contradiction that although water is on the whole more useful, in terms of survival, than diamonds, diamonds command a higher price in the market. The economist Adam Smith is often considered to be the classic presenter of this paradox. Nicolaus Copernicus, John Locke, John Law and others had previously tried to explain the disparity.

   a. 130-30 fund
   b. Paradox of value
   c. St. Petersburg paradox
   d. 100-year flood

41. _____ is the a method of technical and economic research of the systems for purpose to optimize a parity between system's consumer functions or properties and expenses to achieve those functions or properties.

This methodology for continuous perfection of production, industrial technologies, organizational structures was developed by Juryj Sobolev in 1948 at the 'Perm telephone factory'

- 1948 Juryj Sobolev - the first success in application of a method analysis at the 'Perm telephone factory'.
- 1949 - the first application for the invention as result of use of the new method.

Today in economically developed countries practically each enterprise or the company use methodology of the kind of functional-cost analysis as a practice of the quality management, most full satisfying to principles of standards of series ISO 9000.

- Interest of consumer not in products itself, but the advantage which it will receive from its usage.
- The consumer aspires to reduce his expenses
- Functions needed by consumer can be executed in the various ways, and, hence, with various efficiency and expenses. Among possible alternatives of realization of functions exist such in which the parity of quality and the price is the optimal for the consumer.

The goal of _____ is achievement of the highest consumer satisfaction of production at simultaneous decrease in all kinds of industrial expenses Classical _____ has three English synonyms - Value Engineering, Value Management, Value Analysis.

   a. Willingness to pay
   b. Function cost analysis
   c. Staple financing
   d. Monopoly wage

42. An Inquiry into the Nature and Causes of the _____ is the magnum opus of the Scottish economist Adam Smith. It is a clearly written account of economics at the dawn of the Industrial Revolution, as well as a rhetorical piece written for the generally educated individual of the 18th century - advocating a free market economy as more productive and more beneficial to society.

The work is credited as a watershed in history and economics due to its comprehensive, largely accurate characterization of economic mechanisms that survive in modern economics; and also for its effective use of rhetorical technique, including structuring the work to contrast real world examples of free and fettered markets.

   a. Black Book of Communism
   b. The Rise and Fall of the Great Powers
   c. The Bell Curve
   d. Wealth of Nations

58 *Chapter 5. Demand and Consumer Behavior*

43. The term surplus is used in economics for several related quantities. The _____ is the amount that consumers benefit by being able to purchase a product for a price that is less than they would be willing to pay. The producer surplus is the amount that producers benefit by selling at a market price mechanism that is higher than they would be willing to sell for.
   a. Microeconomic reform
   b. Marginal rate of technical substitution
   c. Consumer surplus
   d. Necessity good

44. _____ is a term that refers both to:

   - a formal discipline used to help appraise, or assess, the case for a project or proposal, which itself is a process known as project appraisal; and
   - an informal approach to making decisions of any kind.

   Under both definitions the process involves, whether explicitly or implicitly, weighing the total expected costs against the total expected benefits of one or more actions in order to choose the best or most profitable option. The formal process is often referred to as either CBA (_____) or BCost-benefit analysis

   A hallmark of CBA is that all benefits and all costs are expressed in money terms, and are adjusted for the time value of money, so that all flows of benefits and flows of project costs over time (which tend to occur at different points in time) are expressed on a common basis in terms of their e;present value.e; Closely related, but slightly different, formal techniques include Cost-effectiveness analysis, Economic impact analysis, Fiscal impact analysis and Social Return on Investment(SROI) analysis. The latter builds upon the logic of _____, but differs in that it is explicitly designed to inform the practical decision-making of enterprise managers and investors focused on optimising their social and environmental impacts.

   a. Cost-benefit analysis
   b. Decision theory
   c. 130-30 fund
   d. 100-year flood

45. The _____, a unit of the United States Department of Labor, is the principal fact-finding agency for the U.S. government in the broad field of labor economics and statistics. The BLS is an independent national statistical agency that collects, processes, analyzes, and disseminates essential statistical data to the American public, the U.S. Congress, other Federal agencies, State and local governments, business, and labor representatives. The BLS also serves as a statistical resource to the Department of Labor.
   a. Gross world product
   b. Gross national product
   c. Gross Regional Product
   d. Bureau of Labor Statistics

46. In microeconomic theory a preference map or _____ is the collection of indifference curves possessed by an individual. Similar in nature to a topographical map, the contour lines of such a map demonstrating progressively more desirable options as they move upward or to the right. Because of the nature of indifference curves they cannot intersect and are effectively infinite in number, their sum defining all possible combinations of values.
   a. Elasticity of substitution
   b. Engel curve
   c. Expenditure minimization problem
   d. Indifference map

47. In economics, the _____ is the rate at which a consumer is ready to give up one good in exchange for another good while maintaining the same level of satisfaction.

Chapter 5. Demand and Consumer Behavior

Under the standard assumption of neoclassical economics that goods and services are continuously divisible, the marginal rates of substitution will be the same regardless of the direction of exchange, and will correspond to the slope of an indifference curve (more precisely, to the slope multiplied by -1) passing through the consumption bundle in question, at that point: mathematically, it is the implicit derivative. MRS of Y for X is the amount of Y for which a consumer is willing to exchange for X locally.

a. Demand vacuum
b. Quality bias
c. Marginal rate of substitution
d. Supply and demand

48. A _____ is an expression that compares quantities relative to each other. The most common examples involve two quantities, but any number of quantities can be compared. _____s are represented mathematically by separating each quantity with a colon, for example the _____ 2:3, which is read as the _____ 'two to three'.

a. Y-intercept
b. 130-30 fund
c. Ratio
d. 100-year flood

49. _____ theory is a branch of theoretical economics. It seeks to explain the behavior of supply, demand and prices in a whole economy with several or many markets. It is often assumed that agents are price takers and in that setting two common notions of equilibrium exist: Walrasian (or competitive) equilibrium, and its generalization; a price equilibrium with transfers.

a. Human capital
b. New Keynesian economics
c. General equilibrium
d. Rational choice theory

50. In economics, economic equilibrium is simply a state of the world where economic forces are balanced and in the absence of external influences the (equilibrium) values of economic variables will not change. It is the point at which quantity demanded and quantity supplied are equal. _____, for example, refers to a condition where a market price is established through competition such that the amount of goods or services sought by buyers is equal to the amount of goods or services produced by sellers.

a. Marketization
b. Regulated market
c. Product-Market Growth Matrix
d. Market equilibrium

Chapter 6. Production and Business Organization

1. In microeconomics, _____ is quite simply the conversion of inputs into outputs. It is an economic process that uses resources to create a good or service that is suitable for exchange. This can include manufacturing, storing, shipping, and packaging.
    a. MET
    b. Production
    c. Red Guards
    d. Solved

2. _____ is a term used to define maximum possible output of an economy. According to UNCTAD, no agreed-upon definition exists. UNCTAD itself proposes: 'the productive resources, entrepreneurial capabilities and production linkages which together determine the capacity of a country to produce goods and services.' The term '_____' is also used in binary economics to mean income-generating capacity be it of a factory, land, patent or the labour skills of an individual.
    a. Constant elasticity of substitution
    b. Productive capacity
    c. Price/performance ratio
    d. Multifactor productivity

3. In law and economics, the _____, describes the economic efficiency of an economic allocation or outcome in the presence of externalities. The theorem states that when trade in an externality is possible and there are no transaction costs, bargaining will lead to an efficient outcome regardless of the initial allocation of property rights. In practice, obstacles to bargaining or poorly defined property rights can prevent Coasian bargaining.
    a. Coase theorem
    b. Prior appropriation water rights
    c. General Mining Act of 1872
    d. Means test

4. _____ is the term denoting either an entrance or changes which are inserted into a system and which activate/modify a process. It is an abstract concept, used in the modeling, system(s) design and system(s) exploitation. It is usually connected with other terms, e.g., _____ field, _____ variable, _____ parameter, _____ value, _____ signal, _____ device and _____ file.
    a. ACCRA Cost of Living Index
    b. ACEA agreement
    c. Input
    d. AD-IA Model

5. In economics, the _____ or marginal physical product is the extra output produced by one more unit of an input (for instance, the difference in output when a firm's labour is increased from five to six units.) Assuming that no other inputs to production change, the _____ of a given input (X) can be expressed as:

    _____ = $\Delta Y/\Delta X$ = (the change of Y)/(the change of X.)

-
  -
    - Pending approval by Thomas Sowell***

In neoclassical economics, this is the mathematical derivative of the production function.... Note that the 'product' (Y) is typically defined ignoring external costs and benefits.

    a. Productive capacity
    b. Labor problem
    c. Factor prices
    d. Marginal product

Chapter 6. Production and Business Organization 61

6. The _____ of a variable factor of Production identifies what outputs are possible using various levels of the variable input. This can be displayed in either a chart that lists the output level corresponding to various levels of input, or a graph that summarizes the data into a '_____ curve'. The diagram shows a typical _____ curve. In this example, output increases as more inputs are employed up until point A. The maximum output possible with this Production process is Qm. (If there are other inputs used in the process, they are assumed to be fixed).

    a. Consequence   b. Convexity
    c. Tightness   d. Total product

7. In economics, a _____ is a function that specifies the output of a firm, an industry, or an entire economy for all combinations of inputs. A meta-_____ compares the practice of the existing entities converting inputs X into output y to determine the most efficient practice _____ of the existing entities, whether the most efficient feasible practice production or the most efficient actual practice production. In either case, the maximum output of a technologically-determined production process is a mathematical function of input factors of production.

    a. Production function   b. Short-run
    c. Post-Fordism   d. Constant elasticity of substitution

8. In economics, _____ refers to how the marginal contribution of a factor of production usually decreases as more of the factor is used. According to this relationship, in a production system with fixed and variable inputs, beyond some point, each additional unit of the variable input yields smaller and smaller increases in output. Conversely, producing one more unit of output costs more and more in variable inputs.

    a. Patent troll   b. Diminishing returns
    c. Community property   d. Derivatives law

9. Economics:

- _____,the desire to own something and the ability to pay for it
- _____ curve,a graphic representation of a _____ schedule
- _____ deposit, the money in checking accounts
- _____ pull theory,the theory that inflation occurs when _____ for goods and services exceeds existing supplies
- _____ schedule,a table that lists the quantity of a good a person will buy it each different price
- _____ side economics,the school of economics at believes government spending and tax cuts open economy by raising _____

    a. Production   b. Variability
    c. McKesson ' Robbins scandal   d. Demand

10. In production, returns to scale refers to changes in output subsequent to a proportional change in all inputs (where all inputs increase by a constant factor.) If output increases by that same proportional change then there are _____ If output increases by less than that proportional change, there are decreasing returns to scale (DRS.)

    a. Consumer sovereignty   b. Lexicographic preferences
    c. Long term   d. Constant returns to scale

11. _____, in microeconomics, are the cost advantages that a business obtains due to expansion. They are factors that cause a producere;s average cost per unit to fall as scale is increased. _____ is a long run concept and refers to reductions in unit cost as the size of a facility, or scale, increases.

   a. Isoquant   b. Economic production quantity
   c. Underinvestment employment relationship   d. Economies of scale

12. In economics, _____ are the resources employed to produce goods and services. They facilitate production but do not become part of the product (as with raw materials) or significantly transformed by the production process (as with fuel used to power machinery.) To 19th century economists, the _____ were land (natural resources, gifts from nature), labor (the ability to work), and capital goods (human-made tools and equipment.)

   a. Hicks-neutral technical change   b. Long-run
   c. Product Pipeline   d. Factors of production

13. In calculus, a function f defined on a subset of the real numbers with real values is called _____, if for all x and y such that $x >\leq y$ one has $f(x) >\leq f(y)$, so f preserves the order. In layman's terms, the sign of the slope is always positive (the curve tending upwards) or zero (i.e., non-decreasing, or asymptotic, or depicted as a horizontal, flat line) Likewise, a function is called monotonically decreasing (non-increasing) if, whenever $x >\leq y$, then $f(x) >\geq f(y)$, so it reverses the order.

   a. 100-year flood   b. 130-30 fund
   c. 1921 recession   d. Monotonic

14. In economics, _____ and economies of scale are related terms that describe what happens as the scale of production increases. They are different terms and should not be used interchangeably.

_____ refers to a technical property of production that examines changes in output subsequent to a proportional change in all inputs (where all inputs increase by a constant factor.)

   a. Necessity good   b. Customer equity
   c. Constant returns to scale   d. Returns to scale

15. The _____ consists of a number of economic theories which describe the nature of the firm, company including its existence, its behaviour, and its relationship with the market.

In simplified terms, the _____ aims to answer these questions:

1. Existence - why do firms emerge, why are not all transactions in the economy mediated over the market?
2. Boundaries - why the boundary between firms and the market is located exactly there? Which transactions are performed internally and which are negotiated on the market?
3. Organization - why are firms structured in such specific way? What is the interplay of formal and informal relationships?

Despite looking simple, these questions are not answered by the established economic theory, which usually views firms as given, and treats them as black boxes without any internal structure.

Chapter 6. Production and Business Organization 63

The First World War period saw a change of emphasis in economic theory away from industry-level analysis which mainly included analysing markets to analysis at the level of the firm, as it became increasingly clear that perfect competition was no longer an adequate model of how firms behaved. Economic theory till then had focussed on trying to understand markets alone and there had been little study on understanding why firms or organisations exist.

a. Policy Ineffectiveness Proposition
c. Technology gap
b. Khazzoom-Brookes postulate
d. Theory of the firm

16. _____ , as defined by the _____ Association of America (Information technologyAA), is 'the study, design, development, implementation, support or management of computer-based information systems, particularly software applications and computer hardware.' _____ deals with the use of electronic computers and computer software to convert, store, protect, process, transmit, and securely retrieve information.

Today, the term _____ has ballooned to encompass many aspects of computing and technology, and the term has become very recognizable. The _____ umbrella can be quite large, covering many fields.

a. AD-IA Model
c. ACEA agreement
b. ACCRA Cost of Living Index
d. Information technology

17. _____ is the production of large amounts of standardized products, including and especially on assembly lines. The concepts of _____ are applied to various kinds of products, from fluids and particulates handled in bulk to discrete solid parts to assemblies of such parts

_____ of assemblies typically uses electric-motor-powered moving tracks or conveyor belts to move partially complete products to workers, who perform simple repetitive tasks.

a. 100-year flood
c. 130-30 fund
b. 1921 recession
d. Mass production

18. In economics, _____ is equal to total cost divided by the number of goods produced (the output quantity, Q.) It is also equal to the sum of average variable costs (total variable costs divided by Q) plus average fixed costs (total fixed costs divided by Q.) _____s may be dependent on the time period considered (increasing production may be expensive or impossible in the short term, for example.)

a. Average variable cost
c. Explicit cost
b. Average fixed cost
d. Average cost

19. _____ is a term used in national accounts statistics and macroeconomics. It basically refers to the net additions to the (physical) capital stock in an accounting period, or, to the value of the increase of the capital stock; though it may occasionally also refer to the (growth of the) total stock of capital formed.

Thus, in UNSNA, _____ equals fixed capital investment, the increase in the value of inventories held, plus (net) lending to foreign countries, during an accounting period.

a. Consumption of fixed capital
b. Capital formation
c. Capital flight
d. Capital intensity

20. In economic theory, _____ is the competitive situation in any market where the conditions necessary for perfect competition are not satisfied. It is a market structure that does not meet the conditions of perfect competition.

Forms of _____ include:

- Monopoly, in which there is only one seller of a good.
- Oligopoly, in which there is a small number of sellers.
- Monopolistic competition, in which there are many sellers producing highly differentiated goods.
- Monopsony, in which there is only one buyer of a good.
- Oligopsony, in which there is a small number of buyers.

There may also be _____ in markets due to buyers or sellers lacking information about prices and the goods being traded.

There may also be _____ due to a time lag in a market.

a. AD-IA Model
b. ACCRA Cost of Living Index
c. Imperfect competition
d. ACEA agreement

21. In economic models, the _____ time frame assumes no fixed factors of production. Firms can enter or leave the marketplace, and the cost (and availability) of land, labor, raw materials, and capital goods can be assumed to vary. In contrast, in the short-run time frame, certain factors are assumed to be fixed, because there is not sufficient time for them to change.
a. Long-run
b. Price/performance ratio
c. Productivity world
d. Diseconomies of scale

22. In economics, the concept of the _____ refers to the decision-making time frame of a firm in which at least one factor of production is fixed. Costs which are fixed in the _____ have no impact on a firms decisions. For example a firm can raise output by increasing the amount of labour through overtime.
a. Productivity model
b. Product Pipeline
c. Hicks-neutral technical change
d. Short-run

23. A _____ is an object whose consumption increases the utility of the consumer, for which the quantity demanded exceeds the quantity supplied at zero price. _____s are usually modeled as having diminishing marginal utility. The first individual purchase has high utility; the second has less.
a. Composite good
b. Pie method
c. Merit good
d. Good

24. In economics, economic output is divided into physical goods and intangible services. Consumption of _____ is assumed to produce utility. It is often used when referring to a _____ Tax.
a. Goods and services
b. Manufactured goods
c. Composite good
d. Private good

25. A _____ is an economy based on the division of labor in which the prices of goods and services are determined in a free price system set by supply and demand. This is often contrasted with a planned economy, in which a central government determines the price of goods and services using a fixed price system. Market economies are contrasted with mixed economy where the price system is not entirely free but under some government control that is not extensive enough to constitute a planned economy.

a. Market economy
b. Commons-based peer production
c. Nutritional Economics
d. Network Economy

26. The process of _____ involves the introduction of a good or service that is new or substantially improved. This includes, but is not limited to, improvements in functional characteristics, technical abilities, or ease of use.

a. Refusal to deal
b. Product innovation
c. Microcap stock
d. Dogs of the Dow

27. The _____ is the largest national economy in the world. Its gross domestic product (GDP) was estimated as $14.2 trillion in 2008. The U.S. economy maintains a high level of output per person (GDP per capita, $46,800 in 2008, ranked at around number ten in the world.)

a. AD-IA Model
b. ACCRA Cost of Living Index
c. Economy of the United States
d. ACEA agreement

28. _____ is a term that is used to describe the overall process of invention, innovation and diffusion of technology or processes. The term is redundant with technological development, technological achievement, and technological progress. In essence _____ is the invention of a technology (or a process), the continuous process of improving a technology (in which it often becomes cheaper) and its diffusion throughout industry or society.

a. 1921 recession
b. 130-30 fund
c. 100-year flood
d. Technological change

29. In economics, a _____ exists when the production or use of goods and services by the market is not efficient. That is, there exists another outcome where all involved can be made better off. _____s can be viewed as scenarios where individuals' pursuit of pure self-interest leads to results that are not efficient - that can be improved upon from the societal point-of-view.

a. Market failure
b. Financial economics
c. General equilibrium
d. Fixed exchange rate

30. _____ is a broad label that refers to any individuals or households that use goods and services generated within the economy. The concept of a _____ is used in different contexts, so that the usage and significance of the term may vary.

Typically when business people and economists talk of _____s they are talking about person as _____, an aggregated commodity item with little individuality other than that expressed in the buy/not-buy decision.

a. 1921 recession
b. 130-30 fund
c. 100-year flood
d. Consumer

Chapter 6. Production and Business Organization

31. _____ is the pricing technique of setting a relatively low initial entry price, often lower than the eventual market price, to attract new customers. The strategy works on the expectation that customers will switch to the new brand because of the lower price. _____ is most commonly associated with a marketing objective of increasing market share or sales volume, rather than to make profit in the short term.
    a. Transfer pricing
    b. Contribution margin-based pricing
    c. Fire sale
    d. Penetration pricing

32. _____ is one of the four Ps of the marketing mix. The other three aspects are product, promotion, and place. It is also a key variable in microeconomic price allocation theory.
    a. Premium pricing
    b. Pricing
    c. Guaranteed Maximum Price
    d. Point of total assumption

33. In the theory of artificial neural networks _____ networks are a case of competitive learning in recurrent neural networks. Output nodes in the network inhibit each other and activate themselves through reflexive connections. After some time, only one node in the output layer will be active.
    a. 100-year flood
    b. 1921 recession
    c. 130-30 fund
    d. Winner-take-all

34. In economics, an _____ or spillover of an economic transaction is an impact on a party that is not directly involved in the transaction. In such a case, prices do not reflect the full costs or benefits in production or consumption of a product or service. A positive impact is called an external benefit, while a negative impact is called an external cost.
    a. Environmental tariff
    b. Externality
    c. Environmental impact assessment
    d. Existence value

35. _____ is a type of trade policy that allows traders to act and transact without interference from government. Thus, the policy permits trading partners mutual gains from trade, with goods and services produced according to the theory of comparative advantage.

    Under a _____ policy, prices are a reflection of true supply and demand, and are the sole determinant of resource allocation.

    a. 130-30 fund
    b. Free trade
    c. 100-year flood
    d. 1921 recession

36. _____ in economics refers to metrics and measures of output from production processes, per unit of input. Labor _____, for example, is typically measured as a ratio of output per labor-hour, an input. _____ may be conceived of as a metrics of the technical or engineering efficiency of production.
    a. Production-possibility frontier
    b. Piece work
    c. Fordism
    d. Productivity

37. In economics, _____ (TFP) is a variable which accounts for effects in total output not caused by inputs. For example, a year with unusually good weather will tend to have higher output, because bad weather hinders agricultural output. A variable like weather does not directly relate to unit inputs, so weather is considered a _____ variable.
    a. Human rights
    b. Flow to Equity-Approach
    c. 35-hour working week
    d. Total-factor productivity

Chapter 6. Production and Business Organization

38. _____ was a survey conducted by the U.S. Department of Justice to gauge the prevalence of alcohol and illegal drug use among prior arrestees. It was a reformulation of the prior Drug Use Forecasting (DUF) program, focused on five drugs in particular: cocaine, marijuana, methamphetamine, opiates, and PCP.

Participants were randomly selected from arrest records in major metropolitan areas; because no personally identifying information is taken from each record chosen, the resulting data can be correlated to arrest rates, but not to the total population of persons charged.

a. ACCRA Cost of Living Index
b. Arrestee Drug Abuse Monitoring
c. AD-IA Model
d. ACEA agreement

39. _____ was a Scottish moral philosopher and a pioneer of political economy. One of the key figures of the Scottish Enlightenment, Smith is the author of The Theory of Moral Sentiments and An Inquiry into the Nature and Causes of the Wealth of Nations. The latter, usually abbreviated as The Wealth of Nations, is considered his magnum opus and the first modern work of economics.

a. Alan Greenspan
b. Adolf Hitler
c. Adolph Fischer
d. Adam Smith

40. The _____ is the market for securities, where companies and governments can raise longterm funds. It is a market in which money is lent for periods longer than a year. The _____ includes the stock market and the bond market.

a. Capital market
b. Performance attribution
c. Financial instrument
d. Multi-family office

41. _____s is the social science that studies the production, distribution, and consumption of goods and services. The term _____s comes from the Ancient Greek oá¼°κονομῖα from oá¼¶κος (oikos, 'house') + vῐ́Œμος (nomos, 'custom' or 'law'), hence 'rules of the house(hold)'. Current _____ models developed out of the broader field of political economy in the late 19th century, owing to a desire to use an empirical approach more akin to the physical sciences.

a. Opportunity cost
b. Inflation
c. Energy economics
d. Economic

42. _____ is the increase in the amount of the goods and services produced by an economy over time. It is conventionally measured as the percent rate of increase in real gross domestic product, or real GDP. Growth is usually calculated in real terms, i.e. inflation-adjusted terms, in order to net out the effect of inflation on the price of the goods and services produced.

a. AD-IA Model
b. ACEA agreement
c. ACCRA Cost of Living Index
d. Economic growth

43. In economics, _____ is a rise in the general level of prices of goods and services in an economy over a period of time. When the general price level rises, each unit of currency buys fewer goods and services; consequently, _____ is also a decline in the real value of money--a loss of purchasing power in the medium of exchange which is also the monetary unit of account in the economy. A chief measure of general price-level _____ is the general _____ rate, which is the percentage change in a general price index (normally the Consumer Price Index) over time.

a. Economic
b. Energy economics
c. Opportunity cost
d. Inflation

Chapter 6. Production and Business Organization

44. In economics, the _____ is a measure of inflation, the rate of increase of a price index (for example, a consumer price index.)It is the percentage rate of change in price level over time. The rate of decrease in the purchasing power of money is approximately equal.

It's used to calculate the real interest rate, as well as real increases in wages, and official measurements of this rate act as input variables to COLA adjustments and Inflation derivatives prices.

- a. Inflation rate
- b. Edgeworth paradox
- c. Equity value
- d. Interest rate option

45. In finance, _____ rate of profit or sometimes just return, is the ratio of money gained or lost on an investment relative to the amount of money invested. The amount of money gained or lost may be referred to as interest, profit/loss, gain/loss, or net income/loss. The money invested may be referred to as the asset, capital, principal, or the cost basis of the investment.
- a. Sortino ratio
- b. Rate of return
- c. Current ratio
- d. Cost accrual ratio

46. _____s (economically referred to as land or raw materials) occur naturally within environments that exist relatively undisturbed by mankind, in a natural form. A _____'s is often characterized by amounts of biodiversity existent in various ecosystems.

Mining, petroleum extraction, fishing, hunting, and forestry are generally considered natural-resource industries.

- a. 130-30 fund
- b. 100-year flood
- c. Natural resource
- d. 1921 recession

47. The _____ 4(16) Economica 386-405 by Ronald Coase is a brief but highly influential essay that offers an economic explanation of why individuals choose to form partnerships, companies and other business entities rather than trading bilaterally through contracts on a market.

Given that 'production could be carried on without any organization that is, firms at all', Coase asks, why and under what conditions should we expect firms to emerge? Since modern firms can only emerge when an entrepreneur of some sort begins to hire people, Coase's analysis proceeds by considering the conditions under which it makes sense for an entrepreneur to seek hired help instead of contracting out for some particular task.

The traditional economic theory of the time suggested that, because the market is 'efficient' (that is, those who are best at providing each good or service most cheaply are already doing so), it should always be cheaper to contract out than to hire.

- a. Greenfield agreement
- b. Legal tender
- c. Holder in due course
- d. Nature of the firm

Chapter 6. Production and Business Organization

48. The _____ was an early English joint-stock company that was formed initially for pursuing trade with the East Indies, but that ended up trading with the Indian subcontinent and China. The oldest among several similarly formed European East India Companies, the Company was granted an English Royal Charter, under the name Governor and Company of Merchants of London Trading into the East Indies, by Elizabeth I on 31 December 1600. After a rival English company challenged its monopoly in the late 17th century, the two companies were merged in 1708 to form the United Company of Merchants of England Trading to the East Indies, commonly styled the Honourable _____, and abbreviated, HEast India Company; the Company was colloquially referred to as John Company, and in India as Company Bahadur .
   a. ACCRA Cost of Living Index
   b. East India Company
   c. AD-IA Model
   d. ACEA agreement

49. _____ is a concept whereby a person's financial liability is limited to a fixed sum, most commonly the value of a person's investment in a company or partnership with _____. A shareholder in a limited company is not personally liable for any of the debts of the company, other than for the value of his investment in that company. The same is true for the members of a _____ partnership and the limited partners in a limited partnership.
   a. Deficiency judgment
   b. Nexus of contracts
   c. Personal Responsibility and Work Opportunity Reconciliation Act of 1996
   d. Limited liability

50. _____ is an equity (stock) exchange located at 11 Wall Street in lower Manhattan, New York, USA. It is the largest stock exchange in the world by dollar value of its listed companies' securities. As of October 2008, the combined capitalization of all domestic _____ listed companies was US$10.1 trillion.
   a. 130-30 fund
   b. 1921 recession
   c. 100-year flood
   d. New York Stock Exchange

51. A _____ is a type of business entity in which partners (owners) share with each other the profits or losses of the business _____s are often favored over corporations for taxation purposes, as the _____ structure does not generally incur a tax on profits before it is distributed to the partners (i.e. there is no dividend tax levied.) However, depending on the _____ structure and the jurisdiction in which it operates, owners of a _____ may be exposed to greater personal liability than they would as shareholders of a corporation.

   For a country-by-country listing of types of _____s, companies, etc., see Types of business entity.

   a. Due diligence
   b. Feoffee
   c. Partnership
   d. Minimum wage law

52. A mutual _____ or stockholder is an individual or company (including a corporation) that legally owns one or more shares of stock in a joint stock company. A company's _____s collectively own that company. Thus, the typical goal of such companies is to enhance _____ value.
   a. Prime Standard
   b. Profit warning
   c. Relative valuation
   d. Shareholder

53. A _____ is a corporation or mutual organization which provides trading facilities for stock brokers and traders, to trade stocks and other securities. It may be a physical trading room where the traders gather, or a formalised communications network. Creation of a _____ is a strategy of economic development.

a. 100-year flood
b. Stock Exchange
c. Primary shares
d. SEAQ

54. A _____, or simply proprietorship is a type of business entity which legally has no separate existence from its owner. Hence, the limitations of liability enjoyed by a corporation and limited liability partnerships do not apply to sole proprietors. All debts of the business are debts of the owner.
   a. Sole proprietorship
   b. Golden hello
   c. Golden parachute
   d. Corporate tax

55. _____ is a situation in which the limited resources of a firm are allocated in accordance with the wishes of consumers. An allocatively efficient economy produces an 'optimal mix' of commodities. A firm is allocatively efficient when its price is equal to its marginal costs (that is, P = MC) in a perfect market.
   a. Economic efficiency
   b. Allocative efficiency
   c. ACEA agreement
   d. ACCRA Cost of Living Index

56. _____s are payments made by a corporation to its shareholders. It is the portion of corporate profits paid out to stockholders. When a corporation earns a profit or surplus, that money can be put to two uses: it can either be re-invested in the business (called retained earnings), or it can be paid to the shareholders as a _____.
   a. Dividend yield
   b. Dividend cover
   c. Dividend puzzle
   d. Dividend

57. _____ is subcontracting a process, such as product design or manufacturing, to a third-party company. The decision to outsource is often made in the interest of lowering cost or making better use of time and energy costs, redirecting or conserving energy directed at the competencies of a particular business, or to make more efficient use of land, labor, capital, (information) technology and resources. _____ became part of the business lexicon during the 1980s.
   a. Additional Funds Needed
   b. Averch-Johnson effect
   c. Outsourcing
   d. Electronic business

Chapter 7. Analysis of Costs

1. In economics, and cost accounting, _____ describes the total economic cost of production and is made up of variable costs, which vary according to the quantity of a good produced and include inputs such as labor and raw materials, plus fixed costs, which are independent of the quantity of a good produced and include inputs (capital) that cannot be varied in the short term, such as buildings and machinery. _____ in economics includes the total opportunity cost of each factor of production in addition to fixed and variable costs.

The rate at which _____ changes as the amount produced changes is called marginal cost.

 a. Total cost
 b. 130-30 fund
 c. 100-year flood
 d. 1921 recession

2. In economics, _____ is equal to total cost divided by the number of goods produced (the output quantity, Q.) It is also equal to the sum of average variable costs (total variable costs divided by Q) plus average fixed costs (total fixed costs divided by Q.) _____s may be dependent on the time period considered (increasing production may be expensive or impossible in the short term, for example.)
 a. Average fixed cost
 b. Average variable cost
 c. Average cost
 d. Explicit cost

3. _____s is the social science that studies the production, distribution, and consumption of goods and services. The term _____s comes from the Ancient Greek οἰκονομία from οἶκος (oikos, 'house') + νόμος (nomos, 'custom' or 'law'), hence 'rules of the house(hold)'. Current _____ models developed out of the broader field of political economy in the late 19th century, owing to a desire to use an empirical approach more akin to the physical sciences.
 a. Inflation
 b. Energy economics
 c. Opportunity cost
 d. Economic

4. In microeconomics, _____ is quite simply the conversion of inputs into outputs. It is an economic process that uses resources to create a good or service that is suitable for exchange. This can include manufacturing, storing, shipping, and packaging.
 a. Red Guards
 b. Solved
 c. MET
 d. Production

5. The _____ consists of a number of economic theories which describe the nature of the firm, company including its existence, its behaviour, and its relationship with the market.

In simplified terms, the _____ aims to answer these questions:

 1. Existence - why do firms emerge, why are not all transactions in the economy mediated over the market?
 2. Boundaries - why the boundary between firms and the market is located exactly there? Which transactions are performed internally and which are negotiated on the market?
 3. Organization - why are firms structured in such specific way? What is the interplay of formal and informal relationships?

Despite looking simple, these questions are not answered by the established economic theory, which usually views firms as given, and treats them as black boxes without any internal structure.

Chapter 7. Analysis of Costs

The First World War period saw a change of emphasis in economic theory away from industry-level analysis which mainly included analysing markets to analysis at the level of the firm, as it became increasingly clear that perfect competition was no longer an adequate model of how firms behaved. Economic theory till then had focussed on trying to understand markets alone and there had been little study on understanding why firms or organisations exist.

- a. Khazzoom-Brookes postulate
- b. Policy Ineffectiveness Proposition
- c. Theory of the firm
- d. Technology gap

6. In economics, _____ are business expenses that are not dependent on the activities of the business They tend to be time-related, such as salaries or rents being paid per month. This is in contrast to variable costs, which are volume-related (and are paid per quantity.)

In management accounting, _____ are defined as expenses that do not change in proportion to the activity of a business, within the relevant period or scale of production.

- a. Cost of poor quality
- b. Fixed costs
- c. Cost-Volume-Profit Analysis
- d. Quality costs

7. In economics and finance, _____ is the change in total cost that arises when the quantity produced changes by one unit. It is the cost of producing one more unit of a good. Mathematically, the _____ function is expressed as the first derivative of the total cost (TC) function with respect to quantity (Q.)

- a. Variable cost
- b. Khozraschyot
- c. Quality costs
- d. Marginal cost

8. In business, _____, Overhead cost or _____ expense refers to an ongoing expense of operating a business. The term _____ is usually used to group expenses that are necessary to the continued functioning of the business, but do not directly generate profits.

_____ expenses are all costs on the income statement except for direct labor and direct materials.

- a. ACEA agreement
- b. AD-IA Model
- c. ACCRA Cost of Living Index
- d. Overhead

9. In economics and business decision-making, _____ are costs that cannot be recovered once they have been incurred. _____ are sometimes contrasted with variable costs, which are the costs that will change due to the proposed course of action, and prospective costs which are costs that will be incurred if an action is taken.

In traditional microeconomic theory, only variable costs are relevant to a decision.

- a. Halo effect
- b. Hyperbolic discounting
- c. Post-purchase rationalization
- d. Sunk costs

10. _____s are expenses that change in proportion to the activity of a business. In other words, _____ is the sum of marginal costs. It can also be considered normal costs.

Chapter 7. Analysis of Costs

   a. Cost allocation
   c. Quality costs
   b. Cost-Volume-Profit Analysis
   d. Variable cost

11. _____ is a term used in national accounts statistics and macroeconomics. It basically refers to the net additions to the (physical) capital stock in an accounting period, or, to the value of the increase of the capital stock; though it may occasionally also refer to the (growth of the) total stock of capital formed.

Thus, in UNSNA, _____ equals fixed capital investment, the increase in the value of inventories held, plus (net) lending to foreign countries, during an accounting period.

   a. Capital flight
   c. Capital intensity
   b. Consumption of fixed capital
   d. Capital formation

12. In economics, a _____ is a graph of the costs of production as a function of total quantity produced. In a free market economy, productively efficient firms use these curves to find the optimal point of production, where they make the most profits. There are a few different types of _____s, each relevant to a different area of economics.

   a. Demand curve
   c. Phillips curve
   b. Cost curve
   d. Kuznets curve

Chapter 7. Analysis of Costs

13. A _____ is:

- Rewrite _____, in generative grammar and computer science
- Standardization, a formal and widely-accepted statement, fact, definition, or qualification
- Operation, a determinate _____ for performing a mathematical operation and obtaining a certain result (Mathematics, Logic)
    - Unary operation
    - Binary operation
- _____ of inference, a function from sets of formulae to formulae (Mathematics, Logic)
- _____ of thumb, principle with broad application that is not intended to be strictly accurate or reliable for every situation. Also often simply referred to as a _____
- Moral, an atomic element of a moral code for guiding choices in human behavior
- Heuristic, a quantized '_____' which shows a tendency or probability for successful function
- A regulation, as in sports
- A Production _____, as in computer science
- Procedural law, a _____ set governing the application of laws to cases
    - A law, which may informally be called a '_____'
    - A court ruling, a decision by a court
- In the U.S. Government, a regulation mandated by Congress, but written or expanded upon by the Executive Branch.
- Norm (sociology), an informal but widely accepted _____, concept, truth, definition, or qualification (social norms, legal norms, coding norms)
- Norm (philosophy), a kind of sentence or a reason to act, feel or believe
- 'Rulership' is the concept of governance by a government:
    - Military _____, governance by a military body
    - Monastic _____, a collection of precepts that guides the life of monks or nuns in a religious order where the superior holds the place of Christ
- Slide _____

- '_____,' a song by Ayumi Hamasaki
- '_____,' a song by rapper Nas
- '_____s,' an album by the band The Whitest Boy Alive
- _____s: Pyaar Ka Superhit Formula, a 2003 Bollywood film
- ruler, an instrument for measuring lengths
- _____, a component of an astrolabe, circumferator or similar instrument
- The _____s, a bestselling self-help book
- _____ Project (Run Up-to-date Linux Everywhere), a project that aims to use up-to-date Linux software on old PCs
- _____ engine, a software system that helps managing business _____s
- Ja _____, a hip hop artist
    - R.U.L.E., a 2005 greatest hits album by rapper Ja _____
- '_____s,' a KMFDM song

a. Demand
c. Technocracy
b. Procter ' Gamble
d. Rule

Chapter 7. Analysis of Costs

14. _____ is an economics term used to describe the total fixed costs (TFC) divided by the quantity (Q) of units produced.

$$AFC = \frac{TFC}{Q}$$

_____ is a per-unit measure of fixed costs. As the total number of goods produced increases, the _____ decreases because the same amount of fixed costs are being spread over a larger number of units.

a. Average variable cost
c. Inventory valuation

b. Explicit cost
d. Average fixed cost

15. _____ is an economics term to describe a firms variable costs (labor, electricity, etc.) divided by the quantity (Q) of total units of output.

$$AVC = \frac{TVC}{Q}$$

Where:

- TVC = Total Variable Cost
- _____ = Average variable cost
- Q = Quantity of Units Produced

_____ plus average fixed cost equals average total cost:

_____ + AFC = ATC.

a. Average fixed cost
c. Explicit cost

b. Inventory valuation
d. Average variable cost

16. In law and economics, the _____, describes the economic efficiency of an economic allocation or outcome in the presence of externalities. The theorem states that when trade in an externality is possible and there are no transaction costs, bargaining will lead to an efficient outcome regardless of the initial allocation of property rights. In practice, obstacles to bargaining or poorly defined property rights can prevent Coasian bargaining.

a. Means test
c. Prior appropriation water rights

b. General Mining Act of 1872
d. Coase theorem

17. _____ are the prices that the factors of production of a finished item attract.

There has been some economic debate as to what determines these prices. Classical and Marxist economists argued that the _____ decided the value of a product and so value was intrinsic within the product.

a. Productivity model
b. Marginal product
c. Marginal product of labor
d. Factor prices

18. In algebra, a _____ is a function depending on n that associates a scalar, det(A), to an n×n square matrix A. The fundamental geometric meaning of a _____ is a scale factor for measure when A is regarded as a linear transformation. _____s are important both in calculus, where they enter the substitution rule for several variables, and in multilinear algebra.

For a fixed nonnegative integer n, there is a unique _____ function for the n×n matrices over any commutative ring R. In particular, this function exists when R is the field of real or complex numbers.

a. 130-30 fund
b. 1921 recession
c. 100-year flood
d. Determinant

19. _____ in economics and business is the result of an exchange and from that trade we assign a numerical monetary value to a good, service or asset. If Alice trades Bob 4 apples for an orange, the _____ of an orange is 4 apples. Inversely, the _____ of an apple is 1/4 oranges.

a. Price
b. Price war
c. Price book
d. Premium pricing

20. In economics, _____ refers to how the marginal contribution of a factor of production usually decreases as more of the factor is used. According to this relationship, in a production system with fixed and variable inputs, beyond some point, each additional unit of the variable input yields smaller and smaller increases in output. Conversely, producing one more unit of output costs more and more in variable inputs.

a. Diminishing returns
b. Derivatives law
c. Community property
d. Patent troll

21. _____ is the simplest of the pharmacoeconomics tools and is applied when comparing two drugs of equal efficacy and equal tolerability

Therapeutic equivalence must be referenced by the author conducting the study and should have been done prior to the _____ work. Since equal efficacy and equal tolerability is already demonstrated, there is no requirement to find a common efficacy denominator as would be the case when conducting a cost-effectiveness study. The author is not precluded from doing so through the use of 'cost/cure' or 'cost/year of life gained'.

a. Linkage principle
b. Bord halfpenny
c. Liquidating dividend
d. Cost-minimization

22. _____ is the term denoting either an entrance or changes which are inserted into a system and which activate/modify a process. It is an abstract concept, used in the modeling, system(s) design and system(s) exploitation. It is usually connected with other terms, e.g., _____ field, _____ variable, _____ parameter, _____ value, _____ signal, _____ device and _____ file.

a. Input
b. ACEA agreement
c. ACCRA Cost of Living Index
d. AD-IA Model

23. In economics, the _____ or marginal physical product is the extra output produced by one more unit of an input (for instance, the difference in output when a firm's labour is increased from five to six units.) Assuming that no other inputs to production change, the _____ of a given input (X) can be expressed as:

_____ = ΔY/ΔX = (the change of Y)/(the change of X.)

-
  -
    - Pending approval by Thomas Sowell***

In neoclassical economics, this is the mathematical derivative of the production function.... Note that the 'product' (Y) is typically defined ignoring external costs and benefits.

a. Productive capacity
c. Factor prices
b. Marginal product
d. Labor problem

24. The _____ of a decision depends on both the cost of the alternative chosen and the benefit that the best alternative would have provided if chosen. _____ differs from accounting cost because it includes opportunity cost.

a. Isocost
c. Economic cost
b. Inventory analysis
d. Epstein-Zin preferences

25. _____ is a company's financial statement that indicates how the revenue is transformed into the net income The purpose of the _____ is to show managers and investors whether the company made or lost money during the period being reported.

The important thing to remember about an _____ is that it represents a period of time.

a. AD-IA Model
c. ACEA agreement
b. ACCRA Cost of Living Index
d. Income statement

26. _____ is equal to the income that a firm has after subtracting costs and expenses from the total revenue. _____ can be distributed among holders of common stock as a dividend or held by the firm as retained earnings. _____ is an accounting term.

a. Salvage value
c. Net profit
b. Historical cost
d. Net income

27. In financial accounting, a _____ or statement of financial position is a summary of a person's or organization's balances. Assets, liabilities and ownership equity are listed as of a specific date, such as the end of its financial year. A _____ is often described as a snapshot of a company's financial condition.

a. 100-year flood
c. Balance sheet
b. 130-30 fund
d. 1921 recession

28. In Marxian economics, _____ originally referred to the means of production. Individuals, organizations and governments use _____ in the production of other goods or commodities. _____ include factories, machinery, tools, equipment, and various buildings which are used to produce other products for consumption.

Chapter 7. Analysis of Costs

a. Capital intensive
b. Wealth inequality in the United States
c. Capital goods
d. Capital deepening

29. In financial accounting, _____ or cost of sales includes the direct costs attributable to the production of the goods sold by a company. This amount includes the materials cost used in creating the goods along with the direct labour costs used to produce the good. It excludes indirect expenses such as distribution costs and sales force costs.
   a. 100-year flood
   b. 130-30 fund
   c. Cost of goods sold
   d. 1921 recession

30. _____ is a term used in accounting, economics and finance to spread the cost of an asset over the span of several years.

In simple words we can say that _____ is the reduction in the value of an asset due to usage, passage of time, wear and tear, technological outdating or obsolescence, depletion, inadequacy, rot, rust, decay or other such factors.

In accounting, _____ is a term used to describe any method of attributing the historical or purchase cost of an asset across its useful life, roughly corresponding to normal wear and tear.

   a. Net income per employee
   b. Salvage value
   c. Depreciation
   d. Historical cost

31. A _____ is an object whose consumption increases the utility of the consumer, for which the quantity demanded exceeds the quantity supplied at zero price. _____s are usually modeled as having diminishing marginal utility. The first individual purchase has high utility; the second has less.
   a. Merit good
   b. Composite good
   c. Pie method
   d. Good

32. In business and accounting, _____ are everything of value that is owned by a person or company. It is a claim on the property your income of a borrower. The balance sheet of a firm records the monetary value of the _____ owned by the firm.
   a. ACCRA Cost of Living Index
   b. ACEA agreement
   c. Amortization schedule
   d. Assets

33. The accounting equation relates assets, _____, and owner's equity:

   Assets = _____ + Owner's Equity

The accounting equation is the mathematical structure of the balance sheet.

The Australian Accounting Research Foundation defines _____ as: 'future sacrifice of economic benefits that the entity is presently obliged to make to other entities as a result of past transactions and other past events.'

Chapter 7. Analysis of Costs 79

Probably the most accepted accounting definition of liability is the one used by the International Accounting Standards Board (IASB.) The following is a quotation from IFRS Framework:

A liability is a present obligation of the enterprise arising from past events, the settlement of which is expected to result in an outflow from the enterprise of resources embodying economic benefits

Regulations as to the recognition of _____ are different all over the world, but are roughly similar to those of the IASB.

a. Competition law theory
b. Community property
c. Liabilities
d. Coase theorem

34. In business, _____ is the total liabilitiess minus total outside assets of an individual or a company. For a company, this is called shareholders' prefernce and may be referred to as book value. _____ is stated as at a particular year in time.
a. Sinking fund
b. Bond credit rating
c. Post earnings announcement drift
d. Net worth

35. _____, or corporate _____ are political and business scandals which arise with the disclosure of misdeeds by trusted executives of large public corporations. Such misdeeds typically involve complex methods for misusing or misdirecting funds, overstating revenues, understating expenses, overstating the value of corporate assets or underreporting the existence of liabilities, sometimes with the cooperation of officials in other corporations or affiliates.

In public companies, this type of 'creative accounting' can amount to fraud and investigations are typically launched by government oversight agencies, such as the Securities and Exchange Commission (SEC) in the United States.

a. AD-IA Model
b. ACEA agreement
c. ACCRA Cost of Living Index
d. Accounting scandals

36. In finance, a _____ is a debt security, in which the authorized issuer owes the holders a debt and, depending on the terms of the _____, is obliged to pay interest (the coupon) and/or to repay the principal at a later date, termed maturity. A _____ is a formal contract to repay borrowed money with interest at fixed intervals.

Thus a _____ is like a loan: the issuer is the borrower (debtor), the holder is the lender (creditor), and the coupon is the interest.

a. Prize Bond
b. Bond
c. Callable
d. Zero-coupon

Chapter 7. Analysis of Costs

37. In accounting, _____ is the original monetary value of an economic item. In some circumstances, assets and liabilities may be shown at their _____, as if there had been no change in value since the date of acquisition. The balance sheet value of the item may therefore differ from the 'true' value.

   a. Historical cost
   b. Salvage value
   c. Net income per employee
   d. Deferred financing costs

38. _____ or economic opportunity loss is the value of the next best alternative foregone as the result of making a decision. _____ analysis is an important part of a company's decision-making processes but is not treated as an actual cost in any financial statement. The next best thing that a person can engage in is referred to as the _____ of doing the best thing and ignoring the next best thing to be done.

   a. Economic
   b. Industrial organization
   c. Economic ideology
   d. Opportunity cost

39. _____ is an economic concept with commonplace familiarity. It is the price that a good or service is offered at, or will fetch, in the marketplace. It is of interest mainly in the study of microeconomics.

   a. Market price
   b. Paper trading
   c. Noisy market hypothesis
   d. Market anomaly

40. _____s (economically referred to as land or raw materials) occur naturally within environments that exist relatively undisturbed by mankind, in a natural form. A _____'s is often characterized by amounts of biodiversity existent in various ecosystems.

Mining, petroleum extraction, fishing, hunting, and forestry are generally considered natural-resource industries.

   a. Natural resource
   b. 100-year flood
   c. 1921 recession
   d. 130-30 fund

41. _____ is the a method of technical and economic research of the systems for purpose to optimize a parity between system's consumer functions or properties and expenses to achieve those functions or properties.

This methodology for continuous perfection of production, industrial technologies, organizational structures was developed by Juryj Sobolev in 1948 at the 'Perm telephone factory'

- 1948 Juryj Sobolev - the first success in application of a method analysis at the 'Perm telephone factory'.
- 1949 - the first application for the invention as result of use of the new method.

Chapter 7. Analysis of Costs

Today in economically developed countries practically each enterprise or the company use methodology of the kind of functional-cost analysis as a practice of the quality management, most full satisfying to principles of standards of series ISO 9000.

- Interest of consumer not in products itself, but the advantage which it will receive from its usage.
- The consumer aspires to reduce his expenses
- Functions needed by consumer can be executed in the various ways, and, hence, with various efficiency and expenses. Among possible alternatives of realization of functions exist such in which the parity of quality and the price is the optimal for the consumer.

The goal of _____ is achievement of the highest consumer satisfaction of production at simultaneous decrease in all kinds of industrial expenses Classical _____ has three English synonyms - Value Engineering, Value Management, Value Analysis.

a. Willingness to pay
c. Staple financing
b. Monopoly wage
d. Function cost analysis

42. Competition law, known in the United States as _____ law, has three main elements:

- prohibiting agreements or practices that restrict free trading and competition between business entities. This includes in particular the repression of cartels.
- banning abusive behaviour by a firm dominating a market, or anti-competitive practices that tend to lead to such a dominant position. Practices controlled in this way may include predatory pricing, tying, price gouging, refusal to deal, and many others.
- supervising the mergers and acquisitions of large corporations, including some joint ventures. Transactions that are considered to threaten the competitive process can be prohibited altogether, or approved subject to 'remedies' such as an obligation to divest part of the merged business or to offer licences or access to facilities to enable other businesses to continue competing.

The substance and practice of competition law varies from jurisdiction to jurisdiction. Protecting the interests of consumers (consumer welfare) and ensuring that entrepreneurs have an opportunity to compete in the market economy are often treated as important objectives. Competition law is closely connected with law on deregulation of access to markets, state aids and subsidies, the privatisation of state owned assets and the establishment of independent sector regulators. In recent decades, competition law has been viewed as a way to provide better public services.

a. Intellectual property law
c. Anti-Inflation Act
b. Antitrust
d. United Kingdom competition law

43. _____ is a broad label that refers to any individuals or households that use goods and services generated within the economy. The concept of a _____ is used in different contexts, so that the usage and significance of the term may vary.

Typically when business people and economists talk of _____s they are talking about person as _____, an aggregated commodity item with little individuality other than that expressed in the buy/not-buy decision.

a. 100-year flood
c. 130-30 fund
b. 1921 recession
d. Consumer

44. The term surplus is used in economics for several related quantities. The _____ is the amount that consumers benefit by being able to purchase a product for a price that is less than they would be willing to pay. The producer surplus is the amount that producers benefit by selling at a market price mechanism that is higher than they would be willing to sell for.

a. Necessity good
c. Microeconomic reform
b. Marginal rate of technical substitution
d. Consumer surplus

45. In retail systems, the _____ represents the specific value that represents unit price purchased. This value is used as a key factor in determining profitability and in some stock market theories it is used in establishing the value of stock holding.

_____s appear in several forms, such as Actual Cost, Last Cost, Average Cost and Net realizable value.

a. Ten bagger
c. Facilitation payment
b. Customer Demand Planning
d. Cost Price

46. In economics, _____ are the resources employed to produce goods and services. They facilitate production but do not become part of the product (as with raw materials) or significantly transformed by the production process (as with fuel used to power machinery.) To 19th century economists, the _____ were land (natural resources, gifts from nature), labor (the ability to work), and capital goods (human-made tools and equipment.)

a. Hicks-neutral technical change
c. Long-run
b. Product Pipeline
d. Factors of production

47. A security is a fungible, negotiable instrument representing financial value. _____ are broadly categorized into debt _____; equity _____, e.g., common stocks; and derivative (finance) contracts such as forwards, futures, options and swaps. The company or other entity issuing the security is called the issuer.

a. Red herring prospectus
c. Pass-Through Certificates
b. Settlement risk
d. Securities

48. The U.S. _____ is an independent agency of the United States government which holds primary responsibility for enforcing the federal securities laws and regulating the securities industry, the nation's stock and options exchanges, and other electronic securities markets. The SEC was created by section 4 of the Securities Exchange Act of 1934 (now codified as 15 U.S.C. § 78d and commonly referred to as the 1934 Act.)

a. 100-year flood
c. 1921 recession
b. Securities and Exchange Commission
d. 130-30 fund

49. In economics, the _____ also known as MPL or MPN is the change in output from hiring one additional unit of labor. It is the increase in output added by the last unit of labor. Assuming that no other inputs to production change, the marginal product of a given input (X) can be expressed as:

MP = ΔY/ΔX = (the change of Y)/(the change of X.)

a. Product Pipeline
b. Marginal product of labor
c. Marginal product
d. Production function

50. In economics, a _____ is a function that specifies the output of a firm, an industry, or an entire economy for all combinations of inputs. A meta-_____ compares the practice of the existing entities converting inputs X into output y to determine the most efficient practice _____ of the existing entities, whether the most efficient feasible practice production or the most efficient actual practice production. In either case, the maximum output of a technologically-determined production process is a mathematical function of input factors of production.
   a. Constant elasticity of substitution
   b. Post-Fordism
   c. Short-run
   d. Production function

51. In economics, an _____ is a contour line drawn through the set of points at which the same quantity of output is produced while changing the quantities of two or more inputs. While an indifference curve helps to answer the utility-maximizing problem of consumers, the _____ deals with the cost-minimization problem of producers. _____s are typically drawn on capital-labor graphs, showing the tradeoff between capital and labor in the production function, and the decreasing marginal returns of both inputs.
   a. Economic production quantity
   b. Isoquant
   c. Underinvestment employment relationship
   d. Economies of scale

52. A _____ is an expression that compares quantities relative to each other. The most common examples involve two quantities, but any number of quantities can be compared. _____s are represented mathematically by separating each quantity with a colon, for example the _____ 2:3, which is read as the _____ 'two to three'.
   a. Ratio
   b. 130-30 fund
   c. 100-year flood
   d. Y-intercept

Chapter 8. Analysis of Perfectly Competitive Markets

1. The _____ consists of a number of economic theories which describe the nature of the firm, company including its existence, its behaviour, and its relationship with the market.

In simplified terms, the _____ aims to answer these questions:

1. Existence - why do firms emerge, why are not all transactions in the economy mediated over the market?
2. Boundaries - why the boundary between firms and the market is located exactly there? Which transactions are performed internally and which are negotiated on the market?
3. Organization - why are firms structured in such specific way? What is the interplay of formal and informal relationships?

Despite looking simple, these questions are not answered by the established economic theory, which usually views firms as given, and treats them as black boxes without any internal structure.

The First World War period saw a change of emphasis in economic theory away from industry-level analysis which mainly included analysing markets to analysis at the level of the firm, as it became increasingly clear that perfect competition was no longer an adequate model of how firms behaved. Economic theory till then had focussed on trying to understand markets alone and there had been little study on understanding why firms or organisations exist.

    a. Khazzoom-Brookes postulate   b. Policy Ineffectiveness Proposition
    c. Technology gap   d. Theory of the firm

2. _____ is an economic model based on price, utility and quantity in a market. It predicts that in a competitive market, price will function to equalize the quantity demanded by consumers, and the quantity supplied by producers, resulting in an economic equilibrium of price and quantity. The model incorporates other factors changing equilibrium as a shift of demand and/or supply.

    a. Rational addiction   b. Joint demand
    c. Deferred gratification   d. Supply and demand

3. _____ is a term used in national accounts statistics and macroeconomics. It basically refers to the net additions to the (physical) capital stock in an accounting period, or, to the value of the increase of the capital stock; though it may occasionally also refer to the (growth of the) total stock of capital formed.

Thus, in UNSNA, _____ equals fixed capital investment, the increase in the value of inventories held, plus (net) lending to foreign countries, during an accounting period.

    a. Capital formation   b. Capital flight
    c. Capital intensity   d. Consumption of fixed capital

Chapter 8. Analysis of Perfectly Competitive Markets

4. Economics:

   - _____, the desire to own something and the ability to pay for it
   - _____ curve, a graphic representation of a _____ schedule
   - _____ deposit, the money in checking accounts
   - _____ pull theory, the theory that inflation occurs when _____ for goods and services exceeds existing supplies
   - _____ schedule, a table that lists the quantity of a good a person will buy it each different price
   - _____ side economics, the school of economics at believes government spending and tax cuts open economy by raising _____

   a. Production
   b. Variability
   c. McKesson ' Robbins scandal
   d. Demand

5. In economics, the _____ can be defined as the graph depicting the relationship between the price of a certain commodity, and the amount of it that consumers are willing and able to purchase at that given price. It is a graphic representation of a demand schedule. The _____ for all consumers together follows from the _____ of every individual consumer: the individual demands at each price are added together.
   a. Kuznets curve
   b. Demand curve
   c. Wage curve
   d. Cost curve

6. In neoclassical economics and microeconomics, _____ describes the perfect being a market in which there are many small firms, all producing homogeneous goods. In the short term, such markets are productively inefficient as output will not occur where mc is equal to ac, but allocatively efficient, as output under _____ will always occur where mc is equal to mr, and therefore where mc equals ar. However, in the long term, such markets are both allocatively and productively efficient.
   a. General equilibrium
   b. Perfect competition
   c. Law of supply
   d. Co-operative economics

7. In economics, _____ is the process by which a firm determines the price and output level that returns the greatest profit. There are several approaches to this problem. The total revenue--total cost method relies on the fact that profit equals revenue minus cost, and the marginal revenue--marginal cost method is based on the fact that total profit in a perfectly competitive market reaches its maximum point where marginal revenue equals marginal cost.
   a. Profit margin
   b. Normal profit
   c. 100-year flood
   d. Profit maximization

Chapter 8. Analysis of Perfectly Competitive Markets

8. A _____ is:

- Rewrite _____, in generative grammar and computer science
- Standardization, a formal and widely-accepted statement, fact, definition, or qualification
- Operation, a determinate _____ for performing a mathematical operation and obtaining a certain result (Mathematics, Logic)
    - Unary operation
    - Binary operation
- _____ of inference, a function from sets of formulae to formulae (Mathematics, Logic)
- _____ of thumb, principle with broad application that is not intended to be strictly accurate or reliable for every situation. Also often simply referred to as a _____
- Moral, an atomic element of a moral code for guiding choices in human behavior
- Heuristic, a quantized '_____' which shows a tendency or probability for successful function
- A regulation, as in sports
- A Production _____, as in computer science
- Procedural law, a _____ set governing the application of laws to cases
    - A law, which may informally be called a '_____'
    - A court ruling, a decision by a court
- In the U.S. Government, a regulation mandated by Congress, but written or expanded upon by the Executive Branch.
- Norm (sociology), an informal but widely accepted _____, concept, truth, definition, or qualification (social norms, legal norms, coding norms)
- Norm (philosophy), a kind of sentence or a reason to act, feel or believe
- 'Rulership' is the concept of governance by a government:
    - Military _____, governance by a military body
    - Monastic _____, a collection of precepts that guides the life of monks or nuns in a religious order where the superior holds the place of Christ
- Slide _____

- '_____,' a song by Ayumi Hamasaki
- '_____,' a song by rapper Nas
- '_____s,' an album by the band The Whitest Boy Alive
- _____s: Pyaar Ka Superhit Formula, a 2003 Bollywood film
- ruler, an instrument for measuring lengths
- _____, a component of an astrolabe, circumferator or similar instrument
- The _____s, a bestselling self-help book
- _____ Project (Run Up-to-date Linux Everywhere), a project that aims to use up-to-date Linux software on old PCs
- _____ engine, a software system that helps managing business _____s
- Ja _____, a hip hop artist
    - R.U.L.E., a 2005 greatest hits album by rapper Ja _____
- '_____s,' a KMFDM song

a. Demand
b. Technocracy
c. Procter ' Gamble
d. Rule

Chapter 8. Analysis of Perfectly Competitive Markets

9. In economic theory, _____ is the competitive situation in any market where the conditions necessary for perfect competition are not satisfied. It is a market structure that does not meet the conditions of perfect competition.

Forms of _____ include:

- Monopoly, in which there is only one seller of a good.
- Oligopoly, in which there is a small number of sellers.
- Monopolistic competition, in which there are many sellers producing highly differentiated goods.
- Monopsony, in which there is only one buyer of a good.
- Oligopsony, in which there is a small number of buyers.

There may also be _____ in markets due to buyers or sellers lacking information about prices and the goods being traded.

There may also be _____ due to a time lag in a market.

a. Imperfect competition
b. ACCRA Cost of Living Index
c. AD-IA Model
d. ACEA agreement

10. In economics and finance, _____ is the change in total cost that arises when the quantity produced changes by one unit. It is the cost of producing one more unit of a good. Mathematically, the _____ function is expressed as the first derivative of the total cost (TC) function with respect to quantity (Q.)

a. Quality costs
b. Marginal cost
c. Variable cost
d. Khozraschyot

11. _____ in economics and business is the result of an exchange and from that trade we assign a numerical monetary value to a good, service or asset. If Alice trades Bob 4 apples for an orange, the _____ of an orange is 4 apples. Inversely, the _____ of an apple is 1/4 oranges.

a. Price book
b. Price
c. Price war
d. Premium pricing

12. Monopoly power is an example of market failure which occurs when one or more of the participants has the ability to influence the price or other outcomes in some general or specialized market. The most commonly discussed form of market power is that of a monopoly, but other forms such as monopsony, and more moderate versions of these two extremes, exist. Market participants that have market power are sometimes referred to as 'price makers', while those without are sometimes called '_____'.

a. Market concentration
b. Market power
c. Monopolization
d. Price takers

13. In economics, an _____ or spillover of an economic transaction is an impact on a party that is not directly involved in the transaction. In such a case, prices do not reflect the full costs or benefits in production or consumption of a product or service. A positive impact is called an external benefit, while a negative impact is called an external cost.

a. Existence value
b. Environmental impact assessment
c. Environmental tariff
d. Externality

Chapter 8. Analysis of Perfectly Competitive Markets

14. In law and economics, the _____, describes the economic efficiency of an economic allocation or outcome in the presence of externalities. The theorem states that when trade in an externality is possible and there are no transaction costs, bargaining will lead to an efficient outcome regardless of the initial allocation of property rights. In practice, obstacles to bargaining or poorly defined property rights can prevent Coasian bargaining.
   a. General Mining Act of 1872
   b. Prior appropriation water rights
   c. Coase theorem
   d. Means test

15. _____s is the social science that studies the production, distribution, and consumption of goods and services. The term _____s comes from the Ancient Greek οá¼°κονομῖα from οá¼¶κος (oikos, 'house') + vΐŒμος (nomos, 'custom' or 'law'), hence 'rules of the house(hold)'. Current _____ models developed out of the broader field of political economy in the late 19th century, owing to a desire to use an empirical approach more akin to the physical sciences.
   a. Inflation
   b. Energy economics
   c. Economic
   d. Opportunity cost

16. In economics, _____ is the difference between a company's total revenue and its opportunity costs. It is the increase in wealth that an investor has from making an investment, taking into consideration all costs associated with that investment including the opportunity cost of capital.

    Profit is the factor income of the entrepreneur.

   a. Operating profit
   b. ACCRA Cost of Living Index
   c. Accounting profit
   d. Economic profit

17. In economics, and cost accounting, _____ describes the total economic cost of production and is made up of variable costs, which vary according to the quantity of a good produced and include inputs such as labor and raw materials, plus fixed costs, which are independent of the quantity of a good produced and include inputs (capital) that cannot be varied in the short term, such as buildings and machinery. _____ in economics includes the total opportunity cost of each factor of production in addition to fixed and variable costs.

    The rate at which _____ changes as the amount produced changes is called marginal cost.

   a. Total cost
   b. 100-year flood
   c. 1921 recession
   d. 130-30 fund

18. In economics, a _____ is a graph of the costs of production as a function of total quantity produced. In a free market economy, productively efficient firms use these curves to find the optimal point of production, where they make the most profits. There are a few different types of _____s, each relevant to a different area of economics.
   a. Demand curve
   b. Kuznets curve
   c. Phillips curve
   d. Cost curve

19. In microeconomics, _____ is quite simply the conversion of inputs into outputs. It is an economic process that uses resources to create a good or service that is suitable for exchange. This can include manufacturing, storing, shipping, and packaging.
   a. MET
   b. Production
   c. Solved
   d. Red Guards

Chapter 8. Analysis of Perfectly Competitive Markets

20. _____ is an economic concept with commonplace familiarity. It is the price that a good or service is offered at, or will fetch, in the marketplace. It is of interest mainly in the study of microeconomics.
    a. Paper trading
    b. Noisy market hypothesis
    c. Market anomaly
    d. Market price

21. Competition law, known in the United States as _____ law, has three main elements:

    - prohibiting agreements or practices that restrict free trading and competition between business entities. This includes in particular the repression of cartels.
    - banning abusive behaviour by a firm dominating a market, or anti-competitive practices that tend to lead to such a dominant position. Practices controlled in this way may include predatory pricing, tying, price gouging, refusal to deal, and many others.
    - supervising the mergers and acquisitions of large corporations, including some joint ventures. Transactions that are considered to threaten the competitive process can be prohibited altogether, or approved subject to 'remedies' such as an obligation to divest part of the merged business or to offer licences or access to facilities to enable other businesses to continue competing.

    The substance and practice of competition law varies from jurisdiction to jurisdiction. Protecting the interests of consumers (consumer welfare) and ensuring that entrepreneurs have an opportunity to compete in the market economy are often treated as important objectives. Competition law is closely connected with law on deregulation of access to markets, state aids and subsidies, the privatisation of state owned assets and the establishment of independent sector regulators. In recent decades, competition law has been viewed as a way to provide better public services.

    a. Intellectual property law
    b. Anti-Inflation Act
    c. Antitrust
    d. United Kingdom competition law

22. _____ theory is a branch of theoretical economics. It seeks to explain the behavior of supply, demand and prices in a whole economy with several or many markets. It is often assumed that agents are price takers and in that setting two common notions of equilibrium exist: Walrasian (or competitive) equilibrium, and its generalization; a price equilibrium with transfers.
    a. Human capital
    b. New Keynesian economics
    c. Rational choice theory
    d. General equilibrium

23. In economic models, the _____ time frame assumes no fixed factors of production. Firms can enter or leave the marketplace, and the cost (and availability) of land, labor, raw materials, and capital goods can be assumed to vary. In contrast, in the short-run time frame, certain factors are assumed to be fixed, because there is not sufficient time for them to change.
    a. Long-run
    b. Price/performance ratio
    c. Diseconomies of scale
    d. Productivity world

24. In economics, economic equilibrium is simply a state of the world where economic forces are balanced and in the absence of external influences the (equilibrium) values of economic variables will not change. It is the point at which quantity demanded and quantity supplied are equal. _____, for example, refers to a condition where a market price is established through competition such that the amount of goods or services sought by buyers is equal to the amount of goods or services produced by sellers.

Chapter 8. Analysis of Perfectly Competitive Markets

a. Marketization
b. Product-Market Growth Matrix
c. Regulated market
d. Market equilibrium

25. In economics, the concept of the _____ refers to the decision-making time frame of a firm in which at least one factor of production is fixed. Costs which are fixed in the _____ have no impact on a firms decisions. For example a firm can raise output by increasing the amount of labour through overtime.
   a. Hicks-neutral technical change
   b. Short-run
   c. Productivity model
   d. Product Pipeline

26. _____ is defined as the measure of responsiveness in the quantity demanded for a commodity as a result of change in price of the same commodity. It is a measure of how consumers react to a change in price. In other words, it is percentage change in quantity demanded as per the percentage change in price of the same commodity.
   a. 130-30 fund
   b. 100-year flood
   c. 1921 recession
   d. Price elasticity of demand

27. In economics, _____ is the ratio of the percent change in one variable to the percent change in another variable. It is a tool for measuring the responsiveness of a function to changes in parameters in a relative way. Commonly analyzed are _____ of substitution, price and wealth.
   a. Elasticity
   b. Elasticity of demand
   c. ACEA agreement
   d. ACCRA Cost of Living Index

28. Price _____ is defined as the measure of responsiveness in the quantity demanded for a commodity as a result of change in price of the same commodity. It is a measure of how consumers react to a change in price. In other words, it is percentage change in quantity demanded by the percentage change in price of the same commodity.
   a. ACEA agreement
   b. Elasticity of demand
   c. ACCRA Cost of Living Index
   d. Elasticity

29. _____ is a term used by economists to describe a condition in which firms can freely enter the market for an economic good by establishing production and beginning to sell the product.

   _____ is implied by the perfect competition condition that there is an unlimited number of buyers and sellers in a market. In comparison to perfect competition, however, _____ is a condition often more applicable to real world conditions.

   a. 100-year flood
   b. Free entry
   c. 1921 recession
   d. 130-30 fund

30. _____ is a situation in which the limited resources of a firm are allocated in accordance with the wishes of consumers. An allocatively efficient economy produces an 'optimal mix' of commodities. A firm is allocatively efficient when its price is equal to its marginal costs (that is, P = MC) in a perfect market.
   a. ACCRA Cost of Living Index
   b. ACEA agreement
   c. Economic efficiency
   d. Allocative efficiency

Chapter 8. Analysis of Perfectly Competitive Markets

31. In economics, _____ refers to how the marginal contribution of a factor of production usually decreases as more of the factor is used. According to this relationship, in a production system with fixed and variable inputs, beyond some point, each additional unit of the variable input yields smaller and smaller increases in output. Conversely, producing one more unit of output costs more and more in variable inputs.
    a. Derivatives law
    b. Patent troll
    c. Community property
    d. Diminishing returns

32. In economics supernormal profit _____ or pure profit or excess profits, is a profit exceeding the normal profit. Normal profit equals the opportunity cost of labour and capital, while supernormal profit is the amount exceeds the normal return from these input factors in production.

    _____ is usually generated by an oligopoly or a monopoly; however, these firms often try to hide this from the market to reduce risk of competition or antitrust investigation.

    a. ACCRA Cost of Living Index
    b. Economic profit
    c. Abnormal profit
    d. Accounting profit

33. In economics, _____ are the resources employed to produce goods and services. They facilitate production but do not become part of the product (as with raw materials) or significantly transformed by the production process (as with fuel used to power machinery.) To 19th century economists, the _____ were land (natural resources, gifts from nature), labor (the ability to work), and capital goods (human-made tools and equipment.)
    a. Long-run
    b. Product Pipeline
    c. Hicks-neutral technical change
    d. Factors of production

34. In economics, the _____ is defined as a numerical measure of the responsiveness of the quantity supplied of product (A) to a change in price of product (A) alone. It is the measure of the way quantity supplied reacts to a change in price.

    $\boxed{x}$ >

    For example, if, in response to a 10% rise in the price of a good, the quantity supplied increases by 20%, the _____ would be 20%/10% = 2.

    a. Hedonimetry
    b. Passive income
    c. Demand shaping
    d. Price elasticity of supply

35. Economic _____ is defined as an excess distribution to any factor in a production process above that which is required to induce the factor into the process or any excess above that which is necessary to keep the factor in its current use..

    Classical Factor _____ is primarily concerned with the fee paid for the use of fixed (e.g. natural) resources. The classical definition is expressed as any excess payment above that required to induce or provide for production.

a. 100-year flood
c. 130-30 fund
b. Rent
d. 1921 recession

36. In economics, _____ is equal to total cost divided by the number of goods produced (the output quantity, Q.) It is also equal to the sum of average variable costs (total variable costs divided by Q) plus average fixed costs (total fixed costs divided by Q.) _____s may be dependent on the time period considered (increasing production may be expensive or impossible in the short term, for example.)

   a. Average fixed cost
   c. Explicit cost
   b. Average cost
   d. Average variable cost

37. The supply of labor is the number of total hours that workers wish to work at a given real wage rate.

   _____ curves are derived from the 'labor-leisure' trade-off. More hours worked earn higher incomes but necessitate a cut in the amount of leisure that workers enjoy.

   a. Labor supply
   c. Human trafficking
   b. Creative capitalism
   d. Late capitalism

38. Competitive market equilibrium is the traditional concept of economic equilibrium, appropriate for the analysis of commodity markets with flexible prices and many traders, and serving as the benchmark of efficiency in economic analysis. It relies crucially on the assumption of a competitive environment where each trader decides upon a quantity that is so small compared to the total quantity traded in the market that their individual transactions have no influence on the prices. Competitive markets are an ideal, a standard that other market structures are evaluated by.

   A _____ consists of a vector of prices and an allocation such that given the prices, each trader by maximizing his objective function (profit, preferences) subject to his technological possibilities and resource constraints plans to trade into his part of the proposed allocation, and such that the prices make all net trades compatible with one another ('clear the market') by equating aggregate supply and demand for the commodities which are traded.

   a. Market system
   c. Product-Market Growth Matrix
   b. Partial equilibrium
   d. Competitive equilibrium

39. In economics, the _____ of a good or of a service is the utility of the specific use to which an agent would put a given increase in that good or service, or of the specific use that would be abandoned in response to a given decrease. In other words, _____ is the utility of the marginal use -- which, on the assumption of economic rationality, would be the least urgent use of the good or service, from the best feasible combination of actions in which its use is included. Under the mainstream assumptions, the _____ of a good or service is the posited quantified change in utility obtained by increasing or by decreasing use of that good or service.

   a. 130-30 fund
   c. 1921 recession
   b. 100-year flood
   d. Marginal utility

40. _____ is an important concept in economics with broad applications in game theory, engineering and the social sciences. The term is named after Vilfredo Pareto, an Italian economist who used the concept in his studies of economic efficiency and income distribution. Informally, pareto efficient situations are those in which any change to make any person better off would make someone else worse off.

Chapter 8. Analysis of Perfectly Competitive Markets

a. Lump of labour
b. Matching pennies
c. Perfect rationality
d. Pareto efficiency

41. In economics, _____ is a measure of the relative satisfaction from consumption of various goods and services. Given this measure, one may speak meaningfully of increasing or decreasing _____, and thereby explain economic behavior in terms of attempts to increase one's _____. For illustrative purposes, changes in _____ are sometimes expressed in units called utils.
   a. Utility
   b. Ordinal utility
   c. Expected utility hypothesis
   d. Utility function

42. The term surplus is used in economics for several related quantities. The consumer surplus is the amount that consumers benefit by being able to purchase a product for a price that is less than they would be willing to pay. The _____ is the amount that producers benefit by selling at a market price mechanism that is higher than they would be willing to sell for.
   a. Producer surplus
   b. Schedule delay
   c. Returns to scale
   d. Long term

43. _____ is a broad label that refers to any individuals or households that use goods and services generated within the economy. The concept of a _____ is used in different contexts, so that the usage and significance of the term may vary.

Typically when business people and economists talk of _____s they are talking about person as _____, an aggregated commodity item with little individuality other than that expressed in the buy/not-buy decision.

   a. 130-30 fund
   b. 100-year flood
   c. Consumer
   d. 1921 recession

44. A _____ is an object whose consumption increases the utility of the consumer, for which the quantity demanded exceeds the quantity supplied at zero price. _____s are usually modeled as having diminishing marginal utility. The first individual purchase has high utility; the second has less.
   a. Pie method
   b. Good
   c. Merit good
   d. Composite good

45. In economics, economic output is divided into physical goods and intangible services. Consumption of _____ is assumed to produce utility. It is often used when referring to a _____ Tax.
   a. Composite good
   b. Goods and services
   c. Manufactured goods
   d. Private good

46. A _____ is an economy based on the division of labor in which the prices of goods and services are determined in a free price system set by supply and demand. This is often contrasted with a planned economy, in which a central government determines the price of goods and services using a fixed price system. Market economies are contrasted with mixed economy where the price system is not entirely free but under some government control that is not extensive enough to constitute a planned economy.

a. Network Economy
b. Nutritional Economics
c. Commons-based peer production
d. Market economy

47. In economics, a _____ exists when the production or use of goods and services by the market is not efficient. That is, there exists another outcome where all involved can be made better off. _____s can be viewed as scenarios where individuals' pursuit of pure self-interest leads to results that are not efficient - that can be improved upon from the societal point-of-view.
   a. General equilibrium
   b. Fixed exchange rate
   c. Market failure
   d. Financial economics

48. _____ refers to various economic systems where the means of production are publicly owned, but the market is utilized. In a traditional market socialist economy, prices would be determined by a government planning ministry, and enterprises would either be state-owned or cooperatively-owned and managed by their employees. The People's Republic of China currently has a form of _____ referred to as the socialist market economy.
   a. Market socialism
   b. Red fist
   c. Democratic socialism
   d. Working class

49. _____ is one of the four Ps of the marketing mix. The other three aspects are product, promotion, and place. It is also a key variable in microeconomic price allocation theory.
   a. Premium pricing
   b. Point of total assumption
   c. Guaranteed Maximum Price
   d. Pricing

50. _____ in political thought refers to economic theories of social organization advocating collective ownership and administration of the means of production and distribution of goods, and a society characterized by equality for all individuals, with an egalitarian method of compensation. Modern _____ originated in the late 19th-century intellectual and working class political movement that criticized the effects of industrialization and private ownership on society. Karl Marx posited that _____ would be achieved via class struggle and a proletarian revolution after a transitional stage from capitalism called the dictatorship of the proletariat.
   a. Socialism
   b. Adolph Fischer
   c. Adam Smith
   d. Adolf Hitler

51. In economics, the _____ is the term economists use to describe the self-regulating nature of the marketplace. The _____ is a metaphor coined by the economist Adam Smith in The Wealth of Nations.

Adam Smith mentions the metaphor in Book IV of The Wealth of Nations, arguing that people in any society will certainly employ their capital in foreign trading only if the profits available by that method far exceed those available locally, and that in such a case it is better for society as a whole if they so did.

   a. AD-IA Model
   b. ACCRA Cost of Living Index
   c. Invisible hand
   d. ACEA agreement

Chapter 8. Analysis of Perfectly Competitive Markets

52. Examples of _____ include:

- A beekeeper keeps the bees for their honey. A side effect or externality associated with his activity is the pollination of surrounding crops by the bees. The value generated by the pollination may be more important than the value of the harvested honey.

- An individual planting an attractive garden in front of his house may provide benefits to others living in the area, and even financial benefits in the form of increased property values for all property owners.

- An individual buying a product that is interconnected in a network (e.g., a video cellphone) will increase the usefulness of such phones to other people who have a video cellphone. When each new user of a product increases the value of the same product owned by others, the phenomenon is called a network externality or a network effect. Network externalities often have 'tipping points' where, suddenly, the product reaches general acceptance and near-universal usage, a phenomenon which can be seen in the near universal take-up of cellphones in some Scandinavian countries.

- Knowledge spillover of inventions and information - once an invention (or most other forms of practical information) is discovered or made more easily accessible, others benefit by exploiting the invention or information. Copyright and intellectual property law are mechanisms to allow the inventor or creator to benefit from a temporary, state-protected monopoly in return for 'sharing' the information through publication or other means.

a. Weighted average cost of carbon
c. Total Economic Value
b. Negative externalities
d. Positive externalities

53. Although information has been bought and sold since ancient times, the idea of an information marketplace is relatively recent. The nature of such markets is still evolving, which complicates development of sustainable business models. However, certain attributes of _____ are beginning to be understood, such as diminished participation costs, opportunities for customization, shifting customer relations, and a need for order.

a. Information markets
c. Underground economy
b. Intention economy
d. Open economy

54. In microeconomics, _____ is the extra revenue that an additional unit of product will bring. It is the additional income from selling one more unit of a good; sometimes equal to price. It can also be described as the change in total revenue/change in number of units sold.

a. Market demand schedule
c. Marginal revenue
b. Long term
d. Reservation price

Chapter 9. Imperfect Competition and Monopoly

1. In economic theory, _____ is the competitive situation in any market where the conditions necessary for perfect competition are not satisfied. It is a market structure that does not meet the conditions of perfect competition.

Forms of _____ include:

- Monopoly, in which there is only one seller of a good.
- Oligopoly, in which there is a small number of sellers.
- Monopolistic competition, in which there are many sellers producing highly differentiated goods.
- Monopsony, in which there is only one buyer of a good.
- Oligopsony, in which there is a small number of buyers.

There may also be _____ in markets due to buyers or sellers lacking information about prices and the goods being traded.

There may also be _____ due to a time lag in a market.

a. ACEA agreement
b. ACCRA Cost of Living Index
c. AD-IA Model
d. Imperfect competition

2. _____ is an economic concept with commonplace familiarity. It is the price that a good or service is offered at, or will fetch, in the marketplace. It is of interest mainly in the study of microeconomics.
   a. Market anomaly
   b. Noisy market hypothesis
   c. Paper trading
   d. Market price

3. _____ is a common market structure where many competing producers sell products that are differentiated from one another (ie. the products are substitutes, but are not exactly alike.) Many markets are monopolistically competitive, common examples include the markets for restaurants, cereal, clothing, shoes and service industries in large cities.
   a. Perfect competition
   b. Financial crisis
   c. Mathematical economics
   d. Monopolistic competition

4. In economics, a _____ exists when a specific individual or enterprise has sufficient control over a particular product or service to determine significantly the terms on which other individuals shall have access to it. Monopolies are thus characterized by a lack of economic competition for the good or service that they provide and a lack of viable substitute goods. The verb 'monopolize' refers to the process by which a firm gains persistently greater market share than what is expected under perfect competition.
   a. 100-year flood
   b. Monopoly
   c. 130-30 fund
   d. 1921 recession

5. An _____ is a market form in which a market or industry is dominated by a small number of sellers (oligopolists.) Because there are few participants in this type of market, each oligopolist is aware of the actions of the others. The decisions of one firm influence, and are influenced by, the decisions of other firms.
   a. ACEA agreement
   b. Oligopsony
   c. ACCRA Cost of Living Index
   d. Oligopoly

6. In economics, _____ and economies of scale are related terms that describe what happens as the scale of production increases. They are different terms and should not be used interchangeably.

Chapter 9. Imperfect Competition and Monopoly

_____ refers to a technical property of production that examines changes in output subsequent to a proportional change in all inputs (where all inputs increase by a constant factor.)

a. Constant returns to scale
b. Necessity good
c. Customer equity
d. Returns to scale

7. _____ is a situation in which the limited resources of a firm are allocated in accordance with the wishes of consumers. An allocatively efficient economy produces an 'optimal mix' of commodities. A firm is allocatively efficient when its price is equal to its marginal costs (that is, P = MC) in a perfect market.

a. ACCRA Cost of Living Index
b. Economic efficiency
c. Allocative efficiency
d. ACEA agreement

8. _____ has several particular meanings:

- in mathematics
    - _____ function
    - Euler _____
    - _____
    - _____ subgroup
    - method of _____s (partial differential equations)
- in physics and engineering
    - any _____ curve that shows the relationship between certain input- and output parameters, e.g.
    - an I-V or current-voltage _____ is the current in a circuit as a function of the applied voltage
    - Receiver-Operator _____
- in fiction
    - in Dungeons ' Dragons, _____ is another name for ability score

a. Russian financial crisis
b. Demand
c. Technocracy
d. Characteristic

9. _____ in economics and business is the result of an exchange and from that trade we assign a numerical monetary value to a good, service or asset. If Alice trades Bob 4 apples for an orange, the _____ of an orange is 4 apples. Inversely, the _____ of an apple is 1/4 oranges.

a. Price
b. Premium pricing
c. Price war
d. Price book

10. Competition law, known in the United States as _____ law, has three main elements:

- prohibiting agreements or practices that restrict free trading and competition between business entities. This includes in particular the repression of cartels.
- banning abusive behaviour by a firm dominating a market, or anti-competitive practices that tend to lead to such a dominant position. Practices controlled in this way may include predatory pricing, tying, price gouging, refusal to deal, and many others.
- supervising the mergers and acquisitions of large corporations, including some joint ventures. Transactions that are considered to threaten the competitive process can be prohibited altogether, or approved subject to 'remedies' such as an obligation to divest part of the merged business or to offer licences or access to facilities to enable other businesses to continue competing.

The substance and practice of competition law varies from jurisdiction to jurisdiction. Protecting the interests of consumers (consumer welfare) and ensuring that entrepreneurs have an opportunity to compete in the market economy are often treated as important objectives. Competition law is closely connected with law on deregulation of access to markets, state aids and subsidies, the privatisation of state owned assets and the establishment of independent sector regulators. In recent decades, competition law has been viewed as a way to provide better public services.

a. United Kingdom competition law
b. Anti-Inflation Act
c. Intellectual property law
d. Antitrust

11. Economics:

- _____ ,the desire to own something and the ability to pay for it
- _____ curve, a graphic representation of a _____ schedule
- _____ deposit, the money in checking accounts
- _____ pull theory, the theory that inflation occurs when _____ for goods and services exceeds existing supplies
- _____ schedule, a table that lists the quantity of a good a person will buy it each different price
- _____ side economics, the school of economics at believes government spending and tax cuts open economy by raising _____

a. McKesson ' Robbins scandal
b. Variability
c. Production
d. Demand

12. In economics, the _____ can be defined as the graph depicting the relationship between the price of a certain commodity, and the amount of it that consumers are willing and able to purchase at that given price. It is a graphic representation of a demand schedule. The _____ for all consumers together follows from the _____ of every individual consumer: the individual demands at each price are added together.

a. Cost curve
b. Kuznets curve
c. Wage curve
d. Demand curve

13. A _____ is a set of exclusive rights granted by a state to an inventor or his assignee for a limited period of time in exchange for a disclosure of an invention.

Chapter 9. Imperfect Competition and Monopoly

The procedure for granting _____s, the requirements placed on the _____ee and the extent of the exclusive rights vary widely between countries according to national laws and international agreements. Typically, however, a _____ application must include one or more claims defining the invention which must be new, inventive, and useful or industrially applicable.

a. Bona fide occupational qualification
b. Patent
c. Long service leave
d. Bank regulation

14. _____ is defined as the measure of responsiveness in the quantity demanded for a commodity as a result of change in price of the same commodity. It is a measure of how consumers react to a change in price. In other words, it is percentage change in quantity demanded as per the percentage change in price of the same commodity.

a. 1921 recession
b. 130-30 fund
c. 100-year flood
d. Price elasticity of demand

15. In marketing, _____ is the process of distinguishing the differences of a product or offering from others, to make it more attractive to a particular target market. This involves differentiating it from competitors' products as well as one's own product offerings.

Differentiation is a source of competitive advantage.

a. Market segment
b. Technology acceptance model
c. Pricing science
d. Product differentiation

16. In economics, _____ is the ratio of the percent change in one variable to the percent change in another variable. It is a tool for measuring the responsiveness of a function to changes in parameters in a relative way. Commonly analyzed are _____ of substitution, price and wealth.

a. ACCRA Cost of Living Index
b. Elasticity
c. ACEA agreement
d. Elasticity of demand

17. Price _____ is defined as the measure of responsiveness in the quantity demanded for a commodity as a result of change in price of the same commodity. It is a measure of how consumers react to a change in price. In other words, it is percentage change in quantity demanded by the percentage change in price of the same commodity.

a. ACEA agreement
b. Elasticity
c. ACCRA Cost of Living Index
d. Elasticity of demand

Chapter 9. Imperfect Competition and Monopoly

18. A _____ is:

   - Rewrite _____, in generative grammar and computer science
   - Standardization, a formal and widely-accepted statement, fact, definition, or qualification
   - Operation, a determinate _____ for performing a mathematical operation and obtaining a certain result (Mathematics, Logic)
     - Unary operation
     - Binary operation
   - _____ of inference, a function from sets of formulae to formulae (Mathematics, Logic)
   - _____ of thumb, principle with broad application that is not intended to be strictly accurate or reliable for every situation. Also often simply referred to as a _____
   - Moral, an atomic element of a moral code for guiding choices in human behavior
   - Heuristic, a quantized '_____' which shows a tendency or probability for successful function
   - A regulation, as in sports
   - A Production _____, as in computer science
   - Procedural law, a _____ set governing the application of laws to cases
     - A law, which may informally be called a '_____'
     - A court ruling, a decision by a court
   - In the U.S. Government, a regulation mandated by Congress, but written or expanded upon by the Executive Branch.
   - Norm (sociology), an informal but widely accepted _____, concept, truth, definition, or qualification (social norms, legal norms, coding norms)
   - Norm (philosophy), a kind of sentence or a reason to act, feel or believe
   - 'Rulership' is the concept of governance by a government:
     - Military _____, governance by a military body
     - Monastic _____, a collection of precepts that guides the life of monks or nuns in a religious order where the superior holds the place of Christ
   - Slide _____

   - '_____,' a song by Ayumi Hamasaki
   - '_____,' a song by rapper Nas
   - '_____s,' an album by the band The Whitest Boy Alive
   - _____s: Pyaar Ka Superhit Formula, a 2003 Bollywood film
   - ruler, an instrument for measuring lengths
   - _____, a component of an astrolabe, circumferator or similar instrument
   - The _____s, a bestselling self-help book
   - _____ Project (Run Up-to-date Linux Everywhere), a project that aims to use up-to-date Linux software on old PCs
   - _____ engine, a software system that helps managing business _____s
   - Ja _____, a hip hop artist
     - R.U.L.E., a 2005 greatest hits album by rapper Ja _____
   - '_____s,' a KMFDM song

a. Rule
b. Technocracy
c. Procter ' Gamble
d. Demand

Chapter 9. Imperfect Competition and Monopoly 101

19. In economics, _____ is a measure of the relative satisfaction from consumption of various goods and services. Given this measure, one may speak meaningfully of increasing or decreasing _____, and thereby explain economic behavior in terms of attempts to increase one's _____. For illustrative purposes, changes in _____ are sometimes expressed in units called utils.
    a. Utility function
    b. Ordinal utility
    c. Expected utility hypothesis
    d. Utility

20. A _____ is an object whose consumption increases the utility of the consumer, for which the quantity demanded exceeds the quantity supplied at zero price. _____s are usually modeled as having diminishing marginal utility. The first individual purchase has high utility; the second has less.
    a. Merit good
    b. Pie method
    c. Composite good
    d. Good

21. In economics, economic output is divided into physical goods and intangible services. Consumption of _____ is assumed to produce utility. It is often used when referring to a _____ Tax.
    a. Manufactured goods
    b. Private good
    c. Composite good
    d. Goods and services

22. In economics, _____ describes the state of a market with respect to competition.

    - Perfect competition, in which the market consists of a very large number of firms producing a homogeneous product.
    - Monopolistic competition where there are a large number of independent firms which have a very small proportion of the market share.
    - Oligopoly, in which a market is dominated by a small number of firms which own more than 40% of the market share.
    - Oligopsony, a market dominated by many sellers and a few buyers.
    - Monopoly, where there is only one provider of a product or service.
    - Natural monopoly, a monopoly in which economies of scale cause efficiency to increase continuously with the size of the firm. A firm is a natural monopoly if it is able to serve the entire market demand at a lower cost than any combination of two or more smaller, more specialized firms.
    - Monopsony, when there is only one buyer in a market.

    The imperfectly competitive structure is quite identical to the realistic market conditions where some monopolistic competitors, monopolists, oligopolists, and duopolists exist and dominate the market conditions. The elements of _____ include the number and size distribution of firms, entry conditions, and the extent of differentiation.

    These somewhat abstract concerns tend to determine some but not all details of a specific concrete market system where buyers and sellers actually meet and commit to trade.

    a. Labour economics
    b. Market structure
    c. Human capital
    d. Monopolistic competition

23. In neoclassical economics and microeconomics, _____ describes the perfect being a market in which there are many small firms, all producing homogeneous goods. In the short term, such markets are productively inefficient as output will not occur where mc is equal to ac, but allocatively efficient, as output under _____ will always occur where mc is equal to mr, and therefore where mc equals ar. However, in the long term, such markets are both allocatively and productively efficient.

a. General equilibrium
b. Co-operative economics
c. Law of supply
d. Perfect competition

24. In economics, a _____ is a graph of the costs of production as a function of total quantity produced. In a free market economy, productively efficient firms use these curves to find the optimal point of production, where they make the most profits. There are a few different types of _____s, each relevant to a different area of economics.
   a. Demand curve
   b. Kuznets curve
   c. Cost curve
   d. Phillips curve

25. In calculus, a function f defined on a subset of the real numbers with real values is called _____, if for all x and y such that x >≤ y one has f(x) >≤ f(y), so f preserves the order. In layman's terms, the sign of the slope is always positive (the curve tending upwards) or zero (i.e., non-decreasing, or asymptotic, or depicted as a horizontal, flat line) Likewise, a function is called monotonically decreasing (non-increasing) if, whenever x >≤ y, then f(x) >≥ f(y), so it reverses the order.
   a. 100-year flood
   b. 130-30 fund
   c. 1921 recession
   d. Monotonic

26. In economics, a _____ occurs when, due to the economies of scale of a particular industry, the maximum efficiency of production and distribution is realized through a single supplier.

Natural monopolies arise where the largest supplier in an industry, often the first supplier in a market, has an overwhelming cost advantage over other actual or potential competitors. This tends to be the case in industries where capital costs predominate, creating economies of scale which are large in relation to the size of the market, and hence high barriers to entry; examples include water services and electricity.

   a. Privatizing profits and socializing losses
   b. Collective goods
   c. Common-pool resource
   d. Natural monopoly

27. In economics, _____ is equal to total cost divided by the number of goods produced (the output quantity, Q.) It is also equal to the sum of average variable costs (total variable costs divided by Q) plus average fixed costs (total fixed costs divided by Q.) _____s may be dependent on the time period considered (increasing production may be expensive or impossible in the short term, for example.)
   a. Average cost
   b. Average fixed cost
   c. Explicit cost
   d. Average variable cost

28. In algebra, a _____ is a function depending on n that associates a scalar, det(A), to an n×n square matrix A. The fundamental geometric meaning of a _____ is a scale factor for measure when A is regarded as a linear transformation. _____s are important both in calculus, where they enter the substitution rule for several variables, and in multilinear algebra.

For a fixed nonnegative integer n, there is a unique _____ function for the n×n matrices over any commutative ring R. In particular, this function exists when R is the field of real or complex numbers.

   a. 1921 recession
   b. Determinant
   c. 100-year flood
   d. 130-30 fund

Chapter 9. Imperfect Competition and Monopoly

29. In microeconomics, _____ is quite simply the conversion of inputs into outputs. It is an economic process that uses resources to create a good or service that is suitable for exchange. This can include manufacturing, storing, shipping, and packaging.
    - a. Red Guards
    - b. Solved
    - c. Production
    - d. MET

30. _____, in strategic management and marketing is, according to Carlton O'Neal, the percentage or proportion of the total available market or market segment that is being serviced by a company. It can be expressed as a company's sales revenue (from that market) divided by the total sales revenue available in that market. It can also be expressed as a company's unit sales volume (in a market) divided by the total volume of units sold in that market.
    - a. Pricing science
    - b. Customer to customer
    - c. Product differentiation
    - d. Market share

31. _____, in microeconomics, are the cost advantages that a business obtains due to expansion. They are factors that cause a producere;s average cost per unit to fall as scale is increased. _____ is a long run concept and refers to reductions in unit cost as the size of a facility, or scale, increases.
    - a. Economies of scale
    - b. Economic production quantity
    - c. Isoquant
    - d. Underinvestment employment relationship

32. In economics and especially in the theory of competition, _____ are obstacles in the path of a firm that make it difficult to enter a given market.

_____ are the source of a firm's pricing power - the ability of a firm to raise prices without losing all its customers.

The term refers to hindrances that an individual may face while trying to gain entrance into a profession or trade.

    - a. Group boycott
    - b. Limit price
    - c. Social dumping
    - d. Barriers to entry

33. The _____ is an economic and political union of 27 member states, located primarily in Europe. It was established by the Treaty of Maastricht on 1 November 1993, upon the foundations of the pre-existing European Economic Community. With a population of almost 500 million, the _____ generates an estimated 30% share (US$18.4 trillion in 2008) of the nominal gross world product.
    - a. European Union
    - b. ACEA agreement
    - c. European Court of Justice
    - d. ACCRA Cost of Living Index

34. _____ is a type of trade policy that allows traders to act and transact without interference from government. Thus, the policy permits trading partners mutual gains from trade, with goods and services produced according to the theory of comparative advantage.

Under a _____ policy, prices are a reflection of true supply and demand, and are the sole determinant of resource allocation.

a. 130-30 fund
b. 100-year flood
c. Free trade
d. 1921 recession

35. _____ is a designated group of countries that have agreed to eliminate tariffs, quotas and preferences on most (if not all) goods and services traded between them. It can be considered the second stage of economic integration. Countries choose this kind of economic integration form if their economical structures are complementary.
   a. MERCOSUR
   b. 130-30 fund
   c. Free trade area
   d. 100-year flood

36. In economics, an _____ is any good (e.g. a commodity) or service brought into one country from another country in a legitimate fashion, typically for use in trade.It is a good that is brought in from another country for sale. _____ goods or services are provided to domestic consumers by foreign producers. An _____ in the receiving country is an export to the sending country.
   a. Incoterms
   b. Import quota
   c. Economic integration
   d. Import

37. _____ is the economic policy of restraining trade between states, through methods such as tariffs on imported goods, restrictive quotas, and a variety of other restrictive government regulations designed to discourage imports, and prevent foreign take-over of local markets and companies. This policy is closely aligned with anti-globalization, and contrasts with free trade, where government barriers to trade are kept to a minimum. The term is mostly used in the context of economics, where _____ refers to policies or doctrines which 'protect' businesses and workers within a country by restricting or regulating trade with foreign nations.
   a. Protectionism
   b. Google economy
   c. Digital economy
   d. Knowledge economy

38. A _____ strategy is the planned method of delivering goods or services to a target market and distributing them there. When importing or exporting services, it refers to establishing and managing contracts in a foreign country.

Many companies successfully operate in a niche market without ever expanding into new markets.

   a. Customer centricity
   b. Forfaiting
   c. Deep discount broker
   d. Market entry

39. The _____ consists of a number of economic theories which describe the nature of the firm, company including its existence, its behaviour, and its relationship with the market.

In simplified terms, the _____ aims to answer these questions:

   1. Existence - why do firms emerge, why are not all transactions in the economy mediated over the market?
   2. Boundaries - why the boundary between firms and the market is located exactly there? Which transactions are performed internally and which are negotiated on the market?
   3. Organization - why are firms structured in such specific way? What is the interplay of formal and informal relationships?

Despite looking simple, these questions are not answered by the established economic theory, which usually views firms as given, and treats them as black boxes without any internal structure.

The First World War period saw a change of emphasis in economic theory away from industry-level analysis which mainly included analysing markets to analysis at the level of the firm, as it became increasingly clear that perfect competition was no longer an adequate model of how firms behaved. Economic theory till then had focussed on trying to understand markets alone and there had been little study on understanding why firms or organisations exist.

- a. Policy Ineffectiveness Proposition
- b. Khazzoom-Brookes postulate
- c. Theory of the firm
- d. Technology gap

40. _____ is the price at which an asset would trade in a competitive Walrasian auction setting. _____ is often used interchangeably with open _____, fair value or fair _____, although these terms have distinct definitions in different standards, and may differ in some circumstances.

International Valuation Standards defines _____ as 'the estimated amount for which a property should exchange on the date of valuation between a willing buyer and a willing seller in an arm's-length transaction after proper marketing wherein the parties had each acted knowledgeably, prudently, and without compulsion.'

_____ is a concept distinct from market price, which is 'the price at which one can transact', while _____ is 'the true underlying value' according to theoretical standards.

- a. Market value
- b. Secured loan
- c. Personal financial management
- d. Netting

41. In microeconomics, _____ is the extra revenue that an additional unit of product will bring. It is the additional income from selling one more unit of a good; sometimes equal to price. It can also be described as the change in total revenue/change in number of units sold.

- a. Market demand schedule
- b. Long term
- c. Reservation price
- d. Marginal revenue

42. _____ is the a method of technical and economic research of the systems for purpose to optimize a parity between system's consumer functions or properties and expenses to achieve those functions or properties.

This methodology for continuous perfection of production, industrial technologies, organizational structures was developed by Juryj Sobolev in 1948 at the 'Perm telephone factory'

- 1948 Juryj Sobolev - the first success in application of a method analysis at the 'Perm telephone factory' .
- 1949 - the first application for the invention as result of use of the new method.

Chapter 9. Imperfect Competition and Monopoly

Today in economically developed countries practically each enterprise or the company use methodology of the kind of functional-cost analysis as a practice of the quality management, most full satisfying to principles of standards of series ISO 9000.

- Interest of consumer not in products itself, but the advantage which it will receive from its usage.
- The consumer aspires to reduce his expenses
- Functions needed by consumer can be executed in the various ways, and, hence, with various efficiency and expenses. Among possible alternatives of realization of functions exist such in which the parity of quality and the price is the optimal for the consumer.

The goal of _____ is achievement of the highest consumer satisfaction of production at simultaneous decrease in all kinds of industrial expenses Classical _____ has three English synonyms - Value Engineering, Value Management, Value Analysis.

a. Function cost analysis
c. Willingness to pay
b. Monopoly wage
d. Staple financing

43. _____ is the total money received from the sale of any given quantity of output.

The _____ is calculated by taking the price of the sale times the quantity sold, i.e.

_____ = price X quantity.

a. Market development funds
c. Ceteris paribus
b. Small numbers game
d. Total revenue

44. _____ is an economic model based on price, utility and quantity in a market. It predicts that in a competitive market, price will function to equalize the quantity demanded by consumers, and the quantity supplied by producers, resulting in an economic equilibrium of price and quantity. The model incorporates other factors changing equilibrium as a shift of demand and/or supply.

a. Supply and demand
c. Deferred gratification
b. Joint demand
d. Rational addiction

45. In economics, _____ is the process by which a firm determines the price and output level that returns the greatest profit. There are several approaches to this problem. The total revenue--total cost method relies on the fact that profit equals revenue minus cost, and the marginal revenue--marginal cost method is based on the fact that total profit in a perfectly competitive market reaches its maximum point where marginal revenue equals marginal cost.

a. Profit maximization
c. Normal profit
b. Profit margin
d. 100-year flood

46. In economics, a firm is said to reap _____s when a lack of viable market competition allows it to set its prices above the equilibrium price for a good or service without losing profits to competitors. _____ is a type of economic profit, that is, it is a profit greater than the normal profit that is typical in a perfectly competitive industry. The resulting price is known as the monopoly price.
- a. Borrowing base
- b. Cleanup clause
- c. First-price sealed-bid auction
- d. Monopoly Profit

47. _____ theory is a branch of theoretical economics. It seeks to explain the behavior of supply, demand and prices in a whole economy with several or many markets. It is often assumed that agents are price takers and in that setting two common notions of equilibrium exist: Walrasian (or competitive) equilibrium, and its generalization; a price equilibrium with transfers.
- a. New Keynesian economics
- b. General equilibrium
- c. Human capital
- d. Rational choice theory

48. In economics, economic equilibrium is simply a state of the world where economic forces are balanced and in the absence of external influences the (equilibrium) values of economic variables will not change. It is the point at which quantity demanded and quantity supplied are equal. _____, for example, refers to a condition where a market price is established through competition such that the amount of goods or services sought by buyers is equal to the amount of goods or services produced by sellers.
- a. Product-Market Growth Matrix
- b. Marketization
- c. Regulated market
- d. Market equilibrium

49. In economics and business decision-making, _____ are costs that cannot be recovered once they have been incurred. _____ are sometimes contrasted with variable costs, which are the costs that will change due to the proposed course of action, and prospective costs which are costs that will be incurred if an action is taken.

In traditional microeconomic theory, only variable costs are relevant to a decision.

- a. Sunk costs
- b. Hyperbolic discounting
- c. Halo effect
- d. Post-purchase rationalization

50. _____ was a Scottish-born American industrialist, businessman, and a major philanthropist. He was an immigrant as a child with his parents. He built Pittsburgh's Carnegie Steel Company, which was later merged with Elbert H. Gary's Federal Steel Company and several smaller companies to create U.S. Steel.
- a. Andrew Carnegie
- b. Eli Whitney
- c. Oskar Morgenstern
- d. Alfred Marshall

51. _____ is a term used to describe the lavish spending on goods and services acquired mainly for the purpose of displaying income or wealth. In the mind of a conspicuous consumer, such display serves as a means of attaining or maintaining social status. A very similar but more colloquial term is 'keeping up with the Joneses'.
- a. Diderot effect
- b. Consumer behavior
- c. Conspicuous consumption
- d. Consumption smoothing

52. In American history, the _____ refers to substantial growth in population in the United States and extravagant displays of wealth and excess of America's upper-class during the post-Civil War and post-Reconstruction era, in the late 19th century (1865-1901.) The wealth polarization derived primarily from industrial and population expansion. The businessmen of the Second Industrial Revolution created industrial towns and cities in the Northeast with new factories, and contributed to the creation of an ethnically diverse industrial working class which produced the wealth owned by rising super-rich industrialists and financiers such as Cornelius Vanderbilt, John D. Rockefeller, Andrew Carnegie, Henry Flagler, and J.P. Morgan.
   a. Adolph Fischer
   b. Gilded Age
   c. Adam Smith
   d. Adolf Hitler

53. _____ was an American industrialist and philanthropist. Rockefeller revolutionized the petroleum industry and defined the structure of modern philanthropy. In 1870, he founded the Standard Oil Company and ran it until he officially retired in 1897.
   a. Adolph Fischer
   b. Adolf Hitler
   c. Adam Smith
   d. John Davison Rockefeller

54. _____ was a predominant American integrated oil producing, transporting, refining, and marketing company. Established in 1870 as an Ohio Corporation, it was the largest oil refiner in the world and operated as a major company trust and was one of the world's first and largest multinational corporations until it was broken up by the United States Supreme Court in 1911. John D. Rockefeller was a founder, chairman and major shareholder, and the company made him a billionaire and eventually the richest man in history.
   a. 1921 recession
   b. 100-year flood
   c. 130-30 fund
   d. Standard Oil

55. _____ is a common concept in economics, and gives rise to derived concepts such as consumer debt. Generally _____ is defined by opposition to production. But the precise definition can vary because different schools of economists define production quite differently.
   a. Foreclosure data providers
   b. Cash or share options
   c. Federal Reserve Bank Notes
   d. Consumption

Chapter 10. Oligopoly and Monopolistic Competition

1. Competition law, known in the United States as _____ law, has three main elements:

   - prohibiting agreements or practices that restrict free trading and competition between business entities. This includes in particular the repression of cartels.
   - banning abusive behaviour by a firm dominating a market, or anti-competitive practices that tend to lead to such a dominant position. Practices controlled in this way may include predatory pricing, tying, price gouging, refusal to deal, and many others.
   - supervising the mergers and acquisitions of large corporations, including some joint ventures. Transactions that are considered to threaten the competitive process can be prohibited altogether, or approved subject to 'remedies' such as an obligation to divest part of the merged business or to offer licences or access to facilities to enable other businesses to continue competing.

   The substance and practice of competition law varies from jurisdiction to jurisdiction. Protecting the interests of consumers (consumer welfare) and ensuring that entrepreneurs have an opportunity to compete in the market economy are often treated as important objectives. Competition law is closely connected with law on deregulation of access to markets, state aids and subsidies, the privatisation of state owned assets and the establishment of independent sector regulators. In recent decades, competition law has been viewed as a way to provide better public services.

   a. Intellectual property law
   b. Anti-Inflation Act
   c. United Kingdom competition law
   d. Antitrust

2. In economics, the _____ of an industry is used as an indicator of the relative size of firms in relation to the industry as a whole. It is calculated as the sum of the percent market share of the top n industries. This may also assist in determining the market structure of the industry.

   a. Quasi-rent
   b. Pacman conjecture
   c. Monopolization
   d. Concentration ratio

3. In economic theory, _____ is the competitive situation in any market where the conditions necessary for perfect competition are not satisfied. It is a market structure that does not meet the conditions of perfect competition.

   Forms of _____ include:

   - Monopoly, in which there is only one seller of a good.
   - Oligopoly, in which there is a small number of sellers.
   - Monopolistic competition, in which there are many sellers producing highly differentiated goods.
   - Monopsony, in which there is only one buyer of a good.
   - Oligopsony, in which there is a small number of buyers.

   There may also be _____ in markets due to buyers or sellers lacking information about prices and the goods being traded.

   There may also be _____ due to a time lag in a market.

Chapter 10. Oligopoly and Monopolistic Competition

a. Imperfect competition
c. AD-IA Model
b. ACCRA Cost of Living Index
d. ACEA agreement

4. In economics, _____ is the ability of a firm to alter the market price of a good or service. A firm with _____ can raise prices without losing all customers to competitors.

When a firm has _____ it faces a downward-sloping demand curve.

a. Market power
c. Revenue-cap regulation
b. Pacman conjecture
d. Price makers

5. In economics, _____ describes the state of a market with respect to competition.

- Perfect competition, in which the market consists of a very large number of firms producing a homogeneous product.
- Monopolistic competition where there are a large number of independent firms which have a very small proportion of the market share.
- Oligopoly, in which a market is dominated by a small number of firms which own more than 40% of the market share.
- Oligopsony, a market dominated by many sellers and a few buyers.
- Monopoly, where there is only one provider of a product or service.
- Natural monopoly, a monopoly in which economies of scale cause efficiency to increase continuously with the size of the firm. A firm is a natural monopoly if it is able to serve the entire market demand at a lower cost than any combination of two or more smaller, more specialized firms.
- Monopsony, when there is only one buyer in a market.

The imperfectly competitive structure is quite identical to the realistic market conditions where some monopolistic competitors, monopolists, oligopolists, and duopolists exist and dominate the market conditions. The elements of _____ include the number and size distribution of firms, entry conditions, and the extent of differentiation.

These somewhat abstract concerns tend to determine some but not all details of a specific concrete market system where buyers and sellers actually meet and commit to trade.

a. Market structure
c. Monopolistic competition
b. Labour economics
d. Human capital

6. _____ is a common market structure where many competing producers sell products that are differentiated from one another (ie. the products are substitutes, but are not exactly alike.) Many markets are monopolistically competitive, common examples include the markets for restaurants, cereal, clothing, shoes and service industries in large cities.

a. Mathematical economics
c. Monopolistic competition
b. Financial crisis
d. Perfect competition

7. In economics, a _____ occurs when, due to the economies of scale of a particular industry, the maximum efficiency of production and distribution is realized through a single supplier.

Chapter 10. Oligopoly and Monopolistic Competition

Natural monopolies arise where the largest supplier in an industry, often the first supplier in a market, has an overwhelming cost advantage over other actual or potential competitors. This tends to be the case in industries where capital costs predominate, creating economies of scale which are large in relation to the size of the market, and hence high barriers to entry; examples include water services and electricity.

a. Collective goods
b. Common-pool resource
c. Privatizing profits and socializing losses
d. Natural monopoly

8. An _____ is a market form in which a market or industry is dominated by a small number of sellers (oligopolists.) Because there are few participants in this type of market, each oligopolist is aware of the actions of the others. The decisions of one firm influence, and are influenced by, the decisions of other firms.

a. ACCRA Cost of Living Index
b. Oligopsony
c. Oligopoly
d. ACEA agreement

9. In economics, a _____ exists when a specific individual or enterprise has sufficient control over a particular product or service to determine significantly the terms on which other individuals shall have access to it. Monopolies are thus characterized by a lack of economic competition for the good or service that they provide and a lack of viable substitute goods. The verb 'monopolize' refers to the process by which a firm gains persistently greater market share than what is expected under perfect competition.

a. 100-year flood
b. Monopoly
c. 1921 recession
d. 130-30 fund

10. A _____ is an expression that compares quantities relative to each other. The most common examples involve two quantities, but any number of quantities can be compared. _____s are represented mathematically by separating each quantity with a colon, for example the _____ 2:3, which is read as the _____ 'two to three'.

a. 100-year flood
b. Y-intercept
c. 130-30 fund
d. Ratio

11. In neoclassical economics and microeconomics, _____ describes the perfect being a market in which there are many small firms, all producing homogeneous goods. In the short term, such markets are productively inefficient as output will not occur where mc is equal to ac, but allocatively efficient, as output under _____ will always occur where mc is equal to mr, and therefore where mc equals ar. However, in the long term, such markets are both allocatively and productively efficient.

a. Co-operative economics
b. General equilibrium
c. Law of supply
d. Perfect competition

12. In economics and especially in the theory of competition, _____ are obstacles in the path of a firm that make it difficult to enter a given market.

_____ are the source of a firm's pricing power - the ability of a firm to raise prices without losing all its customers.

The term refers to hindrances that an individual may face while trying to gain entrance into a profession or trade.

a. Limit price
b. Group boycott
c. Social dumping
d. Barriers to entry

13.

The _____ is an independent agency of the United States government, created, directed, and empowered by Congressional statute , and with the majority of its commissioners appointed by the current President. The _____ works towards six strategic goals in the areas of broadband, competition, the spectrum, the media, public safety and homeland security, and modernizing the _____.

a. 130-30 fund
b. Federal Communications Commission
c. 100-year flood
d. 1921 recession

14. _____ is a field of economics that studies the strategic behavior of firms, the structure of markets and their interactions. The study of _____ adds to the perfectly competitive model real-world frictions such as limited information, transaction cost, cost of adjusting prices, government actions, and barriers to entry by new firms into a market. It then considers how firms are organized and how they compete.

a. Economic
b. Inflation
c. Economic ideology
d. Industrial organization

15. The _____ refers to the 'common well-being' or 'general welfare.' The _____ is central to policy debates, politics, democracy and the nature of government itself. While nearly everyone claims that aiding the common well-being or general welfare is positive, there is little, if any, consensus on what exactly constitutes the _____.

There are different views on how many members of the public must benefit from an action before it can be declared to be in the _____: at one extreme, an action has to benefit every single member of society in order to be truly in the _____; at the other extreme, any action can be in the _____ as long as it benefits some of the population and harms none.

a. Stealth tax
b. Power Elite
c. Second-class citizen
d. Public interest

16. The phrase _____, according to the Organization for Economic Co-operation and Development, refers to 'creative work undertaken on a systematic basis in order to increase the stock of knowledge, including knowledge of man, culture and society, and the use of this stock of knowledge to devise new applications [sic]'

New product design and development is more than often a crucial factor in the survival of a company. In an industry that is fast changing, firms must continually revise their design and range of products. This is necessary due to continuous technology change and development as well as other competitors and the changing preference of customers.

a. 1921 recession
b. 130-30 fund
c. 100-year flood
d. Research and development

Chapter 10. Oligopoly and Monopolistic Competition

17. In economics, _____ is equal to total cost divided by the number of goods produced (the output quantity, Q.) It is also equal to the sum of average variable costs (total variable costs divided by Q) plus average fixed costs (total fixed costs divided by Q.) _____s may be dependent on the time period considered (increasing production may be expensive or impossible in the short term, for example.)

   a. Average cost
   b. Average fixed cost
   c. Average variable cost
   d. Explicit cost

18. _____ refers to the state of not requiring any outside aid, support for survival; it is therefore a type of personal or collective autonomy. On a large scale, a totally self-sufficient economy that does not trade with the outside world is called an autarky.

The term _____ is usually applied to varieties of sustainable living in which nothing is consumed outside of what is produced by the self-sufficient individuals.

   a. Sustainable forest management
   b. Global Reporting Initiative
   c. Sustainability science
   d. Self-sufficiency

19. _____ is a fee paid on borrowed assets. It is the price paid for the use of borrowed money, or, money earned by deposited funds. Assets that are sometimes lent with _____ include money, shares, consumer goods through hire purchase, major assets such as aircraft, and even entire factories in finance lease arrangements.

   a. Internal debt
   b. Asset protection
   c. Insolvency
   d. Interest

20. The phrase _____ and acquisitions refers to the aspect of corporate strategy, corporate finance and management dealing with the buying, selling and combining of different companies that can aid, finance, or help a growing company in a given industry grow rapidly without having to create another business entity.

An acquisition, also known as a takeover or a buyout, is the buying of one company (the 'target') by another. An acquisition may be friendly or hostile.

   a. Peace dividend
   b. Differential accumulation
   c. Political economy
   d. Mergers

21. In microeconomics, _____ is quite simply the conversion of inputs into outputs. It is an economic process that uses resources to create a good or service that is suitable for exchange. This can include manufacturing, storing, shipping, and packaging.

   a. MET
   b. Solved
   c. Red Guards
   d. Production

22. A _____ is a counterfeit agreement among industries. It is an informal organization of producers that agree to coordinate prices and production. _____s usually occur in an oligopolistic industry, where there is a small number of sellers and usually involve homogeneous products.

   a. Shill
   b. Shanzhai
   c. 100-year flood
   d. Cartel

Chapter 10. Oligopoly and Monopolistic Competition

23. _____ is the transition of a national economy from monopoly control by groups of large businesses to a free market economy. This change rarely arises naturally, and is generally the result of regulation by a governing body.

A modern example of _____ is the economic restructuring of Germany after the fall of the Third Reich in 1945.

  a. Market power
  c. Monopolization

  b. Complementary monopoly
  d. Decartelization

24. _____ is an agreement, usually secretive, which occurs between two or more persons to deceive, mislead or to obtain an objective forbidden by law typically involving fraud or gaining an unfair advantage. It is an agreement among firms to divide the market, set prices kickbacks, or misrepresenting the independence of the relationship between the colluding parties.' All acts effected by _____ are considered void.

  a. Net Book Agreement
  c. Dividing territories

  b. Bid rigging
  d. Collusion

25. The _____ consists of a number of economic theories which describe the nature of the firm, company including its existence, its behaviour, and its relationship with the market.

In simplified terms, the _____ aims to answer these questions:

  1. Existence - why do firms emerge, why are not all transactions in the economy mediated over the market?
  2. Boundaries - why the boundary between firms and the market is located exactly there? Which transactions are performed internally and which are negotiated on the market?
  3. Organization - why are firms structured in such specific way? What is the interplay of formal and informal relationships?

Despite looking simple, these questions are not answered by the established economic theory, which usually views firms as given, and treats them as black boxes without any internal structure.

The First World War period saw a change of emphasis in economic theory away from industry-level analysis which mainly included analysing markets to analysis at the level of the firm, as it became increasingly clear that perfect competition was no longer an adequate model of how firms behaved. Economic theory till then had focussed on trying to understand markets alone and there had been little study on understanding why firms or organisations exist.

  a. Khazzoom-Brookes postulate
  c. Technology gap

  b. Theory of the firm
  d. Policy Ineffectiveness Proposition

26. In economics, a firm is said to reap _____s when a lack of viable market competition allows it to set its prices above the equilibrium price for a good or service without losing profits to competitors. _____ is a type of economic profit, that is, it is a profit greater than the normal profit that is typical in a perfectly competitive industry. The resulting price is known as the monopoly price.

a. Borrowing base
b. First-price sealed-bid auction
c. Cleanup clause
d. Monopoly profit

27. _____ in economics and business is the result of an exchange and from that trade we assign a numerical monetary value to a good, service or asset. If Alice trades Bob 4 apples for an orange, the _____ of an orange is 4 apples. Inversely, the _____ of an apple is 1/4 oranges.
   a. Price war
   b. Premium pricing
   c. Price book
   d. Price

28. _____ is an agreement between business competitors to sell the same product or service at the same price. In general, it is an agreement intended to ultimately push the price of a product as high as possible, leading to profits for all the sellers. Price-fixing can also involve any agreement to fix, peg, discount or stabilize prices.
   a. Moral victory
   b. Price fixing
   c. Cut-throat competition
   d. Non-price competition

29. _____ is a term used in business to indicate a state of intense competitive rivalry accompanied by a multi-lateral series of price reduction. One competitor will lower its price, then others will lower their prices to match. If one of them reduces their price again, a new round of reductions starts.
   a. Big ticket item
   b. Transactional Net Margin Method
   c. Discounts and allowances
   d. Price war

30. In economics, _____ is the process by which a firm determines the price and output level that returns the greatest profit. There are several approaches to this problem. The total revenue--total cost method relies on the fact that profit equals revenue minus cost, and the marginal revenue--marginal cost method is based on the fact that total profit in a perfectly competitive market reaches its maximum point where marginal revenue equals marginal cost.
   a. Normal profit
   b. 100-year flood
   c. Profit margin
   d. Profit maximization

31. _____ occurs when cartels are illegal or overt collusion is absent. Put another way, two firms agree to play a certain strategy without explicitly saying so. This is also known as price leadership, as firms may stay within the law but still tacitly collude by monitoring each other's prices and keeping them the same.
   a. Staple port
   b. Poverty penalty
   c. Product innovation
   d. Tacit collusion

32. _____ is a term used in national accounts statistics and macroeconomics. It basically refers to the net additions to the (physical) capital stock in an accounting period, or, to the value of the increase of the capital stock; though it may occasionally also refer to the (growth of the) total stock of capital formed.

Thus, in UNSNA, _____ equals fixed capital investment, the increase in the value of inventories held, plus (net) lending to foreign countries, during an accounting period.

   a. Capital formation
   b. Capital intensity
   c. Capital flight
   d. Consumption of fixed capital

33. Economics:

- _____, the desire to own something and the ability to pay for it
- _____ curve, a graphic representation of a _____ schedule
- _____ deposit, the money in checking accounts
- _____ pull theory, the theory that inflation occurs when _____ for goods and services exceeds existing supplies
- _____ schedule, a table that lists the quantity of a good a person will buy it each different price
- _____ side economics, the school of economics at believes government spending and tax cuts open economy by raising _____

a. Production
b. Demand
c. McKesson ' Robbins scandal
d. Variability

34. In economics, the _____ can be defined as the graph depicting the relationship between the price of a certain commodity, and the amount of it that consumers are willing and able to purchase at that given price. It is a graphic representation of a demand schedule. The _____ for all consumers together follows from the _____ of every individual consumer: the individual demands at each price are added together.

a. Kuznets curve
b. Wage curve
c. Cost curve
d. Demand curve

35. The Organization of the Petroleum Exporting Countries is a cartel of twelve countries made up of Algeria, Angola, Ecuador, Iran, Iraq, Kuwait, Libya, Nigeria, Qatar, Saudi Arabia, the United Arab Emirates, and Venezuela. The cartel has maintained its headquarters in Vienna since 1965, and hosts regular meetings among the oil ministers of its Member Countries. Indonesia withdrew its membership in _____ in 2008 after it became a net importer of oil, but stated it would likely return if it became a net exporter in the world.

a. OPEC
b. AD-IA Model
c. ACCRA Cost of Living Index
d. ACEA agreement

36. In marketing, _____ is the process of distinguishing the differences of a product or offering from others, to make it more attractive to a particular target market. This involves differentiating it from competitors' products as well as one's own product offerings.

Differentiation is a source of competitive advantage.

a. Pricing science
b. Product differentiation
c. Technology acceptance model
d. Market segment

Chapter 10. Oligopoly and Monopolistic Competition   117

37. _____ has several particular meanings:

   - in mathematics
     - _____ function
     - Euler _____
     - _____
     - _____ subgroup
     - method of _____s (partial differential equations)
   - in physics and engineering
     - any _____ curve that shows the relationship between certain input- and output parameters, e.g.
     - an I-V or current-voltage _____ is the current in a circuit as a function of the applied voltage
     - Receiver-Operator _____
   - in fiction
     - in Dungeons ' Dragons, _____ is another name for ability score

   a. Russian financial crisis
   b. Demand
   c. Technocracy
   d. Characteristic

38. _____ - The Concept of Countervailing Power is a book by John Kenneth Galbraith, written in 1952.

Not as well-known as some of his other works, it contains a critique of the view that markets, left to their own devices, will provide socially optimal solutions. Galbraith agrees with F. A. Hayek as far as the assertion goes that 'the price system will fulfil [its] function only if competition prevails, that is, if the individual producer has to adapt to price changes and cannot control them.'

Galbraith builds on work by Prof. E. H.

   a. American capitalism
   b. Assets and Liabilities of Commercial Banks in the United States
   c. Economics in One Lesson
   d. Omnipotent Government

39. _____ is an economic system in which wealth, and the means of producing wealth, are privately owned. Through _____, the land, labor, and capital are owned, operated, and traded for the purpose of generating profits, without force or fraud, by private individuals either singly or jointly, and investments, distribution, income, production, pricing and supply of goods, commodities and services are determined by voluntary private decision in a market economy. A distinguishing feature of _____ is that each person owns his or her own labor and therefore is allowed to sell the use of it to employers.

   a. Socialism for the rich and capitalism for the poor
   b. Capitalism
   c. Late capitalism
   d. Creative capitalism

40. A _____ or directed economy is an economic system in which the government or workers' councils manages the economy. It is an economic system in which the central government makes all decisions on the production and consumption of goods and services. Its most extensive form is referred to as a _____, centrally planned economy, or command and control economy.

a. Transition economy
b. Subsistence economy
c. Command economy
d. Nutritional Economics

41. A true _____ is a specific type of oligopoly where only two producers exist in one market. In reality, this definition is generally used where only two firms have dominant control over a market. In the field of industrial organization, it is the most commonly studied form of oligopoly due to its simplicity.
   a. Duopoly
   b. Megacorpstate
   c. 130-30 fund
   d. 100-year flood

42. _____ is a branch of applied mathematics that is used in the social sciences (most notably economics), biology, engineering, political science, international relations, computer science, and philosophy. _____ attempts to mathematically capture behavior in strategic situations, in which an individual's success in making choices depends on the choices of others. While initially developed to analyze competitions in which one individual does better at another's expense (zero sum games), it has been expanded to treat a wide class of interactions, which are classified according to several criteria.
   a. Game theory
   b. Proper equilibrium
   c. Dollar auction
   d. Discriminatory price auction

43. In economic models, the _____ time frame assumes no fixed factors of production. Firms can enter or leave the marketplace, and the cost (and availability) of land, labor, raw materials, and capital goods can be assumed to vary. In contrast, in the short-run time frame, certain factors are assumed to be fixed, because there is not sufficient time for them to change.
   a. Productivity world
   b. Diseconomies of scale
   c. Price/performance ratio
   d. Long-run

44. _____s is the social science that studies the production, distribution, and consumption of goods and services. The term _____s comes from the Ancient Greek oá¼°κονομῖα from oá¼¶κος (oikos, 'house') + vĭŒμος (nomos, 'custom' or 'law'), hence 'rules of the house(hold)'. Current _____ models developed out of the broader field of political economy in the late 19th century, owing to a desire to use an empirical approach more akin to the physical sciences.
   a. Energy economics
   b. Economic
   c. Opportunity cost
   d. Inflation

45. _____ exists when sales of identical goods or services are transacted at different prices from the same provider. In a theoretical market with perfect information, no transaction costs or prohibition on secondary exchange (or re-selling) to prevent arbitrage, _____ can only be a feature of monopoly and oligopoly markets, where market power can be exercised. Otherwise, the moment the seller tries to sell the same good at different prices, the buyer at the lower price can arbitrage by selling to the consumer buying at the higher price but with a tiny discount.
   a. Lerner Index
   b. Loss leader
   c. Price discrimination
   d. Transfer pricing

46. _____ is exchange of capital, goods, and services across international borders or territories. In most countries, it represents a significant share of gross domestic product (GDP.) While _____ has been present throughout much of history , its economic, social, and political importance has been on the rise in recent centuries.
   a. Incoterms
   b. Intra-industry trade
   c. Import license
   d. International trade

47. _____ is an economic concept with commonplace familiarity. It is the price that a good or service is offered at, or will fetch, in the marketplace. It is of interest mainly in the study of microeconomics.
   a. Market price
   b. Paper trading
   c. Market anomaly
   d. Noisy market hypothesis

48. In mathematics, a _____ system is a system which is not linear, that is, a system which does not satisfy the superposition principle, or whose output is not proportional to its input. Less technically, a _____ system is any problem where the variable(s) to be solved for cannot be written as a linear combination of independent components. A nonhomogeneous system, which is linear apart from the presence of a function of the independent variables, is _____ according to a strict definition, but such systems are usually studied alongside linear systems, because they can be transformed to a linear system of multiple variables.
   a. Nonlinear
   b. 100-year flood
   c. Nonlinear system
   d. 130-30 fund

49. A public utility (usually just utility) is an organization that maintains the infrastructure for a public service (often also providing a service using that infrastructure.) _____ are subject to forms of public control and regulation ranging from local community-based groups to state-wide government monopolies. Common arguments in favor of regulation include the desire to control market power, facilitate competition, promote investment or system expansion, or stabilize markets.
   a. Public utilities
   b. 130-30 fund
   c. 1921 recession
   d. 100-year flood

50. _____ is the removal or simplification of government rules and regulations that constrain the operation of market forces. _____ does not mean elimination of laws against fraud, but eliminating or reducing government control of how business is done, thereby moving toward a more free market.

The stated rationale for '_____' is often that fewer and simpler regulations will lead to a raised level of competitiveness, therefore higher productivity, more efficiency and lower prices overall.

   a. Macroeconomic policy instruments
   b. Fundamental psychological law
   c. Secular basis
   d. Deregulation

51. In economics, an _____ or spillover of an economic transaction is an impact on a party that is not directly involved in the transaction. In such a case, prices do not reflect the full costs or benefits in production or consumption of a product or service. A positive impact is called an external benefit, while a negative impact is called an external cost.
   a. Existence value
   b. Environmental tariff
   c. Environmental impact assessment
   d. Externality

52. _____ is a concept based on the fact that rationality of individuals is limited by the information they have, the cognitive limitations of their minds, and the finite amount of time they have to make decisions. This contrasts with the concept of rationality as optimization. Another way to look at _____ is that, because decision-makers lack the ability and resources to arrive at the optimal solution, they instead apply their rationality only after having greatly simplified the choices available.
   a. Generalized game theory
   b. Dynamic inconsistency
   c. Dollar auction
   d. Bounded rationality

Chapter 10. Oligopoly and Monopolistic Competition

53. _____ is a broad label that refers to any individuals or households that use goods and services generated within the economy. The concept of a _____ is used in different contexts, so that the usage and significance of the term may vary.

Typically when business people and economists talk of _____s they are talking about person as _____, an aggregated commodity item with little individuality other than that expressed in the buy/not-buy decision.

a. Consumer
b. 1921 recession
c. 100-year flood
d. 130-30 fund

Chapter 10. Oligopoly and Monopolistic Competition

54. A _____ is:

- Rewrite _____, in generative grammar and computer science
- Standardization, a formal and widely-accepted statement, fact, definition, or qualification
- Operation, a determinate _____ for performing a mathematical operation and obtaining a certain result (Mathematics, Logic)
    - Unary operation
    - Binary operation
- _____ of inference, a function from sets of formulae to formulae (Mathematics, Logic)
- _____ of thumb, principle with broad application that is not intended to be strictly accurate or reliable for every situation. Also often simply referred to as a _____
- Moral, an atomic element of a moral code for guiding choices in human behavior
- Heuristic, a quantized '_____' which shows a tendency or probability for successful function
- A regulation, as in sports
- A Production _____, as in computer science
- Procedural law, a _____ set governing the application of laws to cases
    - A law, which may informally be called a '_____'
    - A court ruling, a decision by a court
- In the U.S. Government, a regulation mandated by Congress, but written or expanded upon by the Executive Branch.
- Norm (sociology), an informal but widely accepted _____, concept, truth, definition, or qualification (social norms, legal norms, coding norms)
- Norm (philosophy), a kind of sentence or a reason to act, feel or believe
- 'Rulership' is the concept of governance by a government:
    - Military _____, governance by a military body
    - Monastic _____, a collection of precepts that guides the life of monks or nuns in a religious order where the superior holds the place of Christ
- Slide _____

- '_____,' a song by Ayumi Hamasaki
- '_____,' a song by rapper Nas
- '_____s,' an album by the band The Whitest Boy Alive
- _____s: Pyaar Ka Superhit Formula, a 2003 Bollywood film
- ruler, an instrument for measuring lengths
- _____, a component of an astrolabe, circumferator or similar instrument
- The _____s, a bestselling self-help book
- _____ Project (Run Up-to-date Linux Everywhere), a project that aims to use up-to-date Linux software on old PCs
- _____ engine, a software system that helps managing business _____s
- Ja _____, a hip hop artist
    - R.U.L.E., a 2005 greatest hits album by rapper Ja _____
- '_____s,' a KMFDM song

a. Rule
b. Technocracy
c. Procter ' Gamble
d. Demand

Chapter 10. Oligopoly and Monopolistic Competition

55. A mutual _____ or stockholder is an individual or company (including a corporation) that legally owns one or more shares of stock in a joint stock company. A company's _____s collectively own that company. Thus, the typical goal of such companies is to enhance _____ value.
   a. Prime Standard
   b. Shareholder
   c. Profit warning
   d. Relative valuation

56. _____ is a specific term used in companies' financial reporting from the company-whole point of view. Because that use excludes the effects of changing ownership interest, an economic measure of _____ is necessary for financial analysis from the shareholders' point of view

   _____ is defined by the Financial Accounting Standards Board, or FASB, as e;the change in equity [net assets] of a business enterprise during a period from transactions and other events and circumstances from nonowner sources. It includes all changes in equity during a period except those resulting from investments by owners and distributions to owners.e;

   _____ is the sum of net income and other items that must bypass the income statement because they have not been realized, including items like an unrealized holding gain or loss from available for sale securities and foreign currency translation gains or losses.

   a. Windfall gain
   b. Net national income
   c. Comprehensive income
   d. Real income

57. _____ is one of the four Ps of the marketing mix. The other three aspects are product, promotion, and place. It is also a key variable in microeconomic price allocation theory.
   a. Guaranteed Maximum Price
   b. Premium pricing
   c. Pricing
   d. Point of total assumption

58. The _____ is a heterodox school of economics that emphasizes the spontaneous organizing power of the price mechanism. It holds that the complexity of subjective human choices makes mathematical modelling of the evolving market extremely difficult and advocates a laissez faire approach to the economy. _____ economists advocate the enforcement of voluntary contractual agreements between economic agents, but otherwise the smallest imposition of coercive force on commercial transactions.
   a. ACEA agreement
   b. Austrian School
   c. ACCRA Cost of Living Index
   d. Economic calculation problem

59. _____s is concerned with the tasks of developing and applying quantitative or statistical methods to the study and elucidation of economic principles. _____s combines economic theory with statistics to analyze and test economic relationships. Theoretical _____s considers questions about the statistical properties of estimators and tests, while applied _____s is concerned with the application of _____ methods to assess economic theories.
   a. Economic
   b. Experimental economics
   c. Evolutionary economics
   d. Econometric

60. _____ is the development of economic wealth of countries or regions for the well-being of their inhabitants. It is the process by which a nation improves the economic, political, and social well being of its people. From a policy perspective, _____ can be defined as efforts that seek to improve the economic well-being and quality of life for a community by creating and/or retaining jobs and supporting or growing incomes and the tax base.

a. Inflation
b. Experimental economics
c. Economic methodology
d. Economic Development

61. _____, 1st Baron Keynes was a renowned economist from Britain whose many ideas on economic and political theories as well as on many governments' monetary policies influenced America. He advocated a government that played an active role in the lives of people regarding business, economy, etc. In this role, the government would use fiscal measures to reduce the consequences of recessions, economic depressions and booms.
   a. John Maynard Keynes
   b. Adolf Hitler
   c. Adolph Fischer
   d. Adam Smith

62. _____ in political thought refers to economic theories of social organization advocating collective ownership and administration of the means of production and distribution of goods, and a society characterized by equality for all individuals, with an egalitarian method of compensation. Modern _____ originated in the late 19th-century intellectual and working class political movement that criticized the effects of industrialization and private ownership on society. Karl Marx posited that _____ would be achieved via class struggle and a proletarian revolution after a transitional stage from capitalism called the dictatorship of the proletariat.
   a. Adolf Hitler
   b. Adam Smith
   c. Adolph Fischer
   d. Socialism

63. _____ is a defined term that an economy with an increased emphasis on informational activities and information industry.

The vagueness of the term has three major sources. First, not surprisingly, there is no agreed-upon definition regarding the threshold of when an economy is _____ and when it is not.

   a. Information economy
   b. Indicative planning
   c. Intention economy
   d. Autarky

64. _____, as defined by the _____ Association of America (Information technologyAA), is 'the study, design, development, implementation, support or management of computer-based information systems, particularly software applications and computer hardware.' _____ deals with the use of electronic computers and computer software to convert, store, protect, process, transmit, and securely retrieve information.

Today, the term _____ has ballooned to encompass many aspects of computing and technology, and the term has become very recognizable. The _____ umbrella can be quite large, covering many fields.

   a. Information technology
   b. ACCRA Cost of Living Index
   c. AD-IA Model
   d. ACEA agreement

65. _____ are legal property rights over creations of the mind, both artistic and commercial, and the corresponding fields of law. Under _____ law, owners are granted certain exclusive rights to a variety of intangible assets, such as musical, literary, and artistic works; ideas, discoveries and inventions; and words, phrases, symbols, and designs. Common types of _____ include copyrights, trademarks, patents, industrial design rights and trade secrets.
   a. Expedited Funds Availability Act
   b. Intellectual property
   c. Independent contractor
   d. Ease of Doing Business Index

124   *Chapter 10. Oligopoly and Monopolistic Competition*

66. A _____ is a set of exclusive rights granted by a state to an inventor or his assignee for a limited period of time in exchange for a disclosure of an invention.

The procedure for granting _____s, the requirements placed on the _____ee and the extent of the exclusive rights vary widely between countries according to national laws and international agreements. Typically, however, a _____ application must include one or more claims defining the invention which must be new, inventive, and useful or industrially applicable.

- a. Patent
- b. Bank regulation
- c. Bona fide occupational qualification
- d. Long service leave

67. A _____ is the exclusive authority to determine how a resource is used, whether that resource is owned by government or by individuals. All economic goods have a _____s attribute. This attribute has three broad components

1. The right to use the good
2. The right to earn income from the good
3. The right to transfer the good to others

The concept of _____s as used by economists and legal scholars are related but distinct. The distinction is largely seen in the economists' focus on the ability of an individual or collective to control the use of the good.

- a. Property right
- b. Holder in due course
- c. Post-sale restraint
- d. High-reeve

68. The _____ was an evolution of developed countries from an industrial/manufacturing-based wealth producing economy into a service sector asset based economy, brought about by globalization and currency manipulation by governments and their central banks. Some analysts claimed that this change in the economic structure of the United States had created a state of permanent steady growth, low unemployment, and immunity to boom and bust macroeconomic cycles. They believed that the change rendered obsolete many business practices.
- a. 130-30 fund
- b. New economy
- c. 100-year flood
- d. 1921 recession

69. The _____ of a decision depends on both the cost of the alternative chosen and the benefit that the best alternative would have provided if chosen. _____ differs from accounting cost because it includes opportunity cost.
- a. Inventory analysis
- b. Isocost
- c. Epstein-Zin preferences
- d. Economic cost

70. The term surplus is used in economics for several related quantities. The _____ is the amount that consumers benefit by being able to purchase a product for a price that is less than they would be willing to pay. The producer surplus is the amount that producers benefit by selling at a market price mechanism that is higher than they would be willing to sell for.
- a. Necessity good
- b. Marginal rate of technical substitution
- c. Microeconomic reform
- d. Consumer surplus

71. In economics, a _____ is a loss of economic efficiency that can occur when equilibrium for a good or service is not Pareto optimal. In other words, either people who would have more marginal benefit than marginal cost are not buying the good or service, or people who would have more marginal cost than marginal benefit are buying the product.

Causes of _____ can include monopoly pricing, externalities, taxes or subsidies, and binding price ceilings or floors.

   a. Leapfrogging
   c. Deadweight loss
   b. Contract curve
   d. Distributive efficiency

72. _____ was an American economist, statistician and public intellectual, and a recipient of the Nobel Memorial Prize in Economic Sciences. He is best known among scholars for his theoretical and empirical research, especially consumption analysis, monetary history and theory, and for his demonstration of the complexity of stabilization policy. A global public followed his restatement of a political philosophy that insisted on minimizing the role of government in favor of the private sector.

   a. Adolf Hitler
   c. Adolph Fischer
   b. Adam Smith
   d. Milton Friedman

73. In economics, _____ is how a natione;s total economy is distributed among its population. ._____ has always been a central concern of economic theory and economic policy. Classical economists such as Adam Smith, Thomas Malthus and David Ricardo were mainly concerned with factor _____, that is, the distribution of income between the main factors of production, land, labour and capital.

   a. Income distribution
   c. Authorised capital
   b. Eco commerce
   d. Equipment trust certificate

74. _____ is the incidence or process of transferring ownership of a business, enterprise, agency or public service from the public sector (government) to the private sector (business.) In a broader sense, _____ refers to transfer of any government function to the private sector including governmental functions like revenue collection and law enforcement.

The term '_____' also has been used to describe two unrelated transactions.

   a. Privatization
   c. Performance reports
   b. Compound empowerment
   d. Ricardian equivalence

75. In economics, _____ is the transfer of income, wealth or property from some individuals to others.

One premise of _____ is that money should be distributed to benefit the poorer members of society, and that the rich have an obligation to assist the poor, thus creating a more financially egalitarian society. Another argument is that the rich exploit the poor or otherwise gain unfair benefits.

   a. 130-30 fund
   c. 100-year flood
   b. 1921 recession
   d. Redistribution

Chapter 11. Uncertainty and Game Theory

1. _____s is the social science that studies the production, distribution, and consumption of goods and services. The term _____s comes from the Ancient Greek οá¼°κονομῖα from οá¼¶κος (oikos, 'house') + vΐŒμος (nomos, 'custom' or 'law'), hence 'rules of the house(hold)'. Current _____ models developed out of the broader field of political economy in the late 19th century, owing to a desire to use an empirical approach more akin to the physical sciences.
    a. Energy economics
    b. Economic
    c. Inflation
    d. Opportunity cost

2. In game theory, _____ is a solution concept of a game involving two or more players, in which each player is assumed to know the equilibrium strategies of the other players, and no player has anything to gain by changing only his or her own strategy unilaterally. If each player has chosen a strategy and no player can benefit by changing his or her strategy while the other players keep theirs unchanged, then the current set of strategy choices and the corresponding payoffs constitute a _____.

   Stated simply, Amy and Bill are in _____ if Amy is making the best decision she can, taking into account Bill's decision, and Bill is making the best decision he can, taking into account Amy's decision.

    a. Proper equilibrium
    b. Linear production game
    c. Lump of labour
    d. Nash equilibrium

3. The Organization of the Petroleum Exporting Countries is a cartel of twelve countries made up of Algeria, Angola, Ecuador, Iran, Iraq, Kuwait, Libya, Nigeria, Qatar, Saudi Arabia, the United Arab Emirates, and Venezuela. The cartel has maintained its headquarters in Vienna since 1965, and hosts regular meetings among the oil ministers of its Member Countries. Indonesia withdrew its membership in _____ in 2008 after it became a net importer of oil, but stated it would likely return if it became a net exporter in the world.
    a. AD-IA Model
    b. ACCRA Cost of Living Index
    c. ACEA agreement
    d. OPEC

4. _____ is a type of risk faced by investors, corporations, and governments. It is a risk that can be understood and managed with proper aforethought and investment.

   Broadly, _____ refers to the complications businesses and governments may face as a result of what are commonly referred to as political decisions--or e;any political change that alters the expected outcome and value of a given economic action by changing the probability of achieving business objectives.e; .

    a. Capital adequacy ratio
    b. Black-Derman-Toy model
    c. Political risk
    d. Pull to par

5. _____ is a branch of applied mathematics that is used in the social sciences (most notably economics), biology, engineering, political science, international relations, computer science, and philosophy. _____ attempts to mathematically capture behavior in strategic situations, in which an individual's success in making choices depends on the choices of others. While initially developed to analyze competitions in which one individual does better at another's expense (zero sum games), it has been expanded to treat a wide class of interactions, which are classified according to several criteria.
    a. Proper equilibrium
    b. Discriminatory price auction
    c. Dollar auction
    d. Game theory

Chapter 11. Uncertainty and Game Theory

6. In microeconomics, _____ is quite simply the conversion of inputs into outputs. It is an economic process that uses resources to create a good or service that is suitable for exchange. This can include manufacturing, storing, shipping, and packaging.
   - a. MET
   - b. Red Guards
   - c. Solved
   - d. Production

7. In economics and finance, _____ is the practice of taking advantage of a price differential between two or more markets: striking a combination of matching deals that capitalize upon the imbalance, the profit being the difference between the market prices. When used by academics, an _____ is a transaction that involves no negative cash flow at any probabilistic or temporal state and a positive cash flow in at least one state; in simple terms, a risk-free profit. A person who engages in _____ is called an arbitrageur--such as a bank or brokerage firm.
   - a. Alternext
   - b. Arbitrage
   - c. Options Price Reporting Authority
   - d. Electronic trading

8. A _____ is an object whose consumption increases the utility of the consumer, for which the quantity demanded exceeds the quantity supplied at zero price. _____s are usually modeled as having diminishing marginal utility. The first individual purchase has high utility; the second has less.
   - a. Pie method
   - b. Merit good
   - c. Good
   - d. Composite good

9. In economics, economic output is divided into physical goods and intangible services. Consumption of _____ is assumed to produce utility. It is often used when referring to a _____ Tax.
   - a. Composite good
   - b. Private good
   - c. Manufactured goods
   - d. Goods and services

10. _____ is the term denoting either an entrance or changes which are inserted into a system and which activate/modify a process. It is an abstract concept, used in the modeling, system(s) design and system(s) exploitation. It is usually connected with other terms, e.g., _____ field, _____ variable, _____ parameter, _____ value, _____ signal, _____ device and _____ file.
    - a. AD-IA Model
    - b. ACEA agreement
    - c. ACCRA Cost of Living Index
    - d. Input

11. _____ in economics and business is the result of an exchange and from that trade we assign a numerical monetary value to a good, service or asset. If Alice trades Bob 4 apples for an orange, the _____ of an orange is 4 apples. Inversely, the _____ of an apple is 1/4 oranges.
    - a. Premium pricing
    - b. Price war
    - c. Price book
    - d. Price

12. In finance, _____ is a financial action that does not promise safety of the initial investment along with the return on the principal sum. _____ typically involves the lending of money or the purchase of assets, equity or debt but in a manner that has not been given thorough analysis or is deemed to have low margin of safety or a significant risk of the loss of the principal investment. The term, '_____,' which is formally defined as above in Graham and Dodd's 1934 text, Security Analysis, contrasts with the term 'investment,' which is a financial operation that, upon thorough analysis, promises safety of principal and a satisfactory return.

a. Municipal Bond Arbitrage
b. Hybrid market
c. Speculation
d. Global Financial Centres Index

13. In economics, the _____ is the term economists use to describe the self-regulating nature of the marketplace. The _____ is a metaphor coined by the economist Adam Smith in The Wealth of Nations.

Adam Smith mentions the metaphor in Book IV of The Wealth of Nations, arguing that people in any society will certainly employ their capital in foreign trading only if the profits available by that method far exceed those available locally, and that in such a case it is better for society as a whole if they so did.

a. Invisible hand
b. ACEA agreement
c. ACCRA Cost of Living Index
d. AD-IA Model

14. _____ is an economic concept with commonplace familiarity. It is the price that a good or service is offered at, or will fetch, in the marketplace. It is of interest mainly in the study of microeconomics.
a. Market price
b. Market anomaly
c. Paper trading
d. Noisy market hypothesis

15. Competition law, known in the United States as _____ law, has three main elements:

- prohibiting agreements or practices that restrict free trading and competition between business entities. This includes in particular the repression of cartels.
- banning abusive behaviour by a firm dominating a market, or anti-competitive practices that tend to lead to such a dominant position. Practices controlled in this way may include predatory pricing, tying, price gouging, refusal to deal, and many others.
- supervising the mergers and acquisitions of large corporations, including some joint ventures. Transactions that are considered to threaten the competitive process can be prohibited altogether, or approved subject to 'remedies' such as an obligation to divest part of the merged business or to offer licences or access to facilities to enable other businesses to continue competing.

The substance and practice of competition law varies from jurisdiction to jurisdiction. Protecting the interests of consumers (consumer welfare) and ensuring that entrepreneurs have an opportunity to compete in the market economy are often treated as important objectives. Competition law is closely connected with law on deregulation of access to markets, state aids and subsidies, the privatisation of state owned assets and the establishment of independent sector regulators. In recent decades, competition law has been viewed as a way to provide better public services.

a. Antitrust
b. Anti-Inflation Act
c. Intellectual property law
d. United Kingdom competition law

16. _____ is a situation in which the limited resources of a firm are allocated in accordance with the wishes of consumers. An allocatively efficient economy produces an 'optimal mix' of commodities. A firm is allocatively efficient when its price is equal to its marginal costs (that is, P = MC) in a perfect market.
a. ACEA agreement
b. Economic efficiency
c. Allocative efficiency
d. ACCRA Cost of Living Index

Chapter 11. Uncertainty and Game Theory 129

17. _____ is a common concept in economics, and gives rise to derived concepts such as consumer debt. Generally _____ is defined by opposition to production. But the precise definition can vary because different schools of economists define production quite differently.
  a. Cash or share options
  b. Foreclosure data providers
  c. Federal Reserve Bank Notes
  d. Consumption

18. In economics, the _____ of a good or of a service is the utility of the specific use to which an agent would put a given increase in that good or service, or of the specific use that would be abandoned in response to a given decrease. In other words, _____ is the utility of the marginal use -- which, on the assumption of economic rationality, would be the least urgent use of the good or service, from the best feasible combination of actions in which its use is included. Under the mainstream assumptions, the _____ of a good or service is the posited quantified change in utility obtained by increasing or by decreasing use of that good or service.
  a. 100-year flood
  b. 1921 recession
  c. 130-30 fund
  d. Marginal utility

19. In economics, _____ is a measure of the relative satisfaction from consumption of various goods and services. Given this measure, one may speak meaningfully of increasing or decreasing _____, and thereby explain economic behavior in terms of attempts to increase one's _____. For illustrative purposes, changes in _____ are sometimes expressed in units called utils.
  a. Utility function
  b. Expected utility hypothesis
  c. Ordinal utility
  d. Utility

20. A variety of measures of _____ and output are used in economics to estimate total economic activity in a country or region, including gross domestic product (GDP), gross national product (GNP), and net _____

There are three main ways of calculating these numbers; the output approach, the income approach and the expenditure approach. In theory, the three must yield the same, because total expenditures on goods and services must equal the total income paid to the producers (Gnational income), and that must also equal the total value of the output of goods and services (GNP.)

  a. Volume index
  b. National income
  c. Gross world product
  d. GNI per capita

21. A _____ represents the combinations of goods and services that a consumer can purchase given current prices and his income. Consumer theory uses the concepts of a _____ and a preference map to analyze consumer choices. Both concepts have a ready graphical representation in the two-good case.
  a. Quality bias
  b. Revealed preference
  c. Joint demand
  d. Budget constraint

22. _____ is a broad label that refers to any individuals or households that use goods and services generated within the economy. The concept of a _____ is used in different contexts, so that the usage and significance of the term may vary.

Typically when business people and economists talk of _____s they are talking about person as _____, an aggregated commodity item with little individuality other than that expressed in the buy/not-buy decision.

a. Consumer
b. 100-year flood
c. 1921 recession
d. 130-30 fund

23. The term surplus is used in economics for several related quantities. The _____ is the amount that consumers benefit by being able to purchase a product for a price that is less than they would be willing to pay. The producer surplus is the amount that producers benefit by selling at a market price mechanism that is higher than they would be willing to sell for.
   a. Marginal rate of technical substitution
   b. Microeconomic reform
   c. Necessity good
   d. Consumer surplus

24. _____ is a company's financial statement that indicates how the revenue is transformed into the net income The purpose of the _____ is to show managers and investors whether the company made or lost money during the period being reported.

The important thing to remember about an _____ is that it represents a period of time.

   a. AD-IA Model
   b. Income statement
   c. ACEA agreement
   d. ACCRA Cost of Living Index

25. The _____ is a heterodox school of economics that emphasizes the spontaneous organizing power of the price mechanism. It holds that the complexity of subjective human choices makes mathematical modelling of the evolving market extremely difficult and advocates a laissez faire approach to the economy. _____ economists advocate the enforcement of voluntary contractual agreements between economic agents, but otherwise the smallest imposition of coercive force on commercial transactions.
   a. ACEA agreement
   b. Austrian School
   c. ACCRA Cost of Living Index
   d. Economic calculation problem

26. _____ is the branch of economics concerned with 'the allocation and deployment of economic resources, both spatially and across time, in an uncertain environment' . It is additionally characterised by its 'concentration on monetary activities', in which 'money of one type or another is likely to appear on both sides of a trade' . The questions within _____ are typically framed in terms of 'time, uncertainty, options and information' .
   a. Financial economics
   b. Fixed exchange rate
   c. Public economics
   d. Price revolution

27. In economics, a _____ is a mechanism that allows people to easily buy and sell (trade) financial securities (such as stocks and bonds), commodities (such as precious metals or agricultural goods), and other fungible items of value at low transaction costs and at prices that reflect the efficient-market hypothesis.

_____s have evolved significantly over several hundred years and are undergoing constant innovation to improve liquidity.

Both general markets (where many commodities are traded) and specialized markets (where only one commodity is traded) exist.

   a. Convertible arbitrage
   b. Market anomaly
   c. Noise trader
   d. Financial market

28. _____, in law and economics, is a form of risk management primarily used to hedge against the risk of a contingent loss. _____ is defined as the equitable transfer of the risk of a loss, from one entity to another, in exchange for a premium, and can be thought of as a guaranteed small loss to prevent a large, possibly devastating loss. An insurer is a company selling the _____; an insured or policyholder is the person or entity buying the _____.
- a. ACCRA Cost of Living Index
- b. AD-IA Model
- c. Insurance
- d. ACEA agreement

29. In economics, a _____ exists when the production or use of goods and services by the market is not efficient. That is, there exists another outcome where all involved can be made better off. _____s can be viewed as scenarios where individuals' pursuit of pure self-interest leads to results that are not efficient - that can be improved upon from the societal point-of-view.
- a. Financial economics
- b. Fixed exchange rate
- c. General equilibrium
- d. Market failure

30. In general _____ refers to any non-human asset made by humans and then used in production. Often, it refers to economic capital in some ambiguous combination of infrastructural capital and natural capital. As these are combined in process-specific and firm-specific ways that neoclassical macroeconomics does not differentiate at its level of analysis, it is common to refer only to physical vs. human capital and seek so-called 'balanced growth' that develops both in tandem

Such analyses, however, fails to make distinctions considered critical by many modern economists.

- a. Net domestic product
- b. Linkage principle
- c. Physical capital
- d. Factor cost

31. A mutual _____ or stockholder is an individual or company (including a corporation) that legally owns one or more shares of stock in a joint stock company. A company's _____s collectively own that company. Thus, the typical goal of such companies is to enhance _____ value.
- a. Profit warning
- b. Shareholder
- c. Prime Standard
- d. Relative valuation

32. In economics, _____ is a rise in the general level of prices of goods and services in an economy over a period of time. When the general price level rises, each unit of currency buys fewer goods and services; consequently, _____ is also a decline in the real value of money--a loss of purchasing power in the medium of exchange which is also the monetary unit of account in the economy. A chief measure of general price-level _____ is the general _____ rate, which is the percentage change in a general price index (normally the Consumer Price Index) over time.
- a. Inflation
- b. Energy economics
- c. Economic
- d. Opportunity cost

33. _____ or the economics of information is a branch of microeconomic theory that studies how information affects an economy and economic decisions. Information has special characteristics. It is easy to create but hard to trust.
- a. ACCRA Cost of Living Index
- b. AD-IA Model
- c. ACEA agreement
- d. Information Economics

34. Although information has been bought and sold since ancient times, the idea of an information marketplace is relatively recent. The nature of such markets is still evolving, which complicates development of sustainable business models. However, certain attributes of _____ are beginning to be understood, such as diminished participation costs, opportunities for customization, shifting customer relations, and a need for order.
   a. Underground economy
   b. Open economy
   c. Intention economy
   d. Information markets

35. To _____ is to impose a financial charge or other levy upon a taxpayer by a state or the functional equivalent of a state.

_____es are also imposed by many subnational entities. _____es consist of direct _____ or indirect _____, and may be paid in money or as its labour equivalent (often but not always unpaid.)

   a. 1921 recession
   b. 130-30 fund
   c. 100-year flood
   d. Tax

36. To tax is to impose a financial charge or other levy upon a taxpayer by a state or the functional equivalent of a state.

_____ are also imposed by many subnational entities. _____ consist of direct tax or indirect tax, and may be paid in money or as its labour equivalent (often but not always unpaid.)

   a. 100-year flood
   b. 1921 recession
   c. 130-30 fund
   d. Taxes

37. _____, anti-selection insurance, statistics, and risk management. It refers to a market process in which 'bad' results occur when buyers and sellers have asymmetric information (i.e. access to different information): the 'bad' products or customers are more likely to be selected. A bank that sets one price for all its checking account customers runs the risk of being adversely selected against by its low-balance, high-activity (and hence least profitable) customers.
   a. ACEA agreement
   b. Adverse selection
   c. ACCRA Cost of Living Index
   d. AD-IA Model

38. A _____ is a situation in microeconomics where a competitive market allowing the exchange of a commodity would be Pareto-efficient, but no such market exists.

A variety of factors can lead to _____s:

A classic example of a _____ is the case of an externality like pollution, where decision makers are not responsible for some of the consequences of their actions. When a factory discharges polluted water into a river, that pollution can hurt people who fish in or get their drinking water from the river downstream, but the factory owner may have no incentive to consider those consequences.

   a. Deadweight loss
   b. Wage share
   c. Distributive efficiency
   d. Missing market

39. _____ is the prospect that a party insulated from risk may behave differently from the way it would behave if it were fully exposed to the risk. In insurance, _____ that occurs without conscious or malicious action is called morale hazard.

Chapter 11. Uncertainty and Game Theory 133

_____ is related to information asymmetry, a situation in which one party in a transaction has more information than another.

a. 1921 recession
b. 100-year flood
c. 130-30 fund
d. Moral hazard

40. _____ is a policy or ideology of violence intended to intimidate or cause terror for the purpose of 'exerting pressure on decision making by state bodies.' The term 'terror' is largely used to indicate clandestine, low-intensity violence that targets civilians and generates public fear. Thus 'terror' is distinct from asymmetric warfare, and violates the concept of a common law of war in which civilian life is regarded. The term '-ism' is used to indicate an ideology --typically one that claims its attacks are in the domain of a 'just war' concept, though most condemn such as crimes against humanity.

a. 1921 recession
b. 130-30 fund
c. 100-year flood
d. Terrorism

41. _____ refers to a business or organization attempting to acquire goods or services to accomplish the goals of the enterprise. Though there are several organizations that attempt to set standards in the _____ process, processes can vary greatly between organizations. Typically the word '_____' is not used interchangeably with the word 'procurement', since procurement typically includes Expediting, Supplier Quality, and Traffic and Logistics (T'L) in addition to _____.

a. Free port
b. 130-30 fund
c. 100-year flood
d. Purchasing

42. An _____ is a market form in which a market or industry is dominated by a small number of sellers (oligopolists.) Because there are few participants in this type of market, each oligopolist is aware of the actions of the others. The decisions of one firm influence, and are influenced by, the decisions of other firms.

a. Oligopsony
b. ACCRA Cost of Living Index
c. ACEA agreement
d. Oligopoly

43. Wisconsin originated the idea of _____ in the U.S. in 1932. In the United States, there are 50 state _____ programs plus one each in the District of Columbia and Puerto Rico. Through the Social Security Act of 1935, the Federal Government of the United States effectively coerced the individual states into adopting _____ plans.

a. ACCRA Cost of Living Index
b. Unemployment insurance
c. AD-IA Model
d. ACEA agreement

44. _____ is the term for economic policies followed as a part of military operations during wartime. The purpose of _____ is to capture critical economic resources so that the military can operate at full efficiency and/or deprive the enemy forces of those resources so that they cannot fight the war properly. The Russians demonstrated the use of economical warfare in the Battle of Stalingrad by cutting off the Germans' supply lines and starving them to death.

a. ACCRA Cost of Living Index
b. ACEA agreement
c. AD-IA Model
d. Economic warfare

45. A true _____ is a specific type of oligopoly where only two producers exist in one market. In reality, this definition is generally used where only two firms have dominant control over a market. In the field of industrial organization, it is the most commonly studied form of oligopoly due to its simplicity.

a. 100-year flood
b. Duopoly
c. 130-30 fund
d. Megacorpstate

46. _____ is a term used in business to indicate a state of intense competitive rivalry accompanied by a multi-lateral series of price reduction. One competitor will lower its price, then others will lower their prices to match. If one of them reduces their price again, a new round of reductions starts.
   a. Price war
   b. Big ticket item
   c. Transactional Net Margin Method
   d. Discounts and allowances

47. _____ was a survey conducted by the U.S. Department of Justice to gauge the prevalence of alcohol and illegal drug use among prior arrestees. It was a reformulation of the prior Drug Use Forecasting (DUF) program, focused on five drugs in particular: cocaine, marijuana, methamphetamine, opiates, and PCP.

Participants were randomly selected from arrest records in major metropolitan areas; because no personally identifying information is taken from each record chosen, the resulting data can be correlated to arrest rates, but not to the total population of persons charged.

   a. ACCRA Cost of Living Index
   b. AD-IA Model
   c. ACEA agreement
   d. Arrestee Drug Abuse Monitoring

48. A _____ is a counterfeit agreement among industries. It is an informal organization of producers that agree to coordinate prices and production. _____s usually occur in an oligopolistic industry, where there is a small number of sellers and usually involve homogeneous products.
   a. Cartel
   b. Shill
   c. 100-year flood
   d. Shanzhai

49. _____ is the transition of a national economy from monopoly control by groups of large businesses to a free market economy. This change rarely arises naturally, and is generally the result of regulation by a governing body.

A modern example of _____ is the economic restructuring of Germany after the fall of the Third Reich in 1945.

   a. Decartelization
   b. Complementary monopoly
   c. Monopolization
   d. Market power

50. _____ is an agreement, usually secretive, which occurs between two or more persons to deceive, mislead or to obtain an objective forbidden by law typically involving fraud or gaining an unfair advantage. It is an agreement among firms to divide the market, set prices kickbacks, or misrepresenting the independence of the relationship between the colluding parties.' All acts effected by _____ are considered void.
   a. Dividing territories
   b. Bid rigging
   c. Net Book Agreement
   d. Collusion

51. _____ was a Scottish moral philosopher and a pioneer of political economy. One of the key figures of the Scottish Enlightenment, Smith is the author of The Theory of Moral Sentiments and An Inquiry into the Nature and Causes of the Wealth of Nations. The latter, usually abbreviated as The Wealth of Nations, is considered his magnum opus and the first modern work of economics.

Chapter 11. Uncertainty and Game Theory 135

a. Alan Greenspan
c. Adam Smith
b. Adolf Hitler
d. Adolph Fischer

52. A _____ is a group of people who share or are motivated by at least one common issue or interest, or work together on a specific project(s) to achieve a common objective. _____s are also characterised by attempts to share and exercise political and social power and to make decisions on a consensus-driven and egalitarian basis. _____s differ from cooperatives in that they are not necessarily focused upon an economic benefit or saving (but can be that as well.)
   a. 130-30 fund
   b. 1921 recession
   c. 100-year flood
   d. Collective

53. In organized labor, _____ is the method whereby workers organize together (usually in unions) to meet, converse, and negotiate upon the work conditions with their employers normally resulting in a written contract setting forth the wages, hours, and other conditions to be observed for a stipulated period.It is the practice in which union and company representatives meet to negotiate a new labor contract. In various national labor and employment law contexts, _____ takes on a more specific legal meaning and so, in a broad sense, however, it is the coming together of workers to negotiate their employment.

A collective agreement is a labor contract between an employer and one or more unions.

   a. Designated Suppliers Program
   b. Strikebreaker
   c. Demarcation dispute
   d. Collective bargaining

54. Competitive market equilibrium is the traditional concept of economic equilibrium, appropriate for the analysis of commodity markets with flexible prices and many traders, and serving as the benchmark of efficiency in economic analysis. It relies crucially on the assumption of a competitive environment where each trader decides upon a quantity that is so small compared to the total quantity traded in the market that their individual transactions have no influence on the prices.Competitive markets are an ideal, a standard that other market structures are evaluated by.

A _____ consists of a vector of prices and an allocation such that given the prices, each trader by maximizing his objective function (profit, preferences) subject to his technological possibilities and resource constraints plans to trade into his part of the proposed allocation, and such that the prices make all net trades compatible with one another ('clear the market') by equating aggregate supply and demand for the commodities which are traded.

   a. Competitive equilibrium
   b. Partial equilibrium
   c. Market system
   d. Product-Market Growth Matrix

55. In the theory of artificial neural networks _____ networks are a case of competitive learning in recurrent neural networks. Output nodes in the network inhibit each other and activate themselves through reflexive connections. After some time, only one node in the output layer will be active.
   a. 1921 recession
   b. 100-year flood
   c. 130-30 fund
   d. Winner-take-all

56. _____ refers to the objective and subjective components of the believability of a source or message.

Chapter 11. Uncertainty and Game Theory

Traditionally, _____ has two key components: trustworthiness and expertise, which both have objective and subjective components. Trustworthiness is a based more on subjective factors, but can include objective measurements such as established reliability.

a. 130-30 fund
c. 1921 recession

b. 100-year flood
d. Credibility

57. _____ is a type of trade policy that allows traders to act and transact without interference from government. Thus, the policy permits trading partners mutual gains from trade, with goods and services produced according to the theory of comparative advantage.

Under a _____ policy, prices are a reflection of true supply and demand, and are the sole determinant of resource allocation.

a. 130-30 fund
c. 1921 recession

b. 100-year flood
d. Free trade

58. _____ is the economic policy of restraining trade between states, through methods such as tariffs on imported goods, restrictive quotas, and a variety of other restrictive government regulations designed to discourage imports, and prevent foreign take-over of local markets and companies. This policy is closely aligned with anti-globalization, and contrasts with free trade, where government barriers to trade are kept to a minimum. The term is mostly used in the context of economics, where _____ refers to policies or doctrines which 'protect' businesses and workers within a country by restricting or regulating trade with foreign nations.

a. Digital economy
c. Google economy

b. Knowledge economy
d. Protectionism

Chapter 12. How Markets Determine Incomes

1. The _____ consists of a number of economic theories which describe the nature of the firm, company including its existence, its behaviour, and its relationship with the market.

In simplified terms, the _____ aims to answer these questions:

1. Existence - why do firms emerge, why are not all transactions in the economy mediated over the market?
2. Boundaries - why the boundary between firms and the market is located exactly there? Which transactions are performed internally and which are negotiated on the market?
3. Organization - why are firms structured in such specific way? What is the interplay of formal and informal relationships?

Despite looking simple, these questions are not answered by the established economic theory, which usually views firms as given, and treats them as black boxes without any internal structure.

The First World War period saw a change of emphasis in economic theory away from industry-level analysis which mainly included analysing markets to analysis at the level of the firm, as it became increasingly clear that perfect competition was no longer an adequate model of how firms behaved. Economic theory till then had focussed on trying to understand markets alone and there had been little study on understanding why firms or organisations exist.

a. Technology gap
c. Khazzoom-Brookes postulate
b. Policy Ineffectiveness Proposition
d. Theory of the firm

2. _____ is the returns received on factors of production: rent is return on land, wages on labor, interest on capital, and profit on entrepreneurship. It is also known as Net Factor Payments (NFP.)

Part of current account with balance of trade (exports minus imports of goods and services) and net transfer payments (such as foreign aid.)

a. 100-year flood
c. Redistributive justice
b. 130-30 fund
d. Factor income

3. A variety of measures of _____ and output are used in economics to estimate total economic activity in a country or region, including gross domestic product (GDP), gross national product (GNP), and net _____

There are three main ways of calculating these numbers; the output approach, the income approach and the expenditure approach. In theory, the three must yield the same, because total expenditures on goods and services must equal the total income paid to the producers (Gnational income), and that must also equal the total value of the output of goods and services (GNP.)

a. GNI per capita
c. Volume index
b. Gross world product
d. National income

4. The _____ captures an expanded spectrum of values and criteria for measuring organizational (and societal) success: economic, ecological and social. With the ratification of the United Nations and ICLEI _____ standard for urban and community accounting in early 2007, this became the dominant approach to public sector full cost accounting. Similar UN standards apply to natural capital and human capital measurement to assist in measurements required by _____, e.g. the ecoBudget standard for reporting ecological footprint.
- a. Triple bottom line
- b. Leapfrogging
- c. Missing market
- d. Social welfare function

5. A _____ represents the combinations of goods and services that a consumer can purchase given current prices and his income. Consumer theory uses the concepts of a _____ and a preference map to analyze consumer choices. Both concepts have a ready graphical representation in the two-good case.
- a. Quality bias
- b. Revealed preference
- c. Joint demand
- d. Budget constraint

6. _____ is a specific term used in companies' financial reporting from the company-whole point of view. Because that use excludes the effects of changing ownership interest, an economic measure of _____ is necessary for financial analysis from the shareholders' point of view

_____ is defined by the Financial Accounting Standards Board, or FASB, as e;the change in equity [net assets] of a business enterprise during a period from transactions and other events and circumstances from nonowner sources. It includes all changes in equity during a period except those resulting from investments by owners and distributions to owners.e;

_____ is the sum of net income and other items that must bypass the income statement because they have not been realized, including items like an unrealized holding gain or loss from available for sale securities and foreign currency translation gains or losses.

- a. Real income
- b. Comprehensive income
- c. Windfall gain
- d. Net national income

7. In economics, _____ is how a natione;s total economy is distributed among its population. ._____ has always been a central concern of economic theory and economic policy. Classical economists such as Adam Smith, Thomas Malthus and David Ricardo were mainly concerned with factor _____, that is, the distribution of income between the main factors of production, land, labour and capital.
- a. Equipment trust certificate
- b. Eco commerce
- c. Authorised capital
- d. Income distribution

8. A _____ is an economy based on the division of labor in which the prices of goods and services are determined in a free price system set by supply and demand. This is often contrasted with a planned economy, in which a central government determines the price of goods and services using a fixed price system. Market economies are contrasted with mixed economy where the price system is not entirely free but under some government control that is not extensive enough to constitute a planned economy.
- a. Network Economy
- b. Nutritional Economics
- c. Market economy
- d. Commons-based peer production

Chapter 12. How Markets Determine Incomes   139

9. Total _____ is defined by the United States' Bureau of Economic Analysis as

income received by persons from all sources. It includes income received from participation in production as well as from government and business transfer payments. It is the sum of compensation of employees (received), supplements to wages and salaries, proprietors' income with inventory valuation adjustment (IVA) and capital consumption adjustment (CCAdj), rental income of persons with CCAdj, _____ receipts on assets, and personal current transfer receipts, less contributions for government social insurance.

a. Greater fool theory
c. Dividend Discount Model
b. Bidding
d. Personal income

10. The _____ or gross domestic income (GDI), a basic measure of an economy's economic performance, is the market value of all final goods and services produced within the borders of a nation in a year. _____ can be defined in three ways, all of which are conceptually identical. First, it is equal to the total expenditures for all final goods and services produced within the country in a stipulated period of time (usually a 365-day year.)

a. Countercyclical
c. Market structure
b. Monopolistic competition
d. Gross domestic product

11. _____ is a fee paid on borrowed assets. It is the price paid for the use of borrowed money , or, money earned by deposited funds . Assets that are sometimes lent with _____ include money, shares, consumer goods through hire purchase, major assets such as aircraft, and even entire factories in finance lease arrangements.

a. Internal debt
c. Asset protection
b. Insolvency
d. Interest

12. Economic _____ is defined as an excess distribution to any factor in a production process above that which is required to induce the factor into the process or any excess above that which is necessary to keep the factor in its current use..

Classical Factor _____ is primarily concerned with the fee paid for the use of fixed (e.g. natural) resources. The classical definition is expressed as any excess payment above that required to induce or provide for production.

a. 100-year flood
c. 1921 recession
b. 130-30 fund
d. Rent

13. In economics, a _____ is a redistribution of income in the market system. These payments are considered to be nonexhaustive because they do not directly absorb resources or create output. Examples of certain _____s include welfare (financial aid), social security, and government subsidies for certain businesses (firms.)

a. 130-30 fund
c. 1921 recession
b. 100-year flood
d. Transfer payment

14. A _____ is the transfer of wealth from one party (such as a person or company) to another. A _____ is usually made in exchange for the provision of goods, services or both, or to fulfill a legal obligation.

The simplest and oldest form of _____ is barter, the exchange of one good or service for another.

Chapter 12. How Markets Determine Incomes

   a. Soft count
   c. Going concern
   b. Payment
   d. Social gravity

15. In business and accounting, _____ are everything of value that is owned by a person or company. It is a claim on the property your income of a borrower. The balance sheet of a firm records the monetary value of the _____ owned by the firm.

   a. ACEA agreement
   c. ACCRA Cost of Living Index
   b. Assets
   d. Amortization schedule

16. In statistics, the _____ problem occurs when one considers a set of statistical inferences simultaneously. Errors in inference, including confidence intervals that fail to include their corresponding population parameters are more likely to occur when one considers the family as a whole. Several statistical techniques have been developed to prevent this from happening, allowing significance levels for single and _____ to be directly compared.

   a. Familywise error rate
   c. False discovery rate
   b. Multiple comparisons
   d. Hypotheses suggested by the data

17. The _____ is 'the basic residential unit in which economic production, consumption, inheritance, child rearing, and shelter are organized and carried out'; [the _____] 'may or may not be synonomous with family'.

The _____ is the basic unit of analysis in many social, microeconomic and government models. The term refers to all individuals who live in the same dwelling.

   a. 100-year flood
   c. Family economics
   b. Household
   d. 130-30 fund

18. The accounting equation relates assets, _____, and owner's equity:

   Assets = _____ + Owner's Equity

The accounting equation is the mathematical structure of the balance sheet.

The Australian Accounting Research Foundation defines _____ as: 'future sacrifice of economic benefits that the entity is presently obliged to make to other entities as a result of past transactions and other past events.'

Probably the most accepted accounting definition of liability is the one used by the International Accounting Standards Board (IASB.) The following is a quotation from IFRS Framework:

A liability is a present obligation of the enterprise arising from past events, the settlement of which is expected to result in an outflow from the enterprise of resources embodying economic benefits

-

Regulations as to the recognition of _____ are different all over the world, but are roughly similar to those of the IASB.

a. Coase theorem
c. Community property
b. Liabilities
d. Competition law theory

19. In business, _____ is the total liabilitiess minus total outside assets of an individual or a company. For a company, this is called shareholders' prefernce and may be referred to as book value. _____ is stated as at a particular year in time.
   a. Bond credit rating
   b. Sinking fund
   c. Post earnings announcement drift
   d. Net worth

20. _____ is a broad label that refers to any individuals or households that use goods and services generated within the economy. The concept of a _____ is used in different contexts, so that the usage and significance of the term may vary.

Typically when business people and economists talk of _____s they are talking about person as _____, an aggregated commodity item with little individuality other than that expressed in the buy/not-buy decision.

   a. 1921 recession
   b. 130-30 fund
   c. Consumer
   d. 100-year flood

21. _____ is a term in economics, where demand for one good or service occurs as a result of demand for another. This may occur as the former is a part of production of the second. For example, demand for coal leads to _____ for mining, as coal must be mined for coal to be consumed.
   a. Rate risk
   b. Leontief production function
   c. Days Sales Outstanding
   d. Derived demand

22. In economics, _____ are the resources employed to produce goods and services. They facilitate production but do not become part of the product (as with raw materials) or significantly transformed by the production process (as with fuel used to power machinery.) To 19th century economists, the _____ were land (natural resources, gifts from nature), labor (the ability to work), and capital goods (human-made tools and equipment.)
   a. Long-run
   b. Hicks-neutral technical change
   c. Product Pipeline
   d. Factors of production

23. _____ is the term denoting either an entrance or changes which are inserted into a system and which activate/modify a process. It is an abstract concept, used in the modeling, system(s) design and system(s) exploitation. It is usually connected with other terms, e.g., _____ field, _____ variable, _____ parameter, _____ value, _____ signal, _____ device and _____ file.
   a. Input
   b. AD-IA Model
   c. ACCRA Cost of Living Index
   d. ACEA agreement

24. In economics, the _____ is a graphical representation of the cumulative distribution function of a probability distribution; it is a graph showing the proportion of the distribution assumed by the bottom y% of the values. It is a curve that illustrates income distribution. It is often used to represent income distribution, where it shows for the bottom x% of households, what percentage y% of the total income they have.

a. Lorenz curve
b. Phillips curve
c. Kuznets curve
d. Demand curve

25. In economics, the _____ or marginal physical product is the extra output produced by one more unit of an input (for instance, the difference in output when a firm's labour is increased from five to six units.) Assuming that no other inputs to production change, the _____ of a given input (X) can be expressed as:

_____ = ΔY/ΔX = (the change of Y)/(the change of X.)

-
  - ○
    - Pending approval by Thomas Sowell***

In neoclassical economics, this is the mathematical derivative of the production function.... Note that the 'product' (Y) is typically defined ignoring external costs and benefits.

a. Labor problem
b. Factor prices
c. Productive capacity
d. Marginal product

26. In economics, the _____ also known as MPL or MPN is the change in output from hiring one additional unit of labor. It is the increase in output added by the last unit of labor. Assuming that no other inputs to production change, the marginal product of a given input (X) can be expressed as:

MP = ΔY/ΔX = (the change of Y)/(the change of X.)

a. Production function
b. Marginal product
c. Marginal product of labor
d. Product Pipeline

27. _____ in economics and business is the result of an exchange and from that trade we assign a numerical monetary value to a good, service or asset. If Alice trades Bob 4 apples for an orange, the _____ of an orange is 4 apples. Inversely, the _____ of an apple is 1/4 oranges.

a. Price book
b. Premium pricing
c. Price
d. Price war

28. Applied microeconomics includes a range of specialized areas of study, many of which draw on methods from other fields. Applied work often uses little more than the basics of _____, supply and demand. Industrial organization and regulation examines topics such as the entry and exit of firms, innovation, role of trademarks.

a. Financial crises
b. Microeconomics
c. Price theory
d. Monopolistic competition

29. _____ is an economic model based on price, utility and quantity in a market. It predicts that in a competitive market, price will function to equalize the quantity demanded by consumers, and the quantity supplied by producers, resulting in an economic equilibrium of price and quantity. The model incorporates other factors changing equilibrium as a shift of demand and/or supply.

Chapter 12. How Markets Determine Incomes 143

a. Deferred gratification
b. Rational addiction
c. Joint demand
d. Supply and demand

30. In economics, the term _____ of income or _____ refers to a simple economic model which describes the reciprocal circulation of income between producers and consumers. In the _____ model, the inter-dependent entitiés of producer and consumer are referred to as 'firms' and 'households' respectively and provide each other with factors in order to facilitate the flow of income. Firms provide consumers with goods and services in exchange for consumer expenditure and 'factors of production' from households.
   a. 130-30 fund
   b. 1921 recession
   c. Circular flow
   d. 100-year flood

31. Economics:

   - _____, the desire to own something and the ability to pay for it
   - _____ curve, a graphic representation of a _____ schedule
   - _____ deposit, the money in checking accounts
   - _____ pull theory, the theory that inflation occurs when _____ for goods and services exceeds existing supplies
   - _____ schedule, a table that lists the quantity of a good a person will buy it each different price
   - _____ side economics, the school of economics at believes government spending and tax cuts open economy by raising _____

   a. Variability
   b. Demand
   c. Production
   d. McKesson ' Robbins scandal

32. _____ is one of the four Ps of the marketing mix. The other three aspects are product, promotion, and place. It is also a key variable in microeconomic price allocation theory.
   a. Guaranteed Maximum Price
   b. Premium pricing
   c. Point of total assumption
   d. Pricing

33. In microeconomics, _____ is quite simply the conversion of inputs into outputs. It is an economic process that uses resources to create a good or service that is suitable for exchange. This can include manufacturing, storing, shipping, and packaging.
   a. MET
   b. Solved
   c. Red Guards
   d. Production

34. In microeconomics, _____ is the extra revenue that an additional unit of product will bring. It is the additional income from selling one more unit of a good; sometimes equal to price. It can also be described as the change in total revenue/change in number of units sold.
   a. Reservation price
   b. Marginal revenue
   c. Long term
   d. Market demand schedule

35. The marginal revenue productivity theory of wages, also referred to as the _____ of labor, is the change in total revenue earned by a firm that results from employing one more unit of labor. It is a neoclassical model that determines, under some conditions, the optimal number of workers to employ at an exogenously determined market wage rate.

The _____ of a worker is equal to the product of the marginal product of labor (MP) and the marginal revenue (MR), given by MR×MP = _____.

a. Coal depletion
b. Marginal revenue product
c. Real prices and ideal prices
d. Marginal revenue productivity theory of wages

36. In economics, the _____ can be defined as the graph depicting the relationship between the price of a certain commodity, and the amount of it that consumers are willing and able to purchase at that given price. It is a graphic representation of a demand schedule. The _____ for all consumers together follows from the _____ of every individual consumer: the individual demands at each price are added together.

a. Demand curve
b. Wage curve
c. Kuznets curve
d. Cost curve

37. In economics, _____ refers to how the marginal contribution of a factor of production usually decreases as more of the factor is used. According to this relationship, in a production system with fixed and variable inputs, beyond some point, each additional unit of the variable input yields smaller and smaller increases in output. Conversely, producing one more unit of output costs more and more in variable inputs.

a. Derivatives law
b. Community property
c. Diminishing returns
d. Patent troll

38. In economic theory, _____ is the competitive situation in any market where the conditions necessary for perfect competition are not satisfied. It is a market structure that does not meet the conditions of perfect competition.

Forms of _____ include:

- Monopoly, in which there is only one seller of a good.
- Oligopoly, in which there is a small number of sellers.
- Monopolistic competition, in which there are many sellers producing highly differentiated goods.
- Monopsony, in which there is only one buyer of a good.
- Oligopsony, in which there is a small number of buyers.

There may also be _____ in markets due to buyers or sellers lacking information about prices and the goods being traded.

There may also be _____ due to a time lag in a market.

a. Imperfect competition
b. AD-IA Model
c. ACCRA Cost of Living Index
d. ACEA agreement

39. _____ is a situation in which the limited resources of a firm are allocated in accordance with the wishes of consumers. An allocatively efficient economy produces an 'optimal mix' of commodities. A firm is allocatively efficient when its price is equal to its marginal costs (that is, P = MC) in a perfect market.

a. ACEA agreement
b. ACCRA Cost of Living Index
c. Economic efficiency
d. Allocative efficiency

Chapter 12. How Markets Determine Incomes

40. _____ is a term used in national accounts statistics and macroeconomics. It basically refers to the net additions to the (physical) capital stock in an accounting period, or, to the value of the increase of the capital stock; though it may occasionally also refer to the (growth of the) total stock of capital formed.

Thus, in UNSNA, _____ equals fixed capital investment, the increase in the value of inventories held, plus (net) lending to foreign countries, during an accounting period.

a. Capital flight
b. Capital intensity
c. Capital formation
d. Consumption of fixed capital

41. In neoclassical economics and microeconomics, _____ describes the perfect being a market in which there are many small firms, all producing homogeneous goods. In the short term, such markets are productively inefficient as output will not occur where mc is equal to ac, but allocatively efficient, as output under _____ will always occur where mc is equal to mr, and therefore where mc equals ar. However, in the long term, such markets are both allocatively and productively efficient.

a. General equilibrium
b. Law of supply
c. Co-operative economics
d. Perfect competition

42. In economics, _____ is the process by which a firm determines the price and output level that returns the greatest profit. There are several approaches to this problem. The total revenue--total cost method relies on the fact that profit equals revenue minus cost, and the marginal revenue--marginal cost method is based on the fact that total profit in a perfectly competitive market reaches its maximum point where marginal revenue equals marginal cost.

a. Profit margin
b. 100-year flood
c. Profit maximization
d. Normal profit

146   Chapter 12. How Markets Determine Incomes

43. A _____ is:

- Rewrite _____, in generative grammar and computer science
- Standardization, a formal and widely-accepted statement, fact, definition, or qualification
- Operation, a determinate _____ for performing a mathematical operation and obtaining a certain result (Mathematics, Logic)
    - Unary operation
    - Binary operation
- _____ of inference, a function from sets of formulae to formulae (Mathematics, Logic)
- _____ of thumb, principle with broad application that is not intended to be strictly accurate or reliable for every situation. Also often simply referred to as a _____
- Moral, an atomic element of a moral code for guiding choices in human behavior
- Heuristic, a quantized '_____' which shows a tendency or probability for successful function
- A regulation, as in sports
- A Production _____, as in computer science
- Procedural law, a _____ set governing the application of laws to cases
    - A law, which may informally be called a '_____'
    - A court ruling, a decision by a court
- In the U.S. Government, a regulation mandated by Congress, but written or expanded upon by the Executive Branch.
- Norm (sociology), an informal but widely accepted _____, concept, truth, definition, or qualification (social norms, legal norms, coding norms)
- Norm (philosophy), a kind of sentence or a reason to act, feel or believe
- 'Rulership' is the concept of governance by a government:
    - Military _____, governance by a military body
    - Monastic _____, a collection of precepts that guides the life of monks or nuns in a religious order where the superior holds the place of Christ
- Slide _____

- '_____,' a song by Ayumi Hamasaki
- '_____,' a song by rapper Nas
- '_____s,' an album by the band The Whitest Boy Alive
- _____s: Pyaar Ka Superhit Formula, a 2003 Bollywood film
- ruler, an instrument for measuring lengths
- _____, a component of an astrolabe, circumferator or similar instrument
- The _____s, a bestselling self-help book
- _____ Project (Run Up-to-date Linux Everywhere), a project that aims to use up-to-date Linux software on old PCs
- _____ engine, a software system that helps managing business _____s
- Ja _____, a hip hop artist
    - R.U.L.E., a 2005 greatest hits album by rapper Ja _____
- '_____s,' a KMFDM song

a. Procter ' Gamble   b. Demand
c. Rule   d. Technocracy

44. _____ are the prices that the factors of production of a finished item attract.

Chapter 12. How Markets Determine Incomes   147

There has been some economic debate as to what determines these prices. Classical and Marxist economists argued that the _____ decided the value of a product and so value was intrinsic within the product.

- a. Marginal product
- b. Marginal product of labor
- c. Productivity model
- d. Factor prices

45. In economics, _____ is the ratio of the percent change in one variable to the percent change in another variable. It is a tool for measuring the responsiveness of a function to changes in parameters in a relative way. Commonly analyzed are _____ of substitution, price and wealth.
    - a. ACEA agreement
    - b. ACCRA Cost of Living Index
    - c. Elasticity of demand
    - d. Elasticity

46. In economics, the _____ is defined as a numerical measure of the responsiveness of the quantity supplied of product (A) to a change in price of product (A) alone. It is the measure of the way quantity supplied reacts to a change in price.

For example, if, in response to a 10% rise in the price of a good, the quantity supplied increases by 20%, the _____ would be 20%/10% = 2.

- a. Hedonimetry
- b. Demand shaping
- c. Passive income
- d. Price elasticity of supply

47. _____ refers to the stock of skills and knowledge embodied in the ability to perform labor so as to produce economic value. It is the skills and knowledge gained by a worker through education and experience. Many early economic theories refer to it simply as labor, one of three factors of production, and consider it to be a fungible resource -- homogeneous and easily interchangeable. Other conceptions of labor dispense with these assumptions.
    - a. Price theory
    - b. General equilibrium
    - c. Law of increasing costs
    - d. Human capital

48. The supply of labor is the number of total hours that workers wish to work at a given real wage rate.

_____ curves are derived from the 'labor-leisure' trade-off. More hours worked earn higher incomes but necessitate a cut in the amount of leisure that workers enjoy.

- a. Creative capitalism
- b. Late capitalism
- c. Human trafficking
- d. Labor supply

49. In algebra, a _____ is a function depending on n that associates a scalar, det(A), to an n×n square matrix A. The fundamental geometric meaning of a _____ is a scale factor for measure when A is regarded as a linear transformation. _____s are important both in calculus, where they enter the substitution rule for several variables, and in multilinear algebra.

Chapter 12. How Markets Determine Incomes

For a fixed nonnegative integer n, there is a unique _____ function for the n×n matrices over any commutative ring R. In particular, this function exists when R is the field of real or complex numbers.

a. 1921 recession
c. 130-30 fund
b. 100-year flood
d. Determinant

50. _____ in economics refers to metrics and measures of output from production processes, per unit of input. Labor _____, for example, is typically measured as a ratio of output per labor-hour, an input. _____ may be conceived of as a metrics of the technical or engineering efficiency of production.

a. Fordism
c. Piece work
b. Productivity
d. Production-possibility frontier

51. In economics, economic equilibrium is simply a state of the world where economic forces are balanced and in the absence of external influences the (equilibrium) values of economic variables will not change. It is the point at which quantity demanded and quantity supplied are equal. _____, for example, refers to a condition where a market price is established through competition such that the amount of goods or services sought by buyers is equal to the amount of goods or services produced by sellers.

a. Marketization
c. Regulated market
b. Product-Market Growth Matrix
d. Market equilibrium

52. The _____ on a portfolio of investments takes into account not only the capital appreciation on the portfolio, but also the income received on the portfolio. The income typically consists of interest, dividends, and securities lending fees. This contrasts with the price return, which takes into account only the capital gain on an investment.

a. Profitability index
c. Total return
b. Micro venture capital
d. Chinese wall

53. In economics, the _____ is the wage rate that produces neither an access supply of workers nor an excess demand for workers and labor market. See economic equilibrium.

a. International free trade agreement
c. Effective unemployment rate
b. Economic stability
d. Equilibrium wage

54. Competition law, known in the United States as _____ law, has three main elements:

- prohibiting agreements or practices that restrict free trading and competition between business entities. This includes in particular the repression of cartels.
- banning abusive behaviour by a firm dominating a market, or anti-competitive practices that tend to lead to such a dominant position. Practices controlled in this way may include predatory pricing, tying, price gouging, refusal to deal, and many others.
- supervising the mergers and acquisitions of large corporations, including some joint ventures. Transactions that are considered to threaten the competitive process can be prohibited altogether, or approved subject to 'remedies' such as an obligation to divest part of the merged business or to offer licences or access to facilities to enable other businesses to continue competing.

Chapter 12. How Markets Determine Incomes

The substance and practice of competition law varies from jurisdiction to jurisdiction. Protecting the interests of consumers (consumer welfare) and ensuring that entrepreneurs have an opportunity to compete in the market economy are often treated as important objectives. Competition law is closely connected with law on deregulation of access to markets, state aids and subsidies, the privatisation of state owned assets and the establishment of independent sector regulators. In recent decades, competition law has been viewed as a way to provide better public services.

- a. United Kingdom competition law
- b. Intellectual property law
- c. Anti-Inflation Act
- d. Antitrust

55. In mathematics, an _____ is a statement about the relative size or order of two objects, or about whether they are the same or not

- The notation a < b means that a is less than b.
- The notation a > b means that a is greater than b.
- The notation a ≠ b means that a is not equal to b, but does not say that one is greater than the other or even that they can be compared in size.

In each statement above, a is not equal to b. These relations are known as strict inequalities. The notation a < b may also be read as 'a is strictly less than b'.

- a. AD-IA Model
- b. ACCRA Cost of Living Index
- c. ACEA agreement
- d. Inequality

56. In economics, the _____ is the term economists use to describe the self-regulating nature of the marketplace. The _____ is a metaphor coined by the economist Adam Smith in The Wealth of Nations.

Adam Smith mentions the metaphor in Book IV of The Wealth of Nations, arguing that people in any society will certainly employ their capital in foreign trading only if the profits available by that method far exceed those available locally, and that in such a case it is better for society as a whole if they so did.

- a. ACEA agreement
- b. AD-IA Model
- c. Invisible hand
- d. ACCRA Cost of Living Index

57. _____ is a term used to describe a policy of allowing events to take their own course. The term is a French phrase literally meaning 'let do'. It is a doctrine that states that government generally should not intervene in the marketplace.
- a. Laissez-faire
- b. Communization
- c. Theory of Productive Forces
- d. Heroic capitalism

58. _____ is the shortage of common things such as food, clothing, shelter and safe drinking water, all of which determine the quality of life. It may also include the lack of access to opportunities such as education and employment which aid the escape from _____ and/or allow one to enjoy the respect of fellow citizens. According to Mollie Orshansky who developed the _____ measurements used by the U.S. government, 'to be poor is to be deprived of those goods and services and pleasures which others around us take for granted.' Ongoing debates over causes, effects and best ways to measure _____, directly influence the design and implementation of _____-reduction programs and are therefore relevant to the fields of public administration and international development.

a. Growth Elasticity of Poverty
b. Liberal welfare reforms
c. Poverty map
d. Poverty

Chapter 13. The Labor Market

1. The _____ was a period in the late 18th and early 19th centuries when major changes in agriculture, manufacturing, mining, and transportation had a profound effect on the socioeconomic and cultural conditions in Britain. The changes subsequently spread throughout Europe, North America, and eventually the world. The onset of the _____ marked a major turning point in human society; almost every aspect of daily life was eventually influenced in some way.
   - a. Adolf Hitler
   - b. Industrial Revolution
   - c. Adolph Fischer
   - d. Adam Smith

2. The term _____s refers to wages that have been adjusted for inflation. This term is used in contrast to nominal wages or unadjusted wages.

   The use of adjusted figures is in undertaking some form of economic analysis.

   - a. Profit sharing
   - b. Federal Wage System
   - c. Living wage
   - d. Real wage

3. In algebra, a _____ is a function depending on n that associates a scalar, det(A), to an n×n square matrix A. The fundamental geometric meaning of a _____ is a scale factor for measure when A is regarded as a linear transformation. _____s are important both in calculus, where they enter the substitution rule for several variables, and in multilinear algebra.

   For a fixed nonnegative integer n, there is a unique _____ function for the n×n matrices over any commutative ring R. In particular, this function exists when R is the field of real or complex numbers.

   - a. 130-30 fund
   - b. 1921 recession
   - c. 100-year flood
   - d. Determinant

4. In microeconomics, _____ is quite simply the conversion of inputs into outputs. It is an economic process that uses resources to create a good or service that is suitable for exchange. This can include manufacturing, storing, shipping, and packaging.
   - a. Solved
   - b. Red Guards
   - c. MET
   - d. Production

5. _____ is an economic model based on price, utility and quantity in a market. It predicts that in a competitive market, price will function to equalize the quantity demanded by consumers, and the quantity supplied by producers, resulting in an economic equilibrium of price and quantity. The model incorporates other factors changing equilibrium as a shift of demand and/or supply.
   - a. Rational addiction
   - b. Joint demand
   - c. Supply and demand
   - d. Deferred gratification

Chapter 13. The Labor Market

6. Economics:

   - _____, the desire to own something and the ability to pay for it
   - _____ curve, a graphic representation of a _____ schedule
   - _____ deposit, the money in checking accounts
   - _____ pull theory, the theory that inflation occurs when _____ for goods and services exceeds existing supplies
   - _____ schedule, a table that lists the quantity of a good a person will buy it each different price
   - _____ side economics, the school of economics at believes government spending and tax cuts open economy by raising _____

   a. Demand
   c. McKesson ' Robbins scandal
   b. Production
   d. Variability

7. In economics, _____ refers to how the marginal contribution of a factor of production usually decreases as more of the factor is used. According to this relationship, in a production system with fixed and variable inputs, beyond some point, each additional unit of the variable input yields smaller and smaller increases in output. Conversely, producing one more unit of output costs more and more in variable inputs.

   a. Derivatives law
   c. Community property
   b. Diminishing returns
   d. Patent troll

8. _____ in economics refers to metrics and measures of output from production processes, per unit of input. Labor _____, for example, is typically measured as a ratio of output per labor-hour, an input. _____ may be conceived of as a metrics of the technical or engineering efficiency of production.

   a. Productivity
   c. Fordism
   b. Piece work
   d. Production-possibility frontier

9. The _____ is a trilateral trade bloc in North America created by the governments of the United States, Canada, and Mexico. The agreement creating the trade bloc came into force on January 1, 1994. It superseded the Canada-United States Free Trade Agreement between the U.S. and Canada.

   a. Case-Shiller Home Price Indices
   c. Demand-side technologies
   b. North American Free Trade Agreement
   d. Federal Reserve Bank Notes

10. A _____ is a group of people who share or are motivated by at least one common issue or interest, or work together on a specific project(s) to achieve a common objective. _____s are also characterised by attempts to share and exercise political and social power and to make decisions on a consensus-driven and egalitarian basis. _____s differ from cooperatives in that they are not necessarily focused upon an economic benefit or saving (but can be that as well.)

    a. 1921 recession
    c. 130-30 fund
    b. 100-year flood
    d. Collective

11. In organized labor, _____ is the method whereby workers organize together (usually in unions) to meet, converse, and negotiate upon the work conditions with their employers normally resulting in a written contract setting forth the wages, hours, and other conditions to be observed for a stipulated period. It is the practice in which union and company representatives meet to negotiate a new labor contract. In various national labor and employment law contexts, _____ takes on a more specific legal meaning and so, in a broad sense, however, it is the coming together of workers to negotiate their employment.

A collective agreement is a labor contract between an employer and one or more unions.

- a. Collective bargaining
- b. Designated Suppliers Program
- c. Strikebreaker
- d. Demarcation dispute

12. _____s is the social science that studies the production, distribution, and consumption of goods and services. The term _____s comes from the Ancient Greek oá¼°κονομῖα from oá¼¶κος (oikos, 'house') + vĺŒμος (nomos, 'custom' or 'law'), hence 'rules of the house(hold)'. Current _____ models developed out of the broader field of political economy in the late 19th century, owing to a desire to use an empirical approach more akin to the physical sciences.
- a. Economic
- b. Inflation
- c. Opportunity cost
- d. Energy economics

13. _____ is the increase in the amount of the goods and services produced by an economy over time. It is conventionally measured as the percent rate of increase in real gross domestic product, or real GDP. Growth is usually calculated in real terms, i.e. inflation-adjusted terms, in order to net out the effect of inflation on the price of the goods and services produced.
- a. ACEA agreement
- b. ACCRA Cost of Living Index
- c. Economic growth
- d. AD-IA Model

14. _____ or government expenditure is classified by economists into three main types. Government purchases of goods and services for current use are classed as government consumption. Government purchases of goods and services intended to create future benefits, such as infrastructure investment or research spending, are classed as government investment.
- a. 100-year flood
- b. 130-30 fund
- c. 1921 recession
- d. Government spending

15. _____ is the term denoting either an entrance or changes which are inserted into a system and which activate/modify a process. It is an abstract concept, used in the modeling, system(s) design and system(s) exploitation. It is usually connected with other terms, e.g., _____ field, _____ variable, _____ parameter, _____ value, _____ signal, _____ device and _____ file.
- a. ACEA agreement
- b. Input
- c. AD-IA Model
- d. ACCRA Cost of Living Index

16. _____ is a common concept in economics, and gives rise to derived concepts such as consumer debt. Generally _____ is defined by opposition to production. But the precise definition can vary because different schools of economists define production quite differently.
- a. Federal Reserve Bank Notes
- b. Consumption
- c. Foreclosure data providers
- d. Cash or share options

17. In economics, the people in the _____ are the suppliers of labor. The _____ is all the nonmilitary people who are employed or unemployed. In 2005, the worldwide _____ was over 3 billion people.
   a. Grenelle agreements
   b. Departmentalization
   c. Distributed workforce
   d. Labor force

18. The term _____ is applied broadly to a variety of situations in which some financial institutions or assets suddenly lose a large part of their value. In the 19th and early 20th centuries, many financial crises were associated with banking panics, and many recessions coincided with these panics. Other situations that are often called financial crises include stock market crashes and the bursting of other financial bubbles, currency crises, and sovereign defaults.
   a. Co-operative economics
   b. Financial crisis
   c. Market failure
   d. Macroeconomics

19. _____ refers to discriminatory employment practices such as bias in hiring, promotion, job assignment, termination, and compensation, and various types of harassment.

In many countries, laws prohibit employers from discriminating on the basis of race, color, sex, religion, national origin, physical or mental disability, or age. There is also a growing body of law preventing or occasionally justifying _____ based on sexual orientation or gender identity.

   a. Irish competition law
   b. Impotent poor
   c. Energy Independence and Security Act of 2007
   d. Employment discrimination

20. _____ is the period of time that an individual spends at paid occupational labor. Unpaid labors such as housework are not considered part of the working week. Many countries regulate the work week by law, such as stipulating minimum daily rest periods, annual holidays and a maximum number of working hours per week.
   a. Working time
   b. 100-year flood
   c. 1921 recession
   d. 130-30 fund

21. In economics, the _____ is the change in consumption resulting from a change in real income.

Another important item that can change is the money income of the consumer. The _____ is the phenomenon observed through changes in purchasing power.

   a. Export subsidy
   b. Inflation hedge
   c. Equilibrium wage
   d. Income effect

22. The supply of labor is the number of total hours that workers wish to work at a given real wage rate.

_____ curves are derived from the 'labor-leisure' trade-off. More hours worked earn higher incomes but necessitate a cut in the amount of leisure that workers enjoy.

   a. Creative capitalism
   b. Late capitalism
   c. Human trafficking
   d. Labor supply

23. _____ to the arrival of new individuals into a habitat or population. It is a biological concept and is important in population ecology, differentiated from emigration and migration.

Chapter 13. The Labor Market

_____ is a modern phenomenon.

a. ACCRA Cost of Living Index
b. ACEA agreement
c. AD-IA Model
d. Immigration

24. In economic theory, _____ is the competitive situation in any market where the conditions necessary for perfect competition are not satisfied. It is a market structure that does not meet the conditions of perfect competition.

Forms of _____ include:

- Monopoly, in which there is only one seller of a good.
- Oligopoly, in which there is a small number of sellers.
- Monopolistic competition, in which there are many sellers producing highly differentiated goods.
- Monopsony, in which there is only one buyer of a good.
- Oligopsony, in which there is a small number of buyers.

There may also be _____ in markets due to buyers or sellers lacking information about prices and the goods being traded.

There may also be _____ due to a time lag in a market.

a. AD-IA Model
b. ACCRA Cost of Living Index
c. Imperfect competition
d. ACEA agreement

25. _____ is a term used in labor economics to analyze the relation between the wage rate and the unpleasantness, risk, or other undesirable attributes of a particular job. A _____, which is also called a compensating wage differential or an equalizing difference, is defined as the additional amount of income that a given worker must be offered in order to motivate them to accept a given undesirable job, relative to other jobs that worker could perform. One can also speak of the _____ for an especially desirable job, or one that provides special benefits, but in this case the differential would be negative: that is, a given worker would be willing to accept a lower wage for an especially desirable job, relative to other jobs.

a. Search theory
b. 100-year flood
c. Wage dispersion
d. Compensating differential

156   *Chapter 13. The Labor Market*

26. A _____ is:

- Rewrite _____, in generative grammar and computer science
- Standardization, a formal and widely-accepted statement, fact, definition, or qualification
- Operation, a determinate _____ for performing a mathematical operation and obtaining a certain result (Mathematics, Logic)
    - Unary operation
    - Binary operation
- _____ of inference, a function from sets of formulae to formulae (Mathematics, Logic)
- _____ of thumb, principle with broad application that is not intended to be strictly accurate or reliable for every situation. Also often simply referred to as a _____
- Moral, an atomic element of a moral code for guiding choices in human behavior
- Heuristic, a quantized '_____' which shows a tendency or probability for successful function
- A regulation, as in sports
- A Production _____, as in computer science
- Procedural law, a _____ set governing the application of laws to cases
    - A law, which may informally be called a '_____'
    - A court ruling, a decision by a court
- In the U.S. Government, a regulation mandated by Congress, but written or expanded upon by the Executive Branch.
- Norm (sociology), an informal but widely accepted _____, concept, truth, definition, or qualification (social norms, legal norms, coding norms)
- Norm (philosophy), a kind of sentence or a reason to act, feel or believe
- 'Rulership' is the concept of governance by a government:
    - Military _____, governance by a military body
    - Monastic _____, a collection of precepts that guides the life of monks or nuns in a religious order where the superior holds the place of Christ
- Slide _____

- '_____,' a song by Ayumi Hamasaki
- '_____,' a song by rapper Nas
- '_____s,' an album by the band The Whitest Boy Alive
- _____s: Pyaar Ka Superhit Formula, a 2003 Bollywood film
- ruler, an instrument for measuring lengths
- _____, a component of an astrolabe, circumferator or similar instrument
- The _____s, a bestselling self-help book
- _____ Project (Run Up-to-date Linux Everywhere), a project that aims to use up-to-date Linux software on old PCs
- _____ engine, a software system that helps managing business _____s
- Ja _____, a hip hop artist
    - R.U.L.E., a 2005 greatest hits album by rapper Ja _____
- '_____s,' a KMFDM song

a. Demand   b. Technocracy
c. Procter ' Gamble   d. Rule

Chapter 13. The Labor Market

27. _____ refers to the stock of skills and knowledge embodied in the ability to perform labor so as to produce economic value. It is the skills and knowledge gained by a worker through education and experience. Many early economic theories refer to it simply as labor, one of three factors of production, and consider it to be a fungible resource -- homogeneous and easily interchangeable. Other conceptions of labor dispense with these assumptions.
   a. Law of increasing costs
   b. Human capital
   c. Price theory
   d. General equilibrium

28. In economics, _____ is the active redirecting resources from being consumed today so that they may create benefits in the future; the use of assets to earn income or profit. _____ is the process of making an investment in order to earn a profit, for example equity investment either through a fund, a 401k plan, or individually. People often invest in order to build up their estate or to accumulate funds for retirement.

To try to predict good stocks to invest in, two main schools of thought exist: technical analysis and fundamentals analysis.

   a. Investing
   b. ACEA agreement
   c. AD-IA Model
   d. ACCRA Cost of Living Index

29. In economics supernormal profit _____ or pure profit or excess profits, is a profit exceeding the normal profit. Normal profit equals the opportunity cost of labour and capital, while supernormal profit is the amount exceeds the normal return from these input factors in production.

_____ is usually generated by an oligopoly or a monopoly; however, these firms often try to hide this from the market to reduce risk of competition or antitrust investigation.

   a. Economic profit
   b. Abnormal profit
   c. ACCRA Cost of Living Index
   d. Accounting profit

30. The _____ captures an expanded spectrum of values and criteria for measuring organizational (and societal) success: economic, ecological and social. With the ratification of the United Nations and ICLEI _____ standard for urban and community accounting in early 2007, this became the dominant approach to public sector full cost accounting. Similar UN standards apply to natural capital and human capital measurement to assist in measurements required by _____, e.g. the ecoBudget standard for reporting ecological footprint.
   a. Leapfrogging
   b. Social welfare function
   c. Missing market
   d. Triple bottom line

31. Economic _____ is defined as an excess distribution to any factor in a production process above that which is required to induce the factor into the process or any excess above that which is necessary to keep the factor in its current use..

Classical Factor _____ is primarily concerned with the fee paid for the use of fixed (e.g. natural) resources. The classical definition is expressed as any excess payment above that required to induce or provide for production.

a. 130-30 fund
b. Rent
c. 100-year flood
d. 1921 recession

32. The _____ was one of the first federations of labor unions in the United States. It was founded in Columbus, Ohio in 1886 by Samuel Gompers as a reorganization of its predecessor, the Federation of Organized Trades and Labor Unions. Gompers became president of the AFL in 1886 and was reelected every year except one until his death on December 13, 1924.
   a. American Federation of Labor
   b. ACCRA Cost of Living Index
   c. AD-IA Model
   d. ACEA agreement

33. In economics, _____ describes the state of a market with respect to competition.

   - Perfect competition, in which the market consists of a very large number of firms producing a homogeneous product.
   - Monopolistic competition where there are a large number of independent firms which have a very small proportion of the market share.
   - Oligopoly, in which a market is dominated by a small number of firms which own more than 40% of the market share.
   - Oligopsony, a market dominated by many sellers and a few buyers.
   - Monopoly, where there is only one provider of a product or service.
   - Natural monopoly, a monopoly in which economies of scale cause efficiency to increase continuously with the size of the firm. A firm is a natural monopoly if it is able to serve the entire market demand at a lower cost than any combination of two or more smaller, more specialized firms.
   - Monopsony, when there is only one buyer in a market.

The imperfectly competitive structure is quite identical to the realistic market conditions where some monopolistic competitors, monopolists, oligopolists, and duopolists exist and dominate the market conditions. The elements of _____ include the number and size distribution of firms, entry conditions, and the extent of differentiation.

These somewhat abstract concerns tend to determine some but not all details of a specific concrete market system where buyers and sellers actually meet and commit to trade.

   a. Monopolistic competition
   b. Labour economics
   c. Human capital
   d. Market structure

34. The American Federation of Labor and Congress of Industrial Organizations, commonly _____, is a national trade union center, the largest federation of unions in the United States, made up of 65 national and international unions (including Canadian), together representing more than 10 million workers. It was formed in 1955 when the AFL and the CIO merged after a long estrangement. From 1955 until 2005, the _____'s member unions represented nearly all unionized workers in the United States.
   a. AD-IA Model
   b. ACCRA Cost of Living Index
   c. ACEA agreement
   d. AFL-CIO

Chapter 13. The Labor Market

35. Competition law, known in the United States as _____ law, has three main elements:

- prohibiting agreements or practices that restrict free trading and competition between business entities. This includes in particular the repression of cartels.
- banning abusive behaviour by a firm dominating a market, or anti-competitive practices that tend to lead to such a dominant position. Practices controlled in this way may include predatory pricing, tying, price gouging, refusal to deal, and many others.
- supervising the mergers and acquisitions of large corporations, including some joint ventures. Transactions that are considered to threaten the competitive process can be prohibited altogether, or approved subject to 'remedies' such as an obligation to divest part of the merged business or to offer licences or access to facilities to enable other businesses to continue competing.

The substance and practice of competition law varies from jurisdiction to jurisdiction. Protecting the interests of consumers (consumer welfare) and ensuring that entrepreneurs have an opportunity to compete in the market economy are often treated as important objectives. Competition law is closely connected with law on deregulation of access to markets, state aids and subsidies, the privatisation of state owned assets and the establishment of independent sector regulators. In recent decades, competition law has been viewed as a way to provide better public services.

a. United Kingdom competition law
b. Anti-Inflation Act
c. Antitrust
d. Intellectual property law

36. The _____ proposed by John L. Lewis in 1932, was a federation of unions that organized workers in industrial unions in the United States and Canada from 1935 to 1955. The Taft-Hartley Act of 1947 required union leaders to swear that they were not Communists. Many CIO leaders refused to obey that requirement, later found unconstitutional.

a. Multinational corporation
b. Chinese correction
c. Foreign direct investment
d. Congress of Industrial Organizations

37. _____ refers to organizing a union in a manner that seeks to unify workers in a particular industry along the lines of the particular craft or trade that they work in by class or skill level. It contrasts with industrial unionism, in which all workers in the same industry are organized into the same union, regardless of differences in skill.

_____ is perhaps best exemplified by many of the construction unions that formed the backbone of the old American Federation of Labor (which later merged with the industrial unions of the Congress of Industrial Organizations to form the AFL-CIO.)

a. 100-year flood
b. Craft unionism
c. 1921 recession
d. 130-30 fund

38. The _____ of 1938 (_____, ch. 676, 52 Stat. 1060, June 25, 1938, 29 U.S.C.ch.8), also called the Wages and Hours Bill, is United States federal law that applies to employees engaged in interstate commerce or employed by an enterprise engaged in commerce or in the production of goods for commerce, unless the employer can claim an exemption from coverage.

a. Generalized System of Preferences
b. Fair Labor Standards Act
c. Hostile work environment
d. Habitability

Chapter 13. The Labor Market

39. _____ is a field of economics that studies the strategic behavior of firms, the structure of markets and their interactions. The study of _____ adds to the perfectly competitive model real-world frictions such as limited information, transaction cost, cost of adjusting prices, government actions, and barriers to entry by new firms into a market. It then considers how firms are organized and how they compete.
   a. Economic ideology
   b. Industrial Organization
   c. Inflation
   d. Economic

40. A trade union or _____ is an organization of workers who have banded together to achieve common goals in key areas and working conditions. The trade union, through its leadership, bargains with the employer on behalf of union members (rank and file members) and negotiates labor contracts (Collective bargaining) with employers. This may include the negotiation of wages, work rules, complaint procedures, rules governing hiring, firing and promotion of workers, benefits, workplace safety and policies.
   a. Basis of futures
   b. Labor union
   c. Business valuation standards
   d. Demand-side technologies

41. In economics, _____ is the ability of a firm to alter the market price of a good or service. A firm with _____ can raise prices without losing all customers to competitors.

   When a firm has _____ it faces a downward-sloping demand curve.

   a. Revenue-cap regulation
   b. Price makers
   c. Market power
   d. Pacman conjecture

42. In a _____ there is both a monopoly (a single seller) and monopsony (a single buyer) in the same market.

   In such market price and output will be determined by the non economic forces like bargaining power of both buyer and seller. A _____ model is often used in situations where the switching costs of both sides are prohibitively high.

   a. Market concentration
   b. Revenue-cap regulation
   c. Bilateral monopoly
   d. Price takers

43. _____ is a branch of applied mathematics that is used in the social sciences (most notably economics), biology, engineering, political science, international relations, computer science, and philosophy. _____ attempts to mathematically capture behavior in strategic situations, in which an individual's success in making choices depends on the choices of others. While initially developed to analyze competitions in which one individual does better at another's expense (zero sum games), it has been expanded to treat a wide class of interactions, which are classified according to several criteria.
   a. Game theory
   b. Discriminatory price auction
   c. Proper equilibrium
   d. Dollar auction

44. In economics, a _____ exists when a specific individual or enterprise has sufficient control over a particular product or service to determine significantly the terms on which other individuals shall have access to it. Monopolies are thus characterized by a lack of economic competition for the good or service that they provide and a lack of viable substitute goods. The verb 'monopolize' refers to the process by which a firm gains persistently greater market share than what is expected under perfect competition.

a. 1921 recession
b. 130-30 fund
c. 100-year flood
d. Monopoly

45. A _____ or labor union is an organization of workers who have banded together to achieve common goals in key areas and working conditions. The _____, through its leadership, bargains with the employer on behalf of union members (rank and file members) and negotiates labor contracts (Collective bargaining) with employers. This may include the negotiation of wages, work rules, complaint procedures, rules governing hiring, firing and promotion of workers, benefits, workplace safety and policies.

a. Guaranteed investment contracts
b. Consumer goods
c. Trade union
d. Case-Shiller Home Price Indices

46. The term _____ refers to economy-wide fluctuations in production or economic activity over several months or years. These fluctuations occur around a long-term growth trend, and typically involve shifts over time between periods of relatively rapid economic growth (expansion or boom), and periods of relative stagnation or decline (contraction or recession.)

These fluctuations are often measured using the growth rate of real gross domestic product.

a. Tobit model
b. Nominal value
c. Consumer theory
d. Business cycle

47. _____ and Keynesian Theory) is a macroeconomic theory based on the ideas of 20th-century British economist John Maynard Keynes. _____ argues that private sector decisions sometimes lead to inefficient macroeconomic outcomes and therefore advocates active policy responses by the public sector, including monetary policy actions by the central bank and fiscal policy actions by the government to stabilize output over the business cycle.

The theories forming the basis of _____ were first presented in The General Theory of Employment, Interest and Money, published in 1936.

a. Keynesian economics
b. Market failure
c. Deflation
d. Rational choice theory

48. A variety of measures of _____ and output are used in economics to estimate total economic activity in a country or region, including gross domestic product (GDP), gross national product (GNP), and net _____

There are three main ways of calculating these numbers; the output approach, the income approach and the expenditure approach. In theory, the three must yield the same, because total expenditures on goods and services must equal the total income paid to the producers (Gnational income), and that must also equal the total value of the output of goods and services (GNP.)

a. GNI per capita
b. Gross world product
c. National income
d. Volume index

Chapter 13. The Labor Market

49. _____ is used to refer to a number of related concepts. It is the using resources in such a way as to maximize the production of goods and services. A system can be called economically efficient if:

- No one can be made better off without making someone else worse off.
- More output cannot be obtained without increasing the amount of inputs.
- Production proceeds at the lowest possible per-unit cost.

These definitions of efficiency are not equivalent, but they are all encompassed by the idea that nothing more can be achieved given the resources available.

An economic system is more efficient if it can provide more goods and services for society without using more resources.

a. Economic efficiency
c. Efficient contract theory
b. ACEA agreement
d. ACCRA Cost of Living Index

50. _____ is a specific term used in companies' financial reporting from the company-whole point of view. Because that use excludes the effects of changing ownership interest, an economic measure of _____ is necessary for financial analysis from the shareholders' point of view

_____ is defined by the Financial Accounting Standards Board, or FASB, as e;the change in equity [net assets] of a business enterprise during a period from transactions and other events and circumstances from nonowner sources. It includes all changes in equity during a period except those resulting from investments by owners and distributions to owners.e;

_____ is the sum of net income and other items that must bypass the income statement because they have not been realized, including items like an unrealized holding gain or loss from available for sale securities and foreign currency translation gains or losses.

a. Net national income
c. Comprehensive income
b. Real income
d. Windfall gain

51. _____, in law and economics, is a form of risk management primarily used to hedge against the risk of a contingent loss. _____ is defined as the equitable transfer of the risk of a loss, from one entity to another, in exchange for a premium, and can be thought of as a guaranteed small loss to prevent a large, possibly devastating loss. An insurer is a company selling the _____; an insured or policyholder is the person or entity buying the _____.

a. ACEA agreement
c. ACCRA Cost of Living Index
b. Insurance
d. AD-IA Model

52. The _____ was a landmark piece of legislation in the United States that outlawed racial segregation in schools, public places, and employment.

a. Le Chapelier Law
c. Civil Rights Act of 1964
b. Patent portfolio
d. Postcautionary principle

Chapter 13. The Labor Market

53. In statistics, the _____ problem occurs when one considers a set of statistical inferences simultaneously. Errors in inference, including confidence intervals that fail to include their corresponding population parameters are more likely to occur when one considers the family as a whole. Several statistical techniques have been developed to prevent this from happening, allowing significance levels for single and _____ to be directly compared.
   a. Familywise error rate
   b. Multiple comparisons
   c. False discovery rate
   d. Hypotheses suggested by the data

54. The _____, a unit of the United States Department of Labor, is the principal fact-finding agency for the U.S. government in the broad field of labor economics and statistics. The BLS is an independent national statistical agency that collects, processes, analyzes, and disseminates essential statistical data to the American public, the U.S. Congress, other Federal agencies, State and local governments, business, and labor representatives. The BLS also serves as a statistical resource to the Department of Labor.
   a. Gross world product
   b. Gross Regional Product
   c. Bureau of Labor Statistics
   d. Gross national product

Chapter 14. Land and Capital

1. _____s is the social science that studies the production, distribution, and consumption of goods and services. The term _____s comes from the Ancient Greek οἰκονομῖα from οἶκος (oikos, 'house') + νόμος (nomos, 'custom' or 'law'), hence 'rules of the house(hold)'. Current _____ models developed out of the broader field of political economy in the late 19th century, owing to a desire to use an empirical approach more akin to the physical sciences.
    a. Energy economics
    b. Opportunity cost
    c. Inflation
    d. Economic

2. An _____ or Ëconomic system is a system that involves the production, distribution and consumption of goods and services between the entities in a particular society. It is the method used by society to produce and distribute goods and services. The _____ is composed of people and institutions, including their relationships to productive resources, such as through the convention of property.
    a. Economic system
    b. Information economy
    c. Intention economy
    d. Indicative planning

3. _____ is an economic concept with commonplace familiarity. It is the price that a good or service is offered at, or will fetch, in the marketplace. It is of interest mainly in the study of microeconomics.
    a. Market anomaly
    b. Market price
    c. Paper trading
    d. Noisy market hypothesis

4. Economic _____ is defined as an excess distribution to any factor in a production process above that which is required to induce the factor into the process or any excess above that which is necessary to keep the factor in its current use..

    Classical Factor _____ is primarily concerned with the fee paid for the use of fixed (e.g. natural) resources. The classical definition is expressed as any excess payment above that required to induce or provide for production.

    a. 1921 recession
    b. 100-year flood
    c. Rent
    d. 130-30 fund

5. Competition law, known in the United States as _____ law, has three main elements:

    - prohibiting agreements or practices that restrict free trading and competition between business entities. This includes in particular the repression of cartels.
    - banning abusive behaviour by a firm dominating a market, or anti-competitive practices that tend to lead to such a dominant position. Practices controlled in this way may include predatory pricing, tying, price gouging, refusal to deal, and many others.
    - supervising the mergers and acquisitions of large corporations, including some joint ventures. Transactions that are considered to threaten the competitive process can be prohibited altogether, or approved subject to 'remedies' such as an obligation to divest part of the merged business or to offer licences or access to facilities to enable other businesses to continue competing.

The substance and practice of competition law varies from jurisdiction to jurisdiction. Protecting the interests of consumers (consumer welfare) and ensuring that entrepreneurs have an opportunity to compete in the market economy are often treated as important objectives. Competition law is closely connected with law on deregulation of access to markets, state aids and subsidies, the privatisation of state owned assets and the establishment of independent sector regulators. In recent decades, competition law has been viewed as a way to provide better public services.

a. Anti-Inflation Act
b. Antitrust
c. Intellectual property law
d. United Kingdom competition law

6. _____ is an economic system in which wealth, and the means of producing wealth, are privately owned. Through _____, the land, labor, and capital are owned, operated, and traded for the purpose of generating profits, without force or fraud, by private individuals either singly or jointly, and investments, distribution, income, production, pricing and supply of goods, commodities and services are determined by voluntary private decision in a market economy. A distinguishing feature of _____ is that each person owns his or her own labor and therefore is allowed to sell the use of it to employers.

a. Late capitalism
b. Capitalism
c. Socialism for the rich and capitalism for the poor
d. Creative capitalism

7. In economics supernormal profit _____ or pure profit or excess profits, is a profit exceeding the normal profit. Normal profit equals the opportunity cost of labour and capital, while supernormal profit is the amount exceeds the normal return from these input factors in production.

_____ is usually generated by an oligopoly or a monopoly; however, these firms often try to hide this from the market to reduce risk of competition or antitrust investigation.

a. ACCRA Cost of Living Index
b. Accounting profit
c. Economic profit
d. Abnormal profit

8. _____ describes a deliberate attempt to interfere with the free and fair operation of the market and create artificial, false or misleading appearances with respect to the price of a security, commodity or currency. _____ is prohibited under Section 9(a)(2) of the Securities Exchange Act of 1934, and in Australia under Section s 1041A of the Corporations Act 2001. The Act defines _____ as transactions which create an artificial price or maintain an artificial price for a tradable security.

a. Legal monopoly
b. Net domestic product
c. Managerial economics
d. Market manipulation

9. _____ in economics and business is the result of an exchange and from that trade we assign a numerical monetary value to a good, service or asset. If Alice trades Bob 4 apples for an orange, the _____ of an orange is 4 apples. Inversely, the _____ of an apple is 1/4 oranges.

a. Premium pricing
b. Price book
c. Price war
d. Price

10. In microeconomics, _____ is quite simply the conversion of inputs into outputs. It is an economic process that uses resources to create a good or service that is suitable for exchange. This can include manufacturing, storing, shipping, and packaging.

Chapter 14. Land and Capital

a. Solved
b. Production
c. MET
d. Red Guards

11. _____ is a term in economics, where demand for one good or service occurs as a result of demand for another. This may occur as the former is a part of production of the second. For example, demand for coal leads to _____ for mining, as coal must be mined for coal to be consumed.
  a. Days Sales Outstanding
  b. Rate risk
  c. Leontief production function
  d. Derived demand

12. In economics, _____ describes demand that is not very sensitive to a change in price.
  a. Export-led growth
  b. Inflation hedge
  c. Inelastic
  d. Effective unemployment rate

13. In economics, economic equilibrium is simply a state of the world where economic forces are balanced and in the absence of external influences the (equilibrium) values of economic variables will not change. It is the point at which quantity demanded and quantity supplied are equal. _____, for example, refers to a condition where a market price is established through competition such that the amount of goods or services sought by buyers is equal to the amount of goods or services produced by sellers.
  a. Product-Market Growth Matrix
  b. Regulated market
  c. Market equilibrium
  d. Marketization

14. Economics:

  - _____,the desire to own something and the ability to pay for it
  - _____ curve,a graphic representation of a _____ schedule
  - _____ deposit, the money in checking accounts
  - _____ pull theory,the theory that inflation occurs when _____ for goods and services exceeds existing supplies
  - _____ schedule,a table that lists the quantity of a good a person will buy it each different price
  - _____ side economics,the school of economics at believes government spending and tax cuts open economy by raising _____

  a. McKesson ' Robbins scandal
  b. Variability
  c. Production
  d. Demand

15. To _____ is to impose a financial charge or other levy upon a taxpayer by a state or the functional equivalent of a state.

    _____es are also imposed by many subnational entities. _____es consist of direct _____ or indirect _____, and may be paid in money or as its labour equivalent (often but not always unpaid.)

  a. 130-30 fund
  b. Tax
  c. 100-year flood
  d. 1921 recession

16. To tax is to impose a financial charge or other levy upon a taxpayer by a state or the functional equivalent of a state.

_____ are also imposed by many subnational entities. _____ consist of direct tax or indirect tax, and may be paid in money or as its labour equivalent (often but not always unpaid.)

- a. 1921 recession
- b. 130-30 fund
- c. 100-year flood
- d. Taxes

17. _____ is the shortage of common things such as food, clothing, shelter and safe drinking water, all of which determine the quality of life. It may also include the lack of access to opportunities such as education and employment which aid the escape from _____ and/or allow one to enjoy the respect of fellow citizens. According to Mollie Orshansky who developed the _____ measurements used by the U.S. government, 'to be poor is to be deprived of those goods and services and pleasures which others around us take for granted.' Ongoing debates over causes, effects and best ways to measure _____, directly influence the design and implementation of _____-reduction programs and are therefore relevant to the fields of public administration and international development.

- a. Poverty map
- b. Growth Elasticity of Poverty
- c. Liberal welfare reforms
- d. Poverty

Chapter 14. Land and Capital

18. A _____ is:

- Rewrite _____, in generative grammar and computer science
- Standardization, a formal and widely-accepted statement, fact, definition, or qualification
- Operation, a determinate _____ for performing a mathematical operation and obtaining a certain result (Mathematics, Logic)
    - Unary operation
    - Binary operation
- _____ of inference, a function from sets of formulae to formulae (Mathematics, Logic)
- _____ of thumb, principle with broad application that is not intended to be strictly accurate or reliable for every situation. Also often simply referred to as a _____
- Moral, an atomic element of a moral code for guiding choices in human behavior
- Heuristic, a quantized '_____' which shows a tendency or probability for successful function
- A regulation, as in sports
- A Production _____, as in computer science
- Procedural law, a _____ set governing the application of laws to cases
    - A law, which may informally be called a '_____'
    - A court ruling, a decision by a court
- In the U.S. Government, a regulation mandated by Congress, but written or expanded upon by the Executive Branch.
- Norm (sociology), an informal but widely accepted _____, concept, truth, definition, or qualification (social norms, legal norms, coding norms)
- Norm (philosophy), a kind of sentence or a reason to act, feel or believe
- 'Rulership' is the concept of governance by a government:
    - Military _____, governance by a military body
    - Monastic _____, a collection of precepts that guides the life of monks or nuns in a religious order where the superior holds the place of Christ
- Slide _____

- '_____,' a song by Ayumi Hamasaki
- '_____,' a song by rapper Nas
- '_____s,' an album by the band The Whitest Boy Alive
- _____s: Pyaar Ka Superhit Formula, a 2003 Bollywood film
- ruler, an instrument for measuring lengths
- _____, a component of an astrolabe, circumferator or similar instrument
- The _____s, a bestselling self-help book
- _____ Project (Run Up-to-date Linux Everywhere), a project that aims to use up-to-date Linux software on old PCs
- _____ engine, a software system that helps managing business _____s
- Ja _____, a hip hop artist
    - R.U.L.E., a 2005 greatest hits album by rapper Ja _____
- '_____s,' a KMFDM song

a. Demand
c. Rule

b. Procter ' Gamble
d. Technocracy

19. In Marxian economics, _____ originally referred to the means of production. Individuals, organizations and governments use _____ in the production of other goods or commodities. _____ include factories, machinery, tools, equipment, and various buildings which are used to produce other products for consumption.
    a. Capital intensive
    b. Capital deepening
    c. Wealth inequality in the United States
    d. Capital goods

20. In economics, _____ is a rise in the general level of prices of goods and services in an economy over a period of time. When the general price level rises, each unit of currency buys fewer goods and services; consequently, _____ is also a decline in the real value of money--a loss of purchasing power in the medium of exchange which is also the monetary unit of account in the economy. A chief measure of general price-level _____ is the general _____ rate, which is the percentage change in a general price index (normally the Consumer Price Index) over time.
    a. Inflation
    b. Economic
    c. Energy economics
    d. Opportunity cost

21. In economics, the _____ is a measure of inflation, the rate of increase of a price index (for example, a consumer price index.)It is the percentage rate of change in price level over time. The rate of decrease in the purchasing power of money is approximately equal.

    It's used to calculate the real interest rate, as well as real increases in wages, and official measurements of this rate act as input variables to COLA adjustments and Inflation derivatives prices.

    a. Interest rate option
    b. Equity value
    c. Edgeworth paradox
    d. Inflation rate

22. In finance, _____ rate of profit or sometimes just return, is the ratio of money gained or lost on an investment relative to the amount of money invested. The amount of money gained or lost may be referred to as interest, profit/loss, gain/loss, or net income/loss. The money invested may be referred to as the asset, capital, principal, or the cost basis of the investment.
    a. Sortino ratio
    b. Cost accrual ratio
    c. Current ratio
    d. Rate of return

23. In economics and especially in the theory of competition, _____ are obstacles in the path of a firm that make it difficult to enter a given market.

    _____ are the source of a firm's pricing power - the ability of a firm to raise prices without losing all its customers.

    The term refers to hindrances that an individual may face while trying to gain entrance into a profession or trade.

    a. Group boycott
    b. Social dumping
    c. Barriers to entry
    d. Limit price

24. In economics, _____ are the resources employed to produce goods and services. They facilitate production but do not become part of the product (as with raw materials) or significantly transformed by the production process (as with fuel used to power machinery.) To 19th century economists, the _____ were land (natural resources, gifts from nature), labor (the ability to work), and capital goods (human-made tools and equipment.)

a. Product Pipeline
b. Long-run
c. Hicks-neutral technical change
d. Factors of production

25. A _____ is an object whose consumption increases the utility of the consumer, for which the quantity demanded exceeds the quantity supplied at zero price. _____s are usually modeled as having diminishing marginal utility. The first individual purchase has high utility; the second has less.
   a. Merit good
   b. Composite good
   c. Pie method
   d. Good

26. In business and accounting, _____ are everything of value that is owned by a person or company. It is a claim on the property your income of a borrower. The balance sheet of a firm records the monetary value of the _____ owned by the firm.
   a. Amortization schedule
   b. ACCRA Cost of Living Index
   c. Assets
   d. ACEA agreement

27. In financial accounting, a _____ or statement of financial position is a summary of a person's or organization's balances. Assets, liabilities and ownership equity are listed as of a specific date, such as the end of its financial year. A _____ is often described as a snapshot of a company's financial condition.
   a. 1921 recession
   b. Balance sheet
   c. 130-30 fund
   d. 100-year flood

28. _____ is a three-volume work on finance published by Austrian economist Eugen von Böhm-Bawerk.

The first two volumes were published in the 1880s when he was teaching at the University of Innsbruck.

The first volume of _____, titled History and Critique of Interest Theories (1884), is an exhaustive survey of the alternative treatments of the phenomenon of interest: use theories, productivity theories, abstinence theories, and many more.

   a. The General Theory of Employment, Interest and Money
   b. The Bell Curve
   c. Development as Freedom
   d. Capital and interest

29. In finance, the _____ is the system that allows the transfer of money between savers and borrowers.

Put another way: the _____ is a set of complex and closely interconnected financial institutions, markets, instruments, services, practices, and transactions.

   a. Hedonimetry
   b. Financial system
   c. Foreign investment
   d. Lean consumption

30. _____ is a fee paid on borrowed assets. It is the price paid for the use of borrowed money, or, money earned by deposited funds. Assets that are sometimes lent with _____ include money, shares, consumer goods through hire purchase, major assets such as aircraft, and even entire factories in finance lease arrangements.

a. Insolvency
c. Interest
b. Internal debt
d. Asset protection

31. An _____ is the price a borrower pays for the use of money they do not own, for instance a small company might borrow from a bank to kick start their business, and the return a lender receives for deferring the use of funds, by lending it to the borrower. _____s are normally expressed as a percentage rate over the period of one year.

_____s targets are also a vital tool of monetary policy and are used to control variables like investment, inflation, and unemployment.

a. Arrow-Debreu model
c. ACCRA Cost of Living Index
b. Interest rate
d. Enterprise value

32. In finance, a _____ is a debt security, in which the authorized issuer owes the holders a debt and, depending on the terms of the _____, is obliged to pay interest (the coupon) and/or to repay the principal at a later date, termed maturity. A _____ is a formal contract to repay borrowed money with interest at fixed intervals.

Thus a _____ is like a loan: the issuer is the borrower (debtor), the holder is the lender (creditor), and the coupon is the interest.

a. Prize Bond
c. Zero-coupon
b. Callable
d. Bond

33. In finance and economics _____ or nominal rate of interest refers to the rate of interest before adjustment for inflation (in contrast with the real interest rate); or, for interest rates 'as stated' without adjustment for the full effect of compounding (also referred to as the nominal annual rate.) An interest rate is called nominal if the frequency of compounding (e.g. a month) is not identical to the basic time unit (normally a year.)

The real interest rate includes compensation for the lender's lost value due to inflation, whereas the _____ excludes inflation.

a. London Interbank Offered Rate
c. Risk-free interest rate
b. Fixed interest
d. Nominal interest rate

34. _____ is the value on a given date of a future payment or series of future payments, discounted to reflect the time value of money and other factors such as investment risk. _____ calculations are widely used in business and economics to provide a means to compare cash flows at different times on a meaningful 'like to like' basis.

Money value fluctuates over time: $100 today are not worth $100 in five years.

a. Present value
c. Tax shield
b. Present value of costs
d. Future value

35. The '_____' is approximately the nominal interest rate minus the inflation rate Since the inflation rate over the course of a loan is not known initially, volatility in inflation represents a risk to both the lender and the borrower.

Chapter 14. Land and Capital

In economics and finance, an individual who lends money for repayment at a later point in time expects to be compensated for the time value of money, or not having the use of that money while it is lent.

a. Reflation
c. Core inflation
b. Cost-push inflation
d. Real interest rate

36. _____ is the a method of technical and economic research of the systems for purpose to optimize a parity between system's consumer functions or properties and expenses to achieve those functions or properties.

This methodology for continuous perfection of production, industrial technologies, organizational structures was developed by Juryj Sobolev in 1948 at the 'Perm telephone factory'

- 1948 Juryj Sobolev - the first success in application of a method analysis at the 'Perm telephone factory'.
- 1949 - the first application for the invention as result of use of the new method.

Today in economically developed countries practically each enterprise or the company use methodology of the kind of functional-cost analysis as a practice of the quality management, most full satisfying to principles of standards of series ISO 9000.

- Interest of consumer not in products itself, but the advantage which it will receive from its usage.
- The consumer aspires to reduce his expenses
- Functions needed by consumer can be executed in the various ways, and, hence, with various efficiency and expenses. Among possible alternatives of realization of functions exist such in which the parity of quality and the price is the optimal for the consumer.

The goal of _____ is achievement of the highest consumer satisfaction of production at simultaneous decrease in all kinds of industrial expenses Classical _____ has three English synonyms - Value Engineering, Value Management, Value Analysis.

a. Monopoly wage
c. Function cost analysis
b. Willingness to pay
d. Staple financing

37. _____ is a financial mechanism in which a debtor obtains the right to delay payments to a creditor, for a defined period of time, in exchange for a charge or fee. Essentially, the party that owes money in the present purchases the right to delay the payment until some future date. The discount, or charge, is simply the difference between the original amount owed in the present and the amount that has to be paid in the future to settle the debt.
a. Discounting
c. Maximum life span
b. Certified Risk Manager
d. Generalized linear model

38. A _____ is an annuity that has no definite end, or a stream of cash payments that continues forever. There are few actual perpetuities in existence (although the British government has issued them in the past, and they are known and still trade as consols.) A number of types of investments are effectively perpetuities, such as real estate and preferred stock, and techniques for valuing a _____ can be applied to establish price.

Chapter 14. Land and Capital

a. Perpetuity
c. Discount rate

b. Heath-Jarrow-Morton framework
d. Current yield

39. In algebra, a _____ is a function depending on n that associates a scalar, det(A), to an n×n square matrix A. The fundamental geometric meaning of a _____ is a scale factor for measure when A is regarded as a linear transformation. _____s are important both in calculus, where they enter the substitution rule for several variables, and in multilinear algebra.

For a fixed nonnegative integer n, there is a unique _____ function for the n×n matrices over any commutative ring R. In particular, this function exists when R is the field of real or complex numbers.

a. 100-year flood
c. Determinant

b. 130-30 fund
d. 1921 recession

40. An _____ is a person who has possession of an enterprise and assumes significant accountability for the inherent risks and the outcome. It is an ambitious leader who combines land, labor, and capital to create and market new goods or services. The term is a loanword from French and was first defined by the Irish economist Richard Cantillon.

a. Entrepreneur
c. ACCRA Cost of Living Index

b. ACEA agreement
d. Expansionary policies

41. _____ is the concept or idea of fairness in economics, particularly as to taxation or welfare economics.

In welfare economics, _____ may be distinguished from economic efficiency in overall evaluation of social welfare. Although '_____' has broader uses, it may be posed as a counterpart to economic inequality in yielding a 'good' distribution of welfare.

a. Equity
c. ACCRA Cost of Living Index

b. AD-IA Model
d. ACEA agreement

42. An _____ is a risk that meets the ideal criteria for efficient insurance. The concept of _____ underlies nearly all insurance decisions.

For a risk to be insurable, several things need to be true:

- The insurer must be able to charge a premium high enough to cover not only claims expenses, but also to cover the insurer's expenses. In other words, the risk cannot be catastrophic, or so large that no insurer could hope to pay for the loss.

- The nature of the loss must be definite and financially measurable. That is, there should not be room for argument as to whether or not payment is due, nor as to what amount the payment should be.

a. Insurable risk
c. Actuary

b. Extreme value theory
d. Ogden tables

Chapter 14. Land and Capital

43. In economics, a _____ occurs when, due to the economies of scale of a particular industry, the maximum efficiency of production and distribution is realized through a single supplier.

Natural monopolies arise where the largest supplier in an industry, often the first supplier in a market, has an overwhelming cost advantage over other actual or potential competitors. This tends to be the case in industries where capital costs predominate, creating economies of scale which are large in relation to the size of the market, and hence high barriers to entry; examples include water services and electricity.

- a. Collective goods
- b. Common-pool resource
- c. Privatizing profits and socializing losses
- d. Natural monopoly

44. _____ or economic opportunity loss is the value of the next best alternative foregone as the result of making a decision. _____ analysis is an important part of a company's decision-making processes but is not treated as an actual cost in any financial statement. The next best thing that a person can engage in is referred to as the _____ of doing the best thing and ignoring the next best thing to be done.

- a. Economic
- b. Opportunity cost
- c. Industrial organization
- d. Economic ideology

45. In finance, _____, also sometimes called market risk, aggregate risk is the risk associated with aggregate market returns. _____ is a risk of security that cannot be reduced through diversification. It should not be confused with systemic risk, which is the risk that the entire financial system will collapse as a result of some catastrophic event.

- a. Concentration risk
- b. Cleanup clause
- c. Global Depository Receipt
- d. Systematic risk

46. _____ represents the total cash investment that shareholders and debtholders have made in a company. There are two different but completely equivalent methods for calculating _____. The operating approach is calculated as:

_____ = Operating Net Working Capital + Net PP'E + Capitalized Operating Leases + Other Operating Assets + Operating Intangibles - Other Operating Liabilities - Cumulative Adjustment for Amortization of R'D

Equivalently, the financing approach is calculated as:

In symbols:

$$K = D + E - M$$

_____ is used in several important measurements of financial performance, including return on _____, economic value added, and free cash flow.

- a. Asset turnover
- b. Operating margin
- c. Average propensity to consume
- d. Invested capital

47. In economics, _____ is the ability of a firm to alter the market price of a good or service. A firm with _____ can raise prices without losing all customers to competitors.

Chapter 14. Land and Capital

When a firm has _____ it faces a downward-sloping demand curve.

a. Revenue-cap regulation
c. Price makers
b. Pacman conjecture
d. Market power

48. In economics, a _____ exists when a specific individual or enterprise has sufficient control over a particular product or service to determine significantly the terms on which other individuals shall have access to it. Monopolies are thus characterized by a lack of economic competition for the good or service that they provide and a lack of viable substitute goods. The verb 'monopolize' refers to the process by which a firm gains persistently greater market share than what is expected under perfect competition.

a. 130-30 fund
c. 100-year flood
b. 1921 recession
d. Monopoly

49. In law and economics, the _____, describes the economic efficiency of an economic allocation or outcome in the presence of externalities. The theorem states that when trade in an externality is possible and there are no transaction costs, bargaining will lead to an efficient outcome regardless of the initial allocation of property rights. In practice, obstacles to bargaining or poorly defined property rights can prevent Coasian bargaining.

a. Coase theorem
c. Prior appropriation water rights
b. General Mining Act of 1872
d. Means test

50. _____ is a common concept in economics, and gives rise to derived concepts such as consumer debt. Generally _____ is defined by opposition to production. But the precise definition can vary because different schools of economists define production quite differently.

a. Foreclosure data providers
c. Consumption
b. Cash or share options
d. Federal Reserve Bank Notes

51. In economics, _____ refers to how the marginal contribution of a factor of production usually decreases as more of the factor is used. According to this relationship, in a production system with fixed and variable inputs, beyond some point, each additional unit of the variable input yields smaller and smaller increases in output. Conversely, producing one more unit of output costs more and more in variable inputs.

a. Derivatives law
c. Community property
b. Patent troll
d. Diminishing returns

52. The _____ is 'the basic residential unit in which economic production, consumption, inheritance, child rearing, and shelter are organized and carried out'; [the _____] 'may or may not be synonomous with family'.

The _____ is the basic unit of analysis in many social, microeconomic and government models. The term refers to all individuals who live in the same dwelling.

a. 130-30 fund
c. Family economics
b. 100-year flood
d. Household

53. _____ is defined as the measure of responsiveness in the quantity demanded for a commodity as a result of change in price of the same commodity. It is a measure of how consumers react to a change in price. In other words, it is percentage change in quantity demanded as per the percentage change in price of the same commodity.

a. 100-year flood
c. 1921 recession
b. Price elasticity of demand
d. 130-30 fund

54. In economics, the _____ is defined as a numerical measure of the responsiveness of the quantity supplied of product (A) to a change in price of product (A) alone. It is the measure of the way quantity supplied reacts to a change in price.

For example, if, in response to a 10% rise in the price of a good, the quantity supplied increases by 20%, the _____ would be 20%/10% = 2.

a. Price elasticity of supply
c. Demand shaping
b. Passive income
d. Hedonimetry

55. _____ is an economic model based on price, utility and quantity in a market. It predicts that in a competitive market, price will function to equalize the quantity demanded by consumers, and the quantity supplied by producers, resulting in an economic equilibrium of price and quantity. The model incorporates other factors changing equilibrium as a shift of demand and/or supply.

a. Joint demand
c. Supply and demand
b. Deferred gratification
d. Rational addiction

56. In economics, _____ is the ratio of the percent change in one variable to the percent change in another variable. It is a tool for measuring the responsiveness of a function to changes in parameters in a relative way. Commonly analyzed are _____ of substitution, price and wealth.

a. ACEA agreement
c. Elasticity
b. ACCRA Cost of Living Index
d. Elasticity of demand

57. Price _____ is defined as the measure of responsiveness in the quantity demanded for a commodity as a result of change in price of the same commodity. It is a measure of how consumers react to a change in price. In other words, it is percentage change in quantity demanded by the percentage change in price of the same commodity.

a. Elasticity of demand
c. Elasticity
b. ACEA agreement
d. ACCRA Cost of Living Index

58. In economic models, the _____ time frame assumes no fixed factors of production. Firms can enter or leave the marketplace, and the cost (and availability) of land, labor, raw materials, and capital goods can be assumed to vary. In contrast, in the short-run time frame, certain factors are assumed to be fixed, because there is not sufficient time for them to change.

a. Price/performance ratio
c. Diseconomies of scale
b. Long-run
d. Productivity world

59. In economics, the _____ or marginal physical product is the extra output produced by one more unit of an input (for instance, the difference in output when a firm's labour is increased from five to six units.) Assuming that no other inputs to production change, the _____ of a given input (X) can be expressed as:

Chapter 14. Land and Capital

_____ = ΔY/ΔX = (the change of Y)/(the change of X.)

-
  -
    - Pending approval by Thomas Sowell***

In neoclassical economics, this is the mathematical derivative of the production function.... Note that the 'product' (Y) is typically defined ignoring external costs and benefits.

a. Labor problem
c. Factor prices
b. Productive capacity
d. Marginal product

60. _____ is the additional output resulting from the use of an additional unit of capital (ceteris paribus assuming all other factors are fixed.) It equals to 1 divided by the Incremental Capital-Output Ratio.

a. Buy-write
c. CAN SLIM
b. Loan officer
d. Marginal product of capital

61. In economics, the concept of the _____ refers to the decision-making time frame of a firm in which at least one factor of production is fixed. Costs which are fixed in the _____ have no impact on a firms decisions. For example a firm can raise output by increasing the amount of labour through overtime.

a. Hicks-neutral technical change
c. Short-run
b. Productivity model
d. Product Pipeline

62. The term _____s refers to wages that have been adjusted for inflation. This term is used in contrast to nominal wages or unadjusted wages.

The use of adjusted figures is in undertaking some form of economic analysis.

a. Living wage
c. Federal Wage System
b. Profit sharing
d. Real wage

63. A _____ is the minimum difference a person requires to be willing to take an uncertain bet, between the expected value of the bet and the certain value that he is indifferent to.

The certainty equivalent is the guaranteed payoff at which a person is 'indifferent' between accepting the guaranteed payoff and a higher but uncertain payoff. (It is the amount of the higher payout minus the _____.)

a. Workers compensation
c. Ruin theory
b. Linear model
d. Risk premium

64. The term '_____' refers to the concept of collecting information and attempting to spot a pattern in the information. In some fields of study, the term '_____' has more formally-defined meanings.

Chapter 14. Land and Capital

In project management _____ is a mathematical technique that uses historical results to predict future outcome.

a. Coefficient of determination
b. Trend analysis
c. Quantile regression
d. Probit model

65. _____ is a situation in which the limited resources of a firm are allocated in accordance with the wishes of consumers. An allocatively efficient economy produces an 'optimal mix' of commodities. A firm is allocatively efficient when its price is equal to its marginal costs (that is, P = MC) in a perfect market.

a. Economic efficiency
b. Allocative efficiency
c. ACEA agreement
d. ACCRA Cost of Living Index

66. In economics, a _____ is a mechanism that allows people to easily buy and sell (trade) financial securities (such as stocks and bonds), commodities (such as precious metals or agricultural goods), and other fungible items of value at low transaction costs and at prices that reflect the efficient-market hypothesis.

_____s have evolved significantly over several hundred years and are undergoing constant innovation to improve liquidity.

Both general markets (where many commodities are traded) and specialized markets (where only one commodity is traded) exist.

a. Market anomaly
b. Noise trader
c. Convertible arbitrage
d. Financial market

67. In economics, _____ is how a natione;s total economy is distributed among its population. ._____ has always been a central concern of economic theory and economic policy. Classical economists such as Adam Smith, Thomas Malthus and David Ricardo were mainly concerned with factor _____, that is, the distribution of income between the main factors of production, land, labour and capital.

a. Equipment trust certificate
b. Eco commerce
c. Income distribution
d. Authorised capital

68. The _____ is the market for securities, where companies and governments can raise longterm funds. It is a market in which money is lent for periods longer than a year. The _____ includes the stock market and the bond market.

a. Capital market
b. Performance attribution
c. Multi-family office
d. Financial instrument

69. In economics, accounting and Marxian economics, _____ is often equated with investment of profit income, especially in real capital goods. The concentration and centralisation of capital are two of the results of such accumulation

Chapter 14. Land and Capital

But _____ can refer variously to

- working and consuming less than earned
- relying on the effects of compound interest to increase initial capital
- real investment in tangible means of production.
- financial investment in assets represented on paper.
- investment in non-productive physical assets such as residential real estate that appreciate in value.
- consuming less than produced by productive assets like farm land--saving or accumulating the residual
- 'human _____,' i.e., new education and training increasing the skills of the labour force.

Non-financial and financial _____ is usually needed for economic growth, since additional production usually requires additional funds to enlarge the scale of production. Smarter and more productive organization of production can also increase production without increased capital.

a. Marxian economics
c. Productive force

b. Capital accumulation
d. Cultural Marxism

70. _____ are the prices that the factors of production of a finished item attract.

There has been some economic debate as to what determines these prices. Classical and Marxist economists argued that the _____ decided the value of a product and so value was intrinsic within the product.

a. Productivity model
c. Marginal product of labor

b. Factor prices
d. Marginal product

71. In mathematics, an _____ is a statement about the relative size or order of two objects, or about whether they are the same or not

- The notation a < b means that a is less than b.
- The notation a > b means that a is greater than b.
- The notation a ≠ b means that a is not equal to b, but does not say that one is greater than the other or even that they can be compared in size.

In each statement above, a is not equal to b. These relations are known as strict inequalities. The notation a < b may also be read as 'a is strictly less than b'.

a. ACCRA Cost of Living Index
c. AD-IA Model

b. Inequality
d. ACEA agreement

72. A _____ is an economy based on the division of labor in which the prices of goods and services are determined in a free price system set by supply and demand. This is often contrasted with a planned economy, in which a central government determines the price of goods and services using a fixed price system. Market economies are contrasted with mixed economy where the price system is not entirely free but under some government control that is not extensive enough to constitute a planned economy.

Chapter 14. Land and Capital

a. Network Economy
b. Commons-based peer production
c. Nutritional Economics
d. Market economy

73. The _____ is the central banking system of the United States. Created in 1913 by the enactment of the Federal Reserve Act (signed by Woodrow Wilson), it is a quasi-public and quasi-private (government entity with private components) banking system that comprises (1) the presidentially appointed Board of Governors of the _____ in Washington, D.C.; (2) the Federal Open Market Committee; (3) twelve regional Federal Reserve Banks located in major cities throughout the nation acting as fiscal agents for the U.S. Treasury, each with its own nine-member board of directors; (4) numerous other private U.S. member banks, which subscribe to required amounts of non-transferable stock in their regional Federal Reserve Banks; and (5) various advisory councils. Since February 2006, Ben Bernanke has served as the Chairman of the Board of Governors of the _____.

a. Monetary Policy Report to the Congress
b. Term auction facility
c. Federal Reserve System
d. Federal Reserve System Open Market Account

74. _____ was a survey conducted by the U.S. Department of Justice to gauge the prevalence of alcohol and illegal drug use among prior arrestees. It was a reformulation of the prior Drug Use Forecasting (DUF) program, focused on five drugs in particular: cocaine, marijuana, methamphetamine, opiates, and PCP.

Participants were randomly selected from arrest records in major metropolitan areas; because no personally identifying information is taken from each record chosen, the resulting data can be correlated to arrest rates, but not to the total population of persons charged.

a. ACEA agreement
b. ACCRA Cost of Living Index
c. AD-IA Model
d. Arrestee Drug Abuse Monitoring

75. _____ theory is a branch of theoretical economics. It seeks to explain the behavior of supply, demand and prices in a whole economy with several or many markets. It is often assumed that agents are price takers and in that setting two common notions of equilibrium exist: Walrasian (or competitive) equilibrium, and its generalization; a price equilibrium with transfers.

a. New Keynesian economics
b. Human capital
c. General equilibrium
d. Rational choice theory

76. In economic theory, _____ is the competitive situation in any market where the conditions necessary for perfect competition are not satisfied. It is a market structure that does not meet the conditions of perfect competition.

Forms of _____ include:

- Monopoly, in which there is only one seller of a good.
- Oligopoly, in which there is a small number of sellers.
- Monopolistic competition, in which there are many sellers producing highly differentiated goods.
- Monopsony, in which there is only one buyer of a good.
- Oligopsony, in which there is a small number of buyers.

There may also be _____ in markets due to buyers or sellers lacking information about prices and the goods being traded.

Chapter 14. Land and Capital

There may also be _____ due to a time lag in a market.

a. Imperfect competition
c. AD-IA Model
b. ACEA agreement
d. ACCRA Cost of Living Index

77. In economics, the _____ is the term economists use to describe the self-regulating nature of the marketplace. The _____ is a metaphor coined by the economist Adam Smith in The Wealth of Nations.

Adam Smith mentions the metaphor in Book IV of The Wealth of Nations, arguing that people in any society will certainly employ their capital in foreign trading only if the profits available by that method far exceed those available locally, and that in such a case it is better for society as a whole if they so did.

a. AD-IA Model
c. ACCRA Cost of Living Index
b. ACEA agreement
d. Invisible hand

78. _____ is an important concept in economics with broad applications in game theory, engineering and the social sciences. The term is named after Vilfredo Pareto, an Italian economist who used the concept in his studies of economic efficiency and income distribution. Informally, pareto efficient situations are those in which any change to make any person better off would make someone else worse off.

a. Perfect rationality
c. Matching pennies
b. Lump of labour
d. Pareto efficiency

79. The _____ refers to the 'common well-being' or 'general welfare.' The _____ is central to policy debates, politics, democracy and the nature of government itself. While nearly everyone claims that aiding the common well-being or general welfare is positive, there is little, if any, consensus on what exactly constitutes the _____.

There are different views on how many members of the public must benefit from an action before it can be declared to be in the _____: at one extreme, an action has to benefit every single member of society in order to be truly in the _____; at the other extreme, any action can be in the _____ as long as it benefits some of the population and harms none.

a. Power Elite
c. Public interest
b. Stealth tax
d. Second-class citizen

80. _____ was a Scottish moral philosopher and a pioneer of political economy. One of the key figures of the Scottish Enlightenment, Smith is the author of The Theory of Moral Sentiments and An Inquiry into the Nature and Causes of the Wealth of Nations. The latter, usually abbreviated as The Wealth of Nations, is considered his magnum opus and the first modern work of economics.

a. Adam Smith
c. Alan Greenspan
b. Adolf Hitler
d. Adolph Fischer

81. In neoclassical economics and microeconomics, _____ describes the perfect being a market in which there are many small firms, all producing homogeneous goods. In the short term, such markets are productively inefficient as output will not occur where mc is equal to ac, but allocatively efficient, as output under _____ will always occur where mc is equal to mr, and therefore where mc equals ar. However, in the long term, such markets are both allocatively and productively efficient.
   a. Co-operative economics
   b. Law of supply
   c. Perfect competition
   d. General equilibrium

82. In economics, the term _____ of income or _____ refers to a simple economic model which describes the reciprocal circulation of income between producers and consumers. In the _____ model, the inter-dependent entities of producer and consumer are referred to as 'firms' and 'households' respectively and provide each other with factors in order to facilitate the flow of income. Firms provide consumers with goods and services in exchange for consumer expenditure and 'factors of production' from households.
   a. 100-year flood
   b. 130-30 fund
   c. 1921 recession
   d. Circular flow

83. _____ refers to the state of not requiring any outside aid, support for survival; it is therefore a type of personal or collective autonomy. On a large scale, a totally self-sufficient economy that does not trade with the outside world is called an autarky.

The term _____ is usually applied to varieties of sustainable living in which nothing is consumed outside of what is produced by the self-sufficient individuals.

   a. Global Reporting Initiative
   b. Sustainable forest management
   c. Sustainability science
   d. Self-sufficiency

84. A _____ is a type of economic equilibrium, where the clearance on the market of some specific goods is obtained independently from prices and quantities demanded and supplied in other markets. In other words, the prices of all substitutes and complements, as well as income levels of consumers are constant. Here the dynamic process is that prices adjust until supply equals demand.
   a. Market system
   b. Market depth
   c. Horizontal market
   d. Partial equilibrium

85. _____ is a broad label that refers to any individuals or households that use goods and services generated within the economy. The concept of a _____ is used in different contexts, so that the usage and significance of the term may vary.

Typically when business people and economists talk of _____s they are talking about person as _____, an aggregated commodity item with little individuality other than that expressed in the buy/not-buy decision.

   a. Consumer
   b. 1921 recession
   c. 130-30 fund
   d. 100-year flood

86. The _____ consists of a number of economic theories which describe the nature of the firm, company including its existence, its behaviour, and its relationship with the market.

Chapter 14. Land and Capital

In simplified terms, the _____ aims to answer these questions:

1. Existence - why do firms emerge, why are not all transactions in the economy mediated over the market?
2. Boundaries - why the boundary between firms and the market is located exactly there? Which transactions are performed internally and which are negotiated on the market?
3. Organization - why are firms structured in such specific way? What is the interplay of formal and informal relationships?

Despite looking simple, these questions are not answered by the established economic theory, which usually views firms as given, and treats them as black boxes without any internal structure.

The First World War period saw a change of emphasis in economic theory away from industry-level analysis which mainly included analysing markets to analysis at the level of the firm, as it became increasingly clear that perfect competition was no longer an adequate model of how firms behaved. Economic theory till then had focussed on trying to understand markets alone and there had been little study on understanding why firms or organisations exist.

a. Technology gap
b. Theory of the firm
c. Khazzoom-Brookes postulate
d. Policy Ineffectiveness Proposition

87. _____ is the term denoting either an entrance or changes which are inserted into a system and which activate/modify a process. It is an abstract concept, used in the modeling, system(s) design and system(s) exploitation. It is usually connected with other terms, e.g., _____ field, _____ variable, _____ parameter, _____ value, _____ signal, _____ device and _____ file.

a. ACCRA Cost of Living Index
b. ACEA agreement
c. AD-IA Model
d. Input

88. _____ is a term used in national accounts statistics and macroeconomics. It basically refers to the net additions to the (physical) capital stock in an accounting period, or, to the value of the increase of the capital stock; though it may occasionally also refer to the (growth of the) total stock of capital formed.

Thus, in UNSNA, _____ equals fixed capital investment, the increase in the value of inventories held, plus (net) lending to foreign countries, during an accounting period.

a. Consumption of fixed capital
b. Capital intensity
c. Capital flight
d. Capital formation

89. In economics, _____ is the process by which a firm determines the price and output level that returns the greatest profit. There are several approaches to this problem. The total revenue--total cost method relies on the fact that profit equals revenue minus cost, and the marginal revenue--marginal cost method is based on the fact that total profit in a perfectly competitive market reaches its maximum point where marginal revenue equals marginal cost.

a. Profit maximization
b. Normal profit
c. 100-year flood
d. Profit margin

Chapter 14. Land and Capital

90. A _____ is message sent to consumers and producers in the form of a price charged for a commodity; this is seen as indicating a signal for producers to increase supplies and/or consumers to reduce demand.

For example, in a free price system, rising prices may indicate a shortage of supply, increase in demand, or a rise in input costs. Regardless of the underlying reason--and without the consumer needing to know the cause--the price increase communicates the notion that consumer demand (at this new, higher price) should recede or that supplies should increase.

   a. Price signal
   c. Threshold population
   b. Market demand schedule
   d. Mohring effect

91. The _____ is a concept widely used in Welfare Economics, and analogous to the better-known Production-possibility frontier. It is a similar diagram which depicts not production of two goods, but rather the utility possibilities of two individuals.

In a competitive economy, any allocation over the _____ is a Pareto optimum, as the UPF is a representation of the Pareto contract curve in a different dimension (utilities versus goods.)

   a. International Social Security Association
   c. ACCRA Cost of Living Index
   b. Equivalent variation
   d. Utility-possibility frontier

Chapter 15. Comparative Advantage and Protectionism

1. _____ is exchange of capital, goods, and services across international borders or territories. In most countries, it represents a significant share of gross domestic product (GDP.) While _____ has been present throughout much of history, its economic, social, and political importance has been on the rise in recent centuries.
   a. Intra-industry trade
   b. Incoterms
   c. Import license
   d. International trade

2. _____s is the social science that studies the production, distribution, and consumption of goods and services. The term _____s comes from the Ancient Greek oá¼°κονομῖα from oá¼¶κος (oikos, 'house') + vῐΈμος (nomos, 'custom' or 'law'), hence 'rules of the house(hold)'. Current _____ models developed out of the broader field of political economy in the late 19th century, owing to a desire to use an empirical approach more akin to the physical sciences.
   a. Energy economics
   b. Opportunity cost
   c. Economic
   d. Inflation

3. _____ is the increase in the amount of the goods and services produced by an economy over time. It is conventionally measured as the percent rate of increase in real gross domestic product, or real GDP. Growth is usually calculated in real terms, i.e. inflation-adjusted terms, in order to net out the effect of inflation on the price of the goods and services produced.
   a. ACEA agreement
   b. ACCRA Cost of Living Index
   c. AD-IA Model
   d. Economic growth

4. In finance, the _____s between two currencies specifies how much one currency is worth in terms of the other. It is the value of a foreign natione;s currency in terms of the home natione;s currency. For example an _____ of 102 Japanese yen to the United States dollar means that JPY 102 is worth the same as USD 1.
   a. Interbank market
   b. ACCRA Cost of Living Index
   c. Exchange rate
   d. ACEA agreement

5. A _____ is an object whose consumption increases the utility of the consumer, for which the quantity demanded exceeds the quantity supplied at zero price. _____s are usually modeled as having diminishing marginal utility. The first individual purchase has high utility; the second has less.
   a. Pie method
   b. Composite good
   c. Merit good
   d. Good

6. In economics, economic output is divided into physical goods and intangible services. Consumption of _____ is assumed to produce utility. It is often used when referring to a _____ Tax.
   a. Composite good
   b. Private good
   c. Manufactured goods
   d. Goods and services

7. _____s (economically referred to as land or raw materials) occur naturally within environments that exist relatively undisturbed by mankind, in a natural form. A _____'s is often characterized by amounts of biodiversity existent in various ecosystems.

Mining, petroleum extraction, fishing, hunting, and forestry are generally considered natural-resource industries.

   a. 100-year flood
   b. Natural resource
   c. 130-30 fund
   d. 1921 recession

Chapter 15. Comparative Advantage and Protectionism

8. Economics:

   - _____ ,the desire to own something and the ability to pay for it
   - _____ curve, a graphic representation of a _____ schedule
   - _____ deposit, the money in checking accounts
   - _____ pull theory, the theory that inflation occurs when _____ for goods and services exceeds existing supplies
   - _____ schedule, a table that lists the quantity of a good a person will buy it each different price
   - _____ side economics, the school of economics at believes government spending and tax cuts open economy by raising _____

   a. Production
   b. Variability
   c. McKesson ' Robbins scandal
   d. Demand

9. _____ is a term used to describe how different aspects between economies are integrated. The basics of this theory were written by the Hungarian Economist Béla Balassa in the 1960s. As _____ increases, the barriers of trade between markets diminishes.

   a. Import license
   b. Import
   c. Inward investment
   d. Economic integration

10. _____ is the value on a given date of a future payment or series of future payments, discounted to reflect the time value of money and other factors such as investment risk. _____ calculations are widely used in business and economics to provide a means to compare cash flows at different times on a meaningful 'like to like' basis.

    Money value fluctuates over time: $100 today are not worth $100 in five years.

    a. Present value
    b. Future value
    c. Present value of costs
    d. Tax shield

11. The term '_____' refers to the concept of collecting information and attempting to spot a pattern in the information. In some fields of study, the term '_____' has more formally-defined meanings.

    In project management _____ is a mathematical technique that uses historical results to predict future outcome.

    a. Coefficient of determination
    b. Quantile regression
    c. Probit model
    d. Trend analysis

12. _____ is the a method of technical and economic research of the systems for purpose to optimize a parity between system's consumer functions or properties and expenses to achieve those functions or properties.

Chapter 15. Comparative Advantage and Protectionism

This methodology for continuous perfection of production, industrial technologies, organizational structures was developed by Juryj Sobolev in 1948 at the 'Perm telephone factory'

- 1948 Juryj Sobolev - the first success in application of a method analysis at the 'Perm telephone factory'.
- 1949 - the first application for the invention as result of use of the new method.

Today in economically developed countries practically each enterprise or the company use methodology of the kind of functional-cost analysis as a practice of the quality management, most full satisfying to principles of standards of series ISO 9000.

- Interest of consumer not in products itself, but the advantage which it will receive from its usage.
- The consumer aspires to reduce his expenses
- Functions needed by consumer can be executed in the various ways, and, hence, with various efficiency and expenses. Among possible alternatives of realization of functions exist such in which the parity of quality and the price is the optimal for the consumer.

The goal of _____ is achievement of the highest consumer satisfaction of production at simultaneous decrease in all kinds of industrial expenses Classical _____ has three English synonyms - Value Engineering, Value Management, Value Analysis.

a. Monopoly wage
c. Function cost analysis
b. Staple financing
d. Willingness to pay

13. The _____ consists of a number of economic theories which describe the nature of the firm, company including its existence, its behaviour, and its relationship with the market.

In simplified terms, the _____ aims to answer these questions:

1. Existence - why do firms emerge, why are not all transactions in the economy mediated over the market?
2. Boundaries - why the boundary between firms and the market is located exactly there? Which transactions are performed internally and which are negotiated on the market?
3. Organization - why are firms structured in such specific way? What is the interplay of formal and informal relationships?

Despite looking simple, these questions are not answered by the established economic theory, which usually views firms as given, and treats them as black boxes without any internal structure.

The First World War period saw a change of emphasis in economic theory away from industry-level analysis which mainly included analysing markets to analysis at the level of the firm, as it became increasingly clear that perfect competition was no longer an adequate model of how firms behaved. Economic theory till then had focussed on trying to understand markets alone and there had been little study on understanding why firms or organisations exist.

a. Khazzoom-Brookes postulate
b. Technology gap
c. Policy Ineffectiveness Proposition
d. Theory of the firm

14. In economics, _____ and economies of scale are related terms that describe what happens as the scale of production increases. They are different terms and should not be used interchangeably.

_____ refers to a technical property of production that examines changes in output subsequent to a proportional change in all inputs (where all inputs increase by a constant factor.)

a. Customer equity
b. Constant returns to scale
c. Necessity good
d. Returns to scale

15. In economics, _____ is equal to total cost divided by the number of goods produced (the output quantity, Q.) It is also equal to the sum of average variable costs (total variable costs divided by Q) plus average fixed costs (total fixed costs divided by Q.) _____s may be dependent on the time period considered (increasing production may be expensive or impossible in the short term, for example.)

a. Average variable cost
b. Explicit cost
c. Average fixed cost
d. Average cost

16. In economics, _____ refers to the ability of a person or a country to produce a particular good at a lower marginal cost and opportunity cost than another person or country. It is the ability to produce a product most efficiently given all the other products that could be produced. It can be contrasted with absolute advantage which refers to the ability of a person or a country to produce a particular good at a lower absolute cost than another.

a. Triffin dilemma
b. Hot money
c. Gravity model of trade
d. Comparative advantage

17. In economic theory, _____ is the competitive situation in any market where the conditions necessary for perfect competition are not satisfied. It is a market structure that does not meet the conditions of perfect competition.

Forms of _____ include:

- Monopoly, in which there is only one seller of a good.
- Oligopoly, in which there is a small number of sellers.
- Monopolistic competition, in which there are many sellers producing highly differentiated goods.
- Monopsony, in which there is only one buyer of a good.
- Oligopsony, in which there is a small number of buyers.

There may also be _____ in markets due to buyers or sellers lacking information about prices and the goods being traded.

There may also be _____ due to a time lag in a market.

a. ACCRA Cost of Living Index
b. Imperfect competition
c. ACEA agreement
d. AD-IA Model

Chapter 15. Comparative Advantage and Protectionism

18. In microeconomics, _____ is quite simply the conversion of inputs into outputs. It is an economic process that uses resources to create a good or service that is suitable for exchange. This can include manufacturing, storing, shipping, and packaging.
    a. Solved
    b. Red Guards
    c. MET
    d. Production

19. In economics, _____ refers to the ability of a party to produce a good or service using fewer real resources than another entity producing the same good or service..A party has an _____ when using the same input as another party, it can produce a greater output. Since _____ is determined by a simple comparison of labor productivities, it is possible for a a party to have no _____ in anything. It can be contrasted with the concept of comparative advantage which refers to the ability to produce a particular good at a lower opportunity cost.
    a. International economics
    b. Index number
    c. ACCRA Cost of Living Index
    d. Absolute advantage

20. _____ was a survey conducted by the U.S. Department of Justice to gauge the prevalence of alcohol and illegal drug use among prior arrestees. It was a reformulation of the prior Drug Use Forecasting (DUF) program, focused on five drugs in particular: cocaine, marijuana, methamphetamine, opiates, and PCP.

Participants were randomly selected from arrest records in major metropolitan areas; because no personally identifying information is taken from each record chosen, the resulting data can be correlated to arrest rates, but not to the total population of persons charged.

    a. AD-IA Model
    b. ACEA agreement
    c. Arrestee Drug Abuse Monitoring
    d. ACCRA Cost of Living Index

21. _____ was a Scottish moral philosopher and a pioneer of political economy. One of the key figures of the Scottish Enlightenment, Smith is the author of The Theory of Moral Sentiments and An Inquiry into the Nature and Causes of the Wealth of Nations. The latter, usually abbreviated as The Wealth of Nations, is considered his magnum opus and the first modern work of economics.
    a. Adolf Hitler
    b. Adolph Fischer
    c. Alan Greenspan
    d. Adam Smith

22. _____ is a type of trade policy that allows traders to act and transact without interference from government. Thus, the policy permits trading partners mutual gains from trade, with goods and services produced according to the theory of comparative advantage.

Under a _____ policy, prices are a reflection of true supply and demand, and are the sole determinant of resource allocation.

    a. 1921 recession
    b. 100-year flood
    c. Free trade
    d. 130-30 fund

23. _____ in economics and business is the result of an exchange and from that trade we assign a numerical monetary value to a good, service or asset. If Alice trades Bob 4 apples for an orange, the _____ of an orange is 4 apples. Inversely, the _____ of an apple is 1/4 oranges.

a. Price war
b. Price book
c. Price
d. Premium pricing

24. A _____ is a hypothetical measure of overall prices for some set of goods and services, in a given region during a given interval, normalized relative to some base set. Typically, a _____ is approximated with a price index.

The classical dichotomy is the assumption that there is a relatively clean distinction between overall increases or decreases in prices and underlying, e;reale; economic variables.

a. Price elasticity of supply
b. Discretionary spending
c. Discouraged worker
d. Price level

Chapter 15. Comparative Advantage and Protectionism   191

25.   A _____ is:

- Rewrite _____, in generative grammar and computer science
- Standardization, a formal and widely-accepted statement, fact, definition, or qualification
- Operation, a determinate _____ for performing a mathematical operation and obtaining a certain result (Mathematics, Logic)
    - Unary operation
    - Binary operation
- _____ of inference, a function from sets of formulae to formulae (Mathematics, Logic)
- _____ of thumb, principle with broad application that is not intended to be strictly accurate or reliable for every situation. Also often simply referred to as a _____
- Moral, an atomic element of a moral code for guiding choices in human behavior
- Heuristic, a quantized '_____' which shows a tendency or probability for successful function
- A regulation, as in sports
- A Production _____, as in computer science
- Procedural law, a _____ set governing the application of laws to cases
    - A law, which may informally be called a '_____'
    - A court ruling, a decision by a court
- In the U.S. Government, a regulation mandated by Congress, but written or expanded upon by the Executive Branch.
- Norm (sociology), an informal but widely accepted _____, concept, truth, definition, or qualification (social norms, legal norms, coding norms)
- Norm (philosophy), a kind of sentence or a reason to act, feel or believe
- 'Rulership' is the concept of governance by a government:
    - Military _____, governance by a military body
    - Monastic _____, a collection of precepts that guides the life of monks or nuns in a religious order where the superior holds the place of Christ
- Slide _____

- '_____,' a song by Ayumi Hamasaki
- '_____,' a song by rapper Nas
- '_____s,' an album by the band The Whitest Boy Alive
- _____s: Pyaar Ka Superhit Formula, a 2003 Bollywood film
- ruler, an instrument for measuring lengths
- _____, a component of an astrolabe, circumferator or similar instrument
- The _____s, a bestselling self-help book
- _____ Project (Run Up-to-date Linux Everywhere), a project that aims to use up-to-date Linux software on old PCs
- _____ engine, a software system that helps managing business _____s
- Ja _____, a hip hop artist
    - R.U.L.E., a 2005 greatest hits album by rapper Ja _____
- '_____s,' a KMFDM song

a. Technocracy   b. Demand
c. Procter ' Gamble   d. Rule

26. _____ is an economic concept with commonplace familiarity. It is the price that a good or service is offered at, or will fetch, in the marketplace. It is of interest mainly in the study of microeconomics.

   a. Paper trading
   b. Market anomaly
   c. Noisy market hypothesis
   d. Market price

27. The term _____s refers to wages that have been adjusted for inflation. This term is used in contrast to nominal wages or unadjusted wages.

The use of adjusted figures is in undertaking some form of economic analysis.

   a. Living wage
   b. Real wage
   c. Profit sharing
   d. Federal Wage System

28. Competition law, known in the United States as _____ law, has three main elements:

   - prohibiting agreements or practices that restrict free trading and competition between business entities. This includes in particular the repression of cartels.
   - banning abusive behaviour by a firm dominating a market, or anti-competitive practices that tend to lead to such a dominant position. Practices controlled in this way may include predatory pricing, tying, price gouging, refusal to deal, and many others.
   - supervising the mergers and acquisitions of large corporations, including some joint ventures. Transactions that are considered to threaten the competitive process can be prohibited altogether, or approved subject to 'remedies' such as an obligation to divest part of the merged business or to offer licences or access to facilities to enable other businesses to continue competing.

The substance and practice of competition law varies from jurisdiction to jurisdiction. Protecting the interests of consumers (consumer welfare) and ensuring that entrepreneurs have an opportunity to compete in the market economy are often treated as important objectives. Competition law is closely connected with law on deregulation of access to markets, state aids and subsidies, the privatisation of state owned assets and the establishment of independent sector regulators. In recent decades, competition law has been viewed as a way to provide better public services.

   a. Intellectual property law
   b. Antitrust
   c. Anti-Inflation Act
   d. United Kingdom competition law

29. _____ is a common concept in economics, and gives rise to derived concepts such as consumer debt. Generally _____ is defined by opposition to production. But the precise definition can vary because different schools of economists define production quite differently.

   a. Foreclosure data providers
   b. Cash or share options
   c. Federal Reserve Bank Notes
   d. Consumption

30. In international economics and international trade, _____ or _____ is the relative prices of a country's export to import. '_____' are sometimes used as a proxy for the relative social welfare of a country, but this heuristic is technically questionable and should be used with extreme caution. An improvement in a nation's _____ is good for that country in the sense that it has to pay less for the products it import.

a. Commercial invoice
b. Kennedy Round
c. Terms of trade
d. Common market

31. A _____ is an expression that compares quantities relative to each other. The most common examples involve two quantities, but any number of quantities can be compared. _____s are represented mathematically by separating each quantity with a colon, for example the _____ 2:3, which is read as the _____ 'two to three'.
 a. Ratio
 b. 100-year flood
 c. Y-intercept
 d. 130-30 fund

32. _____ or clearing trade is trade exclusively between two states, particularly, barter trade based on bilateral deals between governments, and without using hard currency for payment. _____ agreements often aim to keep trade deficits at minimum by keeping a clearing account where deficit would accumulate.

The Soviet Union conducted _____ with two nations, India and Finland.

 a. 1921 recession
 b. 100-year flood
 c. 130-30 fund
 d. Bilateral trade

33. _____ is a historical term indicating trade among three ports or regions. The trade evolved where a region had an export commodity that was required in the region from which its major imports came. _____ thus provided a mechanism for rectifying trade imbalances.
 a. 130-30 fund
 b. 1921 recession
 c. 100-year flood
 d. Triangular trade

34. _____ is widely regarded as the first modern school of economic thought. It is the idea that free markets can regulate themselves. Its major developers include Adam Smith, David Ricardo, Thomas Malthus and John Stuart Mill. Sometimes the definition of _____ is expanded to include William Petty, Johann Heinrich von Thünen.
 a. Marginalism
 b. Tendency of the rate of profit to fall
 c. Schools of economic thought
 d. Classical economics

35. In economics, _____ are the resources employed to produce goods and services. They facilitate production but do not become part of the product (as with raw materials) or significantly transformed by the production process (as with fuel used to power machinery.) To 19th century economists, the _____ were land (natural resources, gifts from nature), labor (the ability to work), and capital goods (human-made tools and equipment.)
 a. Product Pipeline
 b. Hicks-neutral technical change
 c. Long-run
 d. Factors of production

36. The _____ was a worldwide economic downturn starting in most places in 1929 and ending at different times in the 1930s or early 1940s for different countries. It was the largest and most important economic depression in the 20th century, and is used in the 21st century as an example of how far the world's economy can fall. The _____ originated in the United States; historians most often use as a starting date the stock market crash on October 29, 1929, known as Black Tuesday.
 a. Jarrow March
 b. Wall Street Crash of 1929
 c. British Empire Economic Conference
 d. Great Depression

Chapter 15. Comparative Advantage and Protectionism

37. In economics, _____ is how a natione;s total economy is distributed among its population. . _____ has always been a central concern of economic theory and economic policy. Classical economists such as Adam Smith, Thomas Malthus and David Ricardo were mainly concerned with factor _____, that is, the distribution of income between the main factors of production, land, labour and capital.
    a. Eco commerce
    b. Authorised capital
    c. Equipment trust certificate
    d. Income distribution

38. _____ is the economic policy of restraining trade between states, through methods such as tariffs on imported goods, restrictive quotas, and a variety of other restrictive government regulations designed to discourage imports, and prevent foreign take-over of local markets and companies. This policy is closely aligned with anti-globalization, and contrasts with free trade, where government barriers to trade are kept to a minimum. The term is mostly used in the context of economics, where _____ refers to policies or doctrines which 'protect' businesses and workers within a country by restricting or regulating trade with foreign nations.
    a. Protectionism
    b. Google economy
    c. Knowledge economy
    d. Digital economy

39. The _____ is an economic and political union of 27 member states, located primarily in Europe. It was established by the Treaty of Maastricht on 1 November 1993, upon the foundations of the pre-existing European Economic Community. With a population of almost 500 million, the _____ generates an estimated 30% share (US$18.4 trillion in 2008) of the nominal gross world product.
    a. European Union
    b. European Court of Justice
    c. ACEA agreement
    d. ACCRA Cost of Living Index

40. _____ theory is a branch of theoretical economics. It seeks to explain the behavior of supply, demand and prices in a whole economy with several or many markets. It is often assumed that agents are price takers and in that setting two common notions of equilibrium exist: Walrasian (or competitive) equilibrium, and its generalization; a price equilibrium with transfers.
    a. Human capital
    b. Rational choice theory
    c. New Keynesian economics
    d. General equilibrium

41. In economics, economic equilibrium is simply a state of the world where economic forces are balanced and in the absence of external influences the (equilibrium) values of economic variables will not change. It is the point at which quantity demanded and quantity supplied are equal. _____, for example, refers to a condition where a market price is established through competition such that the amount of goods or services sought by buyers is equal to the amount of goods or services produced by sellers.
    a. Regulated market
    b. Marketization
    c. Product-Market Growth Matrix
    d. Market equilibrium

42. The _____ was an act signed into law on June 17, 1930, that raised U.S. tariffs on over 20,000 imported goods to record levels. In the United States 1,028 economists signed a petition against this legislation, and after it was passed, many countries retaliated with their own increased tariffs on U.S. goods, and American exports and imports were reduced by more than half.

Although rated capacity had increased tremendously, actual output, income, and expenditure had not.

Chapter 15. Comparative Advantage and Protectionism

a. Judgment summons
b. Smoot-Hawley Tariff Act
c. Patent Law Treaty
d. Loss of use

43. _____ is an economic model based on price, utility and quantity in a market. It predicts that in a competitive market, price will function to equalize the quantity demanded by consumers, and the quantity supplied by producers, resulting in an economic equilibrium of price and quantity. The model incorporates other factors changing equilibrium as a shift of demand and/or supply.
   a. Deferred gratification
   b. Joint demand
   c. Supply and demand
   d. Rational addiction

44. A _____ is a general term that describes any government policy or regulation that restricts international trade. The barriers can take many forms, including the following terms that include many restrictions in international trade within multiple countries that import and export any items of trade.

- Import duty
- Import licenses
- Export licenses
- Import quotas
- Tariffs
- Subsidies
- Non-tariff barriers to trade
- Voluntary Export Restraints
- Local Content Requirements
- Embargo

Most _____s work on the same principle: the imposition of some sort of cost on trade that raises the price of the traded products. If two or more nations repeatedly use _____s against each other, then a trade war results.

   a. National Foreign Trade Council
   b. Global financial system
   c. Certificate of origin
   d. Trade barrier

45. A _____ is a duty imposed on goods when they are moved across a political boundary. They are usually associated with protectionism, the economic policy of restraining trade between nations. For political reasons, _____s are usually imposed on imported goods, although they may also be imposed on exported goods.
   a. 1921 recession
   b. 130-30 fund
   c. 100-year flood
   d. Tariff

46. The _____ of a decision depends on both the cost of the alternative chosen and the benefit that the best alternative would have provided if chosen. _____ differs from accounting cost because it includes opportunity cost.
   a. Inventory analysis
   b. Economic cost
   c. Epstein-Zin preferences
   d. Isocost

47. _____ is used to refer to a number of related concepts. It is the using resources in such a way as to maximize the production of goods and services. A system can be called economically efficient if:

- No one can be made better off without making someone else worse off.
- More output cannot be obtained without increasing the amount of inputs.
- Production proceeds at the lowest possible per-unit cost.

These definitions of efficiency are not equivalent, but they are all encompassed by the idea that nothing more can be achieved given the resources available.

An economic system is more efficient if it can provide more goods and services for society without using more resources.

    a. Efficient contract theory   b. ACCRA Cost of Living Index
    c. ACEA agreement   d. Economic efficiency

48. In economics, _____ is the transfer of income, wealth or property from some individuals to others.

One premise of _____ is that money should be distributed to benefit the poorer members of society, and that the rich have an obligation to assist the poor, thus creating a more financially egalitarian society. Another argument is that the rich exploit the poor or otherwise gain unfair benefits.

    a. 130-30 fund   b. 100-year flood
    c. 1921 recession   d. Redistribution

49. _____ is an economic theory that holds that the prosperity of a nation is dependent upon its supply of capital, and that the global volume of international trade is 'unchangeable.' Economic assets or capital, are represented by bullion (gold, silver, and trade value) held by the state, which is best increased through a positive balance of trade with other nations (exports minus imports.) _____ suggests that the ruling government should advance these goals by playing a protectionist role in the economy; by encouraging exports and discouraging imports, notably through the use of tariffs and subsidies.

_____ was the dominant school of thought throughout the early modern period (from the 16th to the 18th century.)

    a. General equilibrium theory   b. Mercantilism
    c. Nominal value   d. Consumer theory

50. The _____ is a term used for industries primarily concerned with the design or manufacture of clothing as well as the distribution and use of textiles.

Prior to the manufacturing processes were mechanized, textiles were produced in the home, and excess sold for extra money. Most cloth was made from either wool, cotton, or flax, depending on the era and location.

Chapter 15. Comparative Advantage and Protectionism 197

    a. 130-30 fund
    b. Textile industry
    c. Textile manufacture during the Industrial Revolution
    d. 100-year flood

51. _____ or government expenditure is classified by economists into three main types. Government purchases of goods and services for current use are classed as government consumption. Government purchases of goods and services intended to create future benefits, such as infrastructure investment or research spending, are classed as government investment.
    a. 100-year flood
    b. 1921 recession
    c. 130-30 fund
    d. Government spending

52. In economics, the people in the _____ are the suppliers of labor. The _____ is all the nonmilitary people who are employed or unemployed. In 2005, the worldwide _____ was over 3 billion people.
    a. Labor force
    b. Grenelle agreements
    c. Distributed workforce
    d. Departmentalization

53. The _____ is a trilateral trade bloc in North America created by the governments of the United States, Canada, and Mexico. The agreement creating the trade bloc came into force on January 1, 1994. It superseded the Canada-United States Free Trade Agreement between the U.S. and Canada.
    a. Federal Reserve Bank Notes
    b. Case-Shiller Home Price Indices
    c. North American Free Trade Agreement
    d. Demand-side technologies

54. In neoclassical economics and microeconomics, _____ describes the perfect being a market in which there are many small firms, all producing homogeneous goods. In the short term, such markets are productively inefficient as output will not occur where mc is equal to ac, but allocatively efficient, as output under _____ will always occur where mc is equal to mr, and therefore where mc equals ar. However, in the long term, such markets are both allocatively and productively efficient.
    a. Law of supply
    b. Perfect competition
    c. General equilibrium
    d. Co-operative economics

55. _____ is a fee paid on borrowed assets. It is the price paid for the use of borrowed money , or, money earned by deposited funds . Assets that are sometimes lent with _____ include money, shares, consumer goods through hire purchase, major assets such as aircraft, and even entire factories in finance lease arrangements.
    a. Insolvency
    b. Interest
    c. Asset protection
    d. Internal debt

56. _____ are duties imposed under WTO Rules to neutralize the negative effects of other duties. They are imposed when a foreign country subsidizes its exports, hurting domestic producers in the importing country
    a. Certificate of origin
    b. Kennedy Round
    c. Market access
    d. Countervailing duties

57. In economics, an _____ is any good (e.g. a commodity) or service brought into one country from another country in a legitimate fashion, typically for use in trade.It is a good that is brought in from another country for sale. _____ goods or services are provided to domestic consumers by foreign producers. An _____ in the receiving country is an export to the sending country.

| a. Import quota | b. Economic integration |
| c. Incoterms | d. Import |

58. _____ was the first United States Secretary of the Treasury, a Founding Father, economist, and political philosopher. He led calls for the Philadelphia Convention, was one of America's first Constitutional lawyers, and cowrote the Federalist Papers, a primary source for Constitutional interpretation.

Born on the British West Indian island of Nevis, Hamilton was educated in the Thirteen Colonies.

| a. Adam Smith | b. American exceptionalism |
| c. Economic impact of immigration | d. Alexander Hamilton |

59. The _____ is an economic reason for protectionism. The crux of the argument is that nascent industries often do not have the economies of scale that their older competitors from other countries may have, and thus need to be protected until they can attain similar economies of scale. It was first used by Alexander Hamilton in 1790 and later by Friedrich List, in 1841, to support protection for German manufacturing against British industry.

| a. ACEA agreement | b. AD-IA Model |
| c. ACCRA Cost of Living Index | d. Infant industry argument |

60. The supply of labor is the number of total hours that workers wish to work at a given real wage rate.

_____ curves are derived from the 'labor-leisure' trade-off. More hours worked earn higher incomes but necessitate a cut in the amount of leisure that workers enjoy.

| a. Human trafficking | b. Late capitalism |
| c. Creative capitalism | d. Labor supply |

61. _____ refers to discriminatory employment practices such as bias in hiring, promotion, job assignment, termination, and compensation, and various types of harassment.

In many countries, laws prohibit employers from discriminating on the basis of race, color, sex, religion, national origin, physical or mental disability, or age. There is also a growing body of law preventing or occasionally justifying _____ based on sexual orientation or gender identity.

| a. Energy Independence and Security Act of 2007 | b. Impotent poor |
| c. Employment discrimination | d. Irish competition law |

62. _____ and Keynesian Theory) is a macroeconomic theory based on the ideas of 20th-century British economist John Maynard Keynes. _____ argues that private sector decisions sometimes lead to inefficient macroeconomic outcomes and therefore advocates active policy responses by the public sector, including monetary policy actions by the central bank and fiscal policy actions by the government to stabilize output over the business cycle.

The theories forming the basis of _____ were first presented in The General Theory of Employment, Interest and Money, published in 1936.

Chapter 15. Comparative Advantage and Protectionism

a. Deflation
b. Keynesian economics
c. Rational choice theory
d. Market failure

63. In economics, an _____ is any good or commodity, transported from one country to another country in a legitimate fashion, typically for use in trade. _____ goods or services are provided to foreign consumers by domestic producers. _____ is an important part of international trade.
 a. ACEA agreement
 b. ACCRA Cost of Living Index
 c. Export
 d. AD-IA Model

64. The _____ is the official currency of 16 of the 27 member states of the European Union (EU.) The states, known collectively as the Eurozone, are Austria, Belgium, Cyprus, Finland, France, Germany, Greece, Ireland, Italy, Luxembourg, Malta, the Netherlands, Portugal, Slovakia, Slovenia, and Spain. The currency is also used in a further five European countries, with and without formal agreements and is consequently used daily by some 327 million Europeans.
 a. Import and Export Price Indices
 b. IRS Code 3401
 c. Equity capital market
 d. Euro

65. The _____ was the outcome of the failure of negotiating governments to create the International Trade Organization (ITO.) GATT was formed in 1947 and lasted until 1994, when it was replaced by the World Trade Organization. The Bretton Woods Conference had introduced the idea for an organization to regulate trade as part of a larger plan for economic recovery after World War II.
 a. General Agreement on Trade in Services
 b. Dutch-Scandinavian Economic Pact
 c. General Agreement on Tariffs and Trade
 d. GATT

66. _____ in its literal sense is the process of transformation of local or regional phenomena into global ones. It can be described as a process by which the people of the world are unified into a single society and function together.

This process is a combination of economic, technological, sociocultural and political forces.

 a. Globally Integrated Enterprise
 b. Global Cosmopolitanism
 c. Helsinki Process on Globalisation and Democracy
 d. Globalization

67. The _____ commenced in September 1986 and continued until April 1994. The round, based on the General Agreement on Tariffs and Trade (GATT) ministerial meeting in Geneva (1982), was launched in Punta del Este in Uruguay (hence the name), followed by negotiations in Montreal, Geneva, Brussels, Washington, D.C., and Tokyo, with the 20 agreements finally being signed in Marrakech - the Marrakesh Agreement. The Round transformed the GATT into the World Trade Organization.
 a. Uruguay Round
 b. ACCRA Cost of Living Index
 c. AD-IA Model
 d. ACEA agreement

68. The _____ is an important selective, mainly private, international organization designed by its founders to supervise and liberalize international trade. The organization officially commenced on 1 January 1995, under the Marrakesh Agreement, succeeding the 1947 General Agreement on Tariffs and Trade (GATT.)

Chapter 15. Comparative Advantage and Protectionism

The _____ deals with regulation of trade between participating countries; it provides a framework for negotiating and formalising trade agreements, and a dispute resolution process aimed at enforcing participants' adherence to _____ agreements which are signed by representatives of member governments and ratified by their parliaments.

a. 2009 G-20 London summit protests
b. Bio-energy village
c. World Trade Organization
d. Backus-Kehoe-Kydland consumption correlation puzzle

69. _____ is a branch of economics with three main subdisciplines international trade, monetary economics and international finance.

- International trade studies goods-and-services flows across international boundaries from supply-and-demand factors, economic integration, and policy variables such as tariff rates and trade quotas.
- International finance studies the flow of capital across international financial markets, and the effects of these movements on exchange rates.
- International monetary economics and macroeconomics studies money and macro flows across countries.
- Stanley W. Black (2008.) 'international monetary institutions,' The New Palgrave Dictionary of Economics. 2nd Edition.

a. ACCRA Cost of Living Index
b. Economic depreciation
c. International Economics
d. Index number

70. The _____ is an international organization that oversees the global financial system by following the macroeconomic policies of its member countries, in particular those with an impact on exchange rates and the balance of payments. It is an organization formed to stabilize international exchange rates and facilitate development. It also offers financial and technical assistance to its members, making it an international lender of last resort.

a. ACEA agreement
b. ACCRA Cost of Living Index
c. International Monetary Fund
d. Office of Thrift Supervision

71. The _____ is an international financial institution that provides financial and technical assistance to developing countries for development programs (e.g. bridges, roads, schools, etc.) with the stated goal of reducing poverty.

The _____ differs from the _____ Group, in that the _____ comprises only two institutions:

- International Bank for Reconstruction and Development (IBRD)
- International Development Association (IDA)

Whereas the latter incorporates these two in addition to three more:

- International Finance Corporation (IFC)
- Multilateral Investment Guarantee Agency (MIGA)
- International Centre for Settlement of Investment Disputes (ICSID)

John Maynard Keynes (right) represented the UK at the conference, and Harry Dexter White represented the US.

The _____ is one of two major financial institutions created as a result of the Bretton Woods Conference in 1944. The International Monetary Fund, a related but separate institution, is the second.

a. Bank-State-Branch
c. Flow to Equity-Approach
b. Financial costs of the 2003 Iraq War
d. World Bank

Chapter 16. Government Taxation and Expenditure

1. The _____ or gross domestic income (GDI), a basic measure of an economy's economic performance, is the market value of all final goods and services produced within the borders of a nation in a year. _____ can be defined in three ways, all of which are conceptually identical. First, it is equal to the total expenditures for all final goods and services produced within the country in a stipulated period of time (usually a 365-day year.)
   a. Monopolistic competition
   b. Market structure
   c. Countercyclical
   d. Gross Domestic Product

2. In economics, a _____ is a redistribution of income in the market system. These payments are considered to be nonexhaustive because they do not directly absorb resources or create output. Examples of certain _____s include welfare (financial aid), social security, and government subsidies for certain businesses (firms.)
   a. 100-year flood
   b. 130-30 fund
   c. Transfer payment
   d. 1921 recession

3. _____ or government expenditure is classified by economists into three main types. Government purchases of goods and services for current use are classed as government consumption. Government purchases of goods and services intended to create future benefits, such as infrastructure investment or research spending, are classed as government investment.
   a. Government spending
   b. 130-30 fund
   c. 1921 recession
   d. 100-year flood

4. A _____ is the transfer of wealth from one party (such as a person or company) to another. A _____ is usually made in exchange for the provision of goods, services or both, or to fulfill a legal obligation.

   The simplest and oldest form of _____ is barter, the exchange of one good or service for another.

   a. Going concern
   b. Payment
   c. Soft count
   d. Social gravity

5. _____ describes a broad class of theories that try to explain the ways in which people form states and/or maintain social order. The notion of the _____ implies that the people give up some rights to a government or other authority in order to receive or maintain social order.

   _____ theory formed a central pillar in the historically important notion that legitimate state authority must be derived from the consent of the governed.

   a. 1921 recession
   b. 130-30 fund
   c. 100-year flood
   d. Social contract

6. _____ is a common concept in economics, and gives rise to derived concepts such as consumer debt. Generally _____ is defined by opposition to production. But the precise definition can vary because different schools of economists define production quite differently.
   a. Federal Reserve Bank Notes
   b. Consumption
   c. Foreclosure data providers
   d. Cash or share options

7. The term '_____' refers to the concept of collecting information and attempting to spot a pattern in the information. In some fields of study, the term '_____' has more formally-defined meanings.

Chapter 16. Government Taxation and Expenditure

In project management _____ is a mathematical technique that uses historical results to predict future outcome.

a. Quantile regression
b. Trend analysis
c. Coefficient of determination
d. Probit model

8. Competition law, known in the United States as _____ law, has three main elements:

- prohibiting agreements or practices that restrict free trading and competition between business entities. This includes in particular the repression of cartels.
- banning abusive behaviour by a firm dominating a market, or anti-competitive practices that tend to lead to such a dominant position. Practices controlled in this way may include predatory pricing, tying, price gouging, refusal to deal, and many others.
- supervising the mergers and acquisitions of large corporations, including some joint ventures. Transactions that are considered to threaten the competitive process can be prohibited altogether, or approved subject to 'remedies' such as an obligation to divest part of the merged business or to offer licences or access to facilities to enable other businesses to continue competing.

The substance and practice of competition law varies from jurisdiction to jurisdiction. Protecting the interests of consumers (consumer welfare) and ensuring that entrepreneurs have an opportunity to compete in the market economy are often treated as important objectives. Competition law is closely connected with law on deregulation of access to markets, state aids and subsidies, the privatisation of state owned assets and the establishment of independent sector regulators. In recent decades, competition law has been viewed as a way to provide better public services.

a. Antitrust
b. Anti-Inflation Act
c. Intellectual property law
d. United Kingdom competition law

9. _____s is the social science that studies the production, distribution, and consumption of goods and services. The term _____s comes from the Ancient Greek oá¼°κονομῖα from oá¼¶κος (oikos, 'house') + vĭŒμος (nomos, 'custom' or 'law'), hence 'rules of the house(hold)'. Current _____ models developed out of the broader field of political economy in the late 19th century, owing to a desire to use an empirical approach more akin to the physical sciences.

a. Opportunity cost
b. Energy economics
c. Economic
d. Inflation

10. The _____ was a regulatory body in the United States created by the Interstate Commerce Act of 1887, which was signed into law by President Grover Cleveland. The agency was abolished in 1995, and the agency's remaining functions were transferred to the Surface Transportation Board.

The Commission's five members were appointed by the President with the consent of the United States Senate.

a. Interstate Commerce Commission
b. Office of Thrift Supervision
c. ACEA agreement
d. ACCRA Cost of Living Index

Chapter 16. Government Taxation and Expenditure

11. _____ is a term used to describe a policy of allowing events to take their own course. The term is a French phrase literally meaning 'let do'. It is a doctrine that states that government generally should not intervene in the marketplace.
    a. Theory of Productive Forces
    b. Laissez-faire
    c. Communization
    d. Heroic capitalism

12. _____, often referred to by his initials _____, was the 32nd President of the United States. He was a central figure of the 20th century during a time of worldwide economic crisis and world war. Elected to four terms in office, he served from 1933 to 1945 and is the only U.S. president to have served more than two terms.
    a. Adolf Hitler
    b. Adam Smith
    c. Adolph Fischer
    d. Franklin Delano Roosevelt

13. _____ , also known as T.R., and to the public as Teddy, was the 26th President of the United States. A leader of the Republican Party and of the Progressive Party, he was a Governor of New York and a professional historian, naturalist, explorer, hunter, author, and soldier. He is most famous for his personality: his energy, his vast range of interests and achievements, his model of masculinity, and his 'cowboy' image.
    a. Adolf Hitler
    b. Adolph Fischer
    c. Adam Smith
    d. Theodore D. Roosevelt

14.

The _____ was the first United States Federal statute to limit cartels and monopolies. It falls under antitrust law.

The Act provides: 'Every contract, combination in the form of trust or otherwise, or conspiracy, in restraint of trade or commerce among the several States, or with foreign nations, is declared to be illegal'. The Act also provides: 'Every person who shall monopolize, or attempt to monopolize, or combine or conspire with any other person or persons, to monopolize any part of the trade or commerce among the several States, or with foreign nations, shall be deemed guilty of a felony [. . .]' The Act put responsibility upon government attorneys and district courts to pursue and investigate trusts, companies and organizations suspected of violating the Act. The Clayton Act extended the right to sue under the antitrust laws to 'any person who shall be injured in his business or property by reason of anything forbidden in the antitrust laws.' Under the Clayton Act, private parties may sue in U.S. district court and should they prevail, they may be awarded treble damages and the cost of suit, including reasonable attorney's fees.

   a. 100-year flood
   b. Sherman Antitrust Act
   c. 130-30 fund
   d. 1921 recession

15. _____ is a situation in which the limited resources of a firm are allocated in accordance with the wishes of consumers. An allocatively efficient economy produces an 'optimal mix' of commodities. A firm is allocatively efficient when its price is equal to its marginal costs (that is, P = MC) in a perfect market.
    a. Allocative efficiency
    b. ACEA agreement
    c. Economic efficiency
    d. ACCRA Cost of Living Index

Chapter 16. Government Taxation and Expenditure

16. _____ is an economic system in which wealth, and the means of producing wealth, are privately owned. Through _____, the land, labor, and capital are owned, operated, and traded for the purpose of generating profits, without force or fraud, by private individuals either singly or jointly, and investments, distribution, income, production, pricing and supply of goods, commodities and services are determined by voluntary private decision in a market economy. A distinguishing feature of _____ is that each person owns his or her own labor and therefore is allowed to sell the use of it to employers.
   a. Socialism for the rich and capitalism for the poor
   b. Creative capitalism
   c. Capitalism
   d. Late capitalism

17. In economic theory, _____ is the competitive situation in any market where the conditions necessary for perfect competition are not satisfied. It is a market structure that does not meet the conditions of perfect competition.

   Forms of _____ include:

   - Monopoly, in which there is only one seller of a good.
   - Oligopoly, in which there is a small number of sellers.
   - Monopolistic competition, in which there are many sellers producing highly differentiated goods.
   - Monopsony, in which there is only one buyer of a good.
   - Oligopsony, in which there is a small number of buyers.

   There may also be _____ in markets due to buyers or sellers lacking information about prices and the goods being traded.

   There may also be _____ due to a time lag in a market.

   a. ACEA agreement
   b. AD-IA Model
   c. ACCRA Cost of Living Index
   d. Imperfect competition

18. In economics, the _____ is the term economists use to describe the self-regulating nature of the marketplace. The _____ is a metaphor coined by the economist Adam Smith in The Wealth of Nations.

   Adam Smith mentions the metaphor in Book IV of The Wealth of Nations, arguing that people in any society will certainly employ their capital in foreign trading only if the profits available by that method far exceed those available locally, and that in such a case it is better for society as a whole if they so did.

   a. Invisible hand
   b. ACEA agreement
   c. ACCRA Cost of Living Index
   d. AD-IA Model

19. _____ is a branch of economics that studies how individuals, households and firms and some states make decisions to allocate limited resources, typically in markets where goods or services are being bought and sold. _____ examines how these decisions and behaviours affect the supply and demand for goods and services, which determines prices; and how prices, in turn, determine the supply and demand of goods and services.

   Whereas macroeconomics involves the 'sum total of economic activity, dealing with the issues of growth, inflation and unemployment, and with national economic policies relating to these issues' and the effects of government actions on them.

a. New Keynesian economics
b. Countercyclical
c. Recession
d. Microeconomics

20. The _____ of June 30, 1906 is a United States federal law that provided federal inspection of meat products and forbade the manufacture, sale, or transportation of adulterated food products and poisonous patent medicines. The Act arose due to public education and exposés from authors such as Upton Sinclair and Samuel Hopkins Adams, social activist Florence Kelley, researcher Harvey W. Wiley, and President Theodore Roosevelt.

The _____ was initially concerned with ensuring products were labeled correctly.

a. Security and Freedom Through Encryption Act
b. Sherman Silver Purchase Act
c. 100-year flood
d. Pure food and drug act

21. _____ is the increase in the amount of the goods and services produced by an economy over time. It is conventionally measured as the percent rate of increase in real gross domestic product, or real GDP. Growth is usually calculated in real terms, i.e. inflation-adjusted terms, in order to net out the effect of inflation on the price of the goods and services produced.

a. ACCRA Cost of Living Index
b. ACEA agreement
c. AD-IA Model
d. Economic growth

22. The _____ is a measure of statistical dispersion, commonly used as a measure of inequality of income distribution or inequality of wealth distribution. It is defined as a ratio with values between 0 and 1: A low _____ indicates more equal income or wealth distribution, while a high _____ indicates more unequal distribution. 0 corresponds to perfect equality (everyone having exactly the same income) and 1 corresponds to perfect inequality (where one person has all the income, while everyone else has zero income.)

a. Suits index
b. Compensating variation
c. Leapfrogging
d. Gini coefficient

23. In economics, _____ is how a natione;s total economy is distributed among its population. ._____ has always been a central concern of economic theory and economic policy. Classical economists such as Adam Smith, Thomas Malthus and David Ricardo were mainly concerned with factor _____, that is, the distribution of income between the main factors of production, land, labour and capital.

a. Income distribution
b. Authorised capital
c. Equipment trust certificate
d. Eco commerce

24. In economics, a _____ exists when the production or use of goods and services by the market is not efficient. That is, there exists another outcome where all involved can be made better off. _____s can be viewed as scenarios where individuals' pursuit of pure self-interest leads to results that are not efficient - that can be improved upon from the societal point-of-view.

a. Financial economics
b. Market failure
c. Fixed exchange rate
d. General equilibrium

Chapter 16. Government Taxation and Expenditure

25. In economics, a _____ is a good that is non-rivaled and non-excludable. This means, respectively, that consumption of the good by one individual does not reduce availability of the good for consumption by others; and that no one can be effectively excluded from using the good. In the real world, there may be no such thing as an absolutely non-rivaled and non-excludable good; but economists think that some goods approximate the concept closely enough for the analysis to be economically useful.

    a. Demand-pull theory
    b. Public good
    c. Neoclassical synthesis
    d. Happiness economics

26. There are two main interpretations of the idea of a _____:

- A model in which the state assumes primary responsibility for the welfare of its citizens. This responsibility in theory ought to be comprehensive, because all aspects of welfare are considered and universally applied to citizens as a 'right'. _____ can also mean the creation of a 'social safety net' of minimum standards of varying forms of welfare. Here is found some confusion between a '_____' and a 'welfare society' in common debate about the definition of the term.
- The provision of welfare in society. In many '_____s', especially in continental Europe, welfare is not actually provided by the state, but by a combination of independent, voluntary, mutualist and government services. The functional provider of benefits and services may be a central or state government, a state-sponsored company or agency, a private corporation, a charity or another form of non-profit organization. However, this phenomenon has been more appropriately termed a 'welfare society,' and the term 'welfare system' has been used to describe the range of _____ and welfare society mixes that are found.

The English term '_____' is believed by Asa Briggs to have been coined by Archbishop William Temple during the Second World War, contrasting wartime Britain with the 'warfare state' of Nazi Germany. Friedrich Hayek contends that the term derived from the older German word Wohlfahrtsstaat, which itself was used by nineteenth century historians to describe a variant of the ideal of Polizeistaat . It was fully developed by the German academic Sozialpolitiker--'socialists of the chair'--from 1870 and first implemented through Bismarck's 'state socialism'. Bismarck's policies have also been seen as the creation of a _____.

    a. Welfare state
    b. 130-30 fund
    c. 1921 recession
    d. 100-year flood

27. In mathematics, a _____ is a constant multiplicative factor of a certain object. For example, in the expression $9x^2$, the _____ of x^2 is 9.

The object can be such things as a variable, a vector, a function, etc.

    a. 1921 recession
    b. 100-year flood
    c. 130-30 fund
    d. Coefficient

Chapter 16. Government Taxation and Expenditure

28. _____ is used to refer to a number of related concepts. It is the using resources in such a way as to maximize the production of goods and services. A system can be called economically efficient if:

- No one can be made better off without making someone else worse off.
- More output cannot be obtained without increasing the amount of inputs.
- Production proceeds at the lowest possible per-unit cost.

These definitions of efficiency are not equivalent, but they are all encompassed by the idea that nothing more can be achieved given the resources available.

An economic system is more efficient if it can provide more goods and services for society without using more resources.

a. ACCRA Cost of Living Index
b. ACEA agreement
c. Efficient contract theory
d. Economic efficiency

29. A _____ is an object whose consumption increases the utility of the consumer, for which the quantity demanded exceeds the quantity supplied at zero price. _____ s are usually modeled as having diminishing marginal utility. The first individual purchase has high utility; the second has less.

a. Pie method
b. Good
c. Merit good
d. Composite good

30. In economics, _____ is the transfer of income, wealth or property from some individuals to others.

One premise of _____ is that money should be distributed to benefit the poorer members of society, and that the rich have an obligation to assist the poor, thus creating a more financially egalitarian society. Another argument is that the rich exploit the poor or otherwise gain unfair benefits.

a. Redistribution
b. 130-30 fund
c. 100-year flood
d. 1921 recession

31. In mathematics, an _____ is a statement about the relative size or order of two objects, or about whether they are the same or not

- The notation a < b means that a is less than b.
- The notation a > b means that a is greater than b.
- The notation a ≠ b means that a is not equal to b, but does not say that one is greater than the other or even that they can be compared in size.

In each statement above, a is not equal to b. These relations are known as strict inequalities. The notation a < b may also be read as 'a is strictly less than b'.

a. AD-IA Model
b. ACCRA Cost of Living Index
c. Inequality
d. ACEA agreement

Chapter 16. Government Taxation and Expenditure

32. The term _____ refers to economy-wide fluctuations in production or economic activity over several months or years. These fluctuations occur around a long-term growth trend, and typically involve shifts over time between periods of relatively rapid economic growth (expansion or boom), and periods of relative stagnation or decline (contraction or recession.)

These fluctuations are often measured using the growth rate of real gross domestic product.

- a. Tobit model
- b. Business cycle
- c. Nominal value
- d. Consumer theory

33. The _____ is an economic and political union of 27 member states, located primarily in Europe. It was established by the Treaty of Maastricht on 1 November 1993, upon the foundations of the pre-existing European Economic Community. With a population of almost 500 million, the _____ generates an estimated 30% share (US$18.4 trillion in 2008) of the nominal gross world product.
- a. ACEA agreement
- b. European Union
- c. European Court of Justice
- d. ACCRA Cost of Living Index

34. The term _____ refers to government debt, expenditures and revenues, or to finance (particularly financial revenue) in general.

- _____ deficit is the budget deficit of federal or local government
- _____ policy is the discretionary spending of governments. Contrasts with monetary policy.
- _____ year and _____ quarter are reporting periods for firms and other agencies.

- a. Bucket shop
- b. Procter ' Gamble
- c. Drawdown
- d. Fiscal

35. In economics, _____ is the use of government spending and revenue collection to influence the economy.

_____ can be contrasted with the other main type of economic policy, monetary policy, which attempts to stabilize the economy by controlling interest rates and the supply of money. The two main instruments of _____ are government spending and taxation.

- a. Sustainable investment rule
- b. 100-year flood
- c. Fiscalism
- d. Fiscal policy

36. The _____ was a worldwide economic downturn starting in most places in 1929 and ending at different times in the 1930s or early 1940s for different countries. It was the largest and most important economic depression in the 20th century, and is used in the 21st century as an example of how far the world's economy can fall. The _____ originated in the United States; historians most often use as a starting date the stock market crash on October 29, 1929, known as Black Tuesday.
- a. Jarrow March
- b. Wall Street Crash of 1929
- c. British Empire Economic Conference
- d. Great Depression

Chapter 16. Government Taxation and Expenditure

37. _____ is exchange of capital, goods, and services across international borders or territories. In most countries, it represents a significant share of gross domestic product (GDP.) While _____ has been present throughout much of history, its economic, social, and political importance has been on the rise in recent centuries.

   a. International trade
   b. Incoterms
   c. Import license
   d. Intra-industry trade

38. _____ is the process by which the government, central bank (ii) availability of money, and (iii) cost of money or rate of interest, in order to attain a set of objectives oriented towards the growth and stability of the economy. Monetary theory provides insight into how to craft optimal _____.

   _____ is referred to as either being an expansionary policy where an expansionary policy increases the total supply of money in the economy, and a contractionary policy decreases the total money supply.

   a. 1921 recession
   b. 130-30 fund
   c. 100-year flood
   d. Monetary policy

39. A _____ is a general term that describes any government policy or regulation that restricts international trade. The barriers can take many forms, including the following terms that include many restrictions in international trade within multiple countries that import and export any items of trade.

   - Import duty
   - Import licenses
   - Export licenses
   - Import quotas
   - Tariffs
   - Subsidies
   - Non-tariff barriers to trade
   - Voluntary Export Restraints
   - Local Content Requirements
   - Embargo

   Most _____s work on the same principle: the imposition of some sort of cost on trade that raises the price of the traded products. If two or more nations repeatedly use _____s against each other, then a trade war results.

   a. National Foreign Trade Council
   b. Trade barrier
   c. Certificate of origin
   d. Global financial system

40. _____ is a voluntary transfer of resources from one country to another, given at least partly with the objective of benefiting the recipient country. It may have other functions as well: it may be given as a signal of diplomatic approval, or to strengthen a military ally, to reward a government for behaviour desired by the donor, to extend the donor's cultural influence, to provide infrastructure needed by the donor for resource extraction from the recipient country, or to gain other kinds of commercial access. Humanitarianism and altruism are, nevertheless, significant motivations for the giving of _____.

   a. AD-IA Model
   b. Aid
   c. ACEA agreement
   d. ACCRA Cost of Living Index

Chapter 16. Government Taxation and Expenditure

41. _____ is any long-term change in the patterns of average weather of a specific region or the Earth as a whole. _____ reflects abnormal variations to the Earth's climate and subsequent effects on other parts of the Earth, such as in the ice caps over durations ranging from decades to millions of years.

In recent usage, especially in the context of environmental policy, _____ usually refers to changes in modern climate

- a. Climate change
- c. 1921 recession
- b. 100-year flood
- d. 130-30 fund

42. _____ refers to the actions that governments take in the economic field. It covers the systems for setting interest rates and government deficit as well as the labour market, national ownership, and many other areas of government.

Such policies are often influenced by international institutions like the International Monetary Fund or World Bank as well as political beliefs and the consequent policies of parties.

- a. ACEA agreement
- c. AD-IA Model
- b. ACCRA Cost of Living Index
- d. Economic policy

43. The term _____ is applied broadly to a variety of situations in which some financial institutions or assets suddenly lose a large part of their value. In the 19th and early 20th centuries, many financial crises were associated with banking panics, and many recessions coincided with these panics. Other situations that are often called financial crises include stock market crashes and the bursting of other financial bubbles, currency crises, and sovereign defaults.

- a. Macroeconomics
- c. Co-operative economics
- b. Financial crisis
- d. Market failure

44. _____ was a survey conducted by the U.S. Department of Justice to gauge the prevalence of alcohol and illegal drug use among prior arrestees. It was a reformulation of the prior Drug Use Forecasting (DUF) program, focused on five drugs in particular: cocaine, marijuana, methamphetamine, opiates, and PCP.

Participants were randomly selected from arrest records in major metropolitan areas; because no personally identifying information is taken from each record chosen, the resulting data can be correlated to arrest rates, but not to the total population of persons charged.

- a. AD-IA Model
- c. ACCRA Cost of Living Index
- b. ACEA agreement
- d. Arrestee Drug Abuse Monitoring

45. As a subfield of public economics, _____ is concerned with 'understanding which functions and instruments are best centralized and which are best placed in the sphere of decentralized levels of government' (Oates, 1999.) In other words, it is the study of how competencies (expenditure side) and fiscal instruments (revenue side) are allocated across different (vertical) layers of the administration.

An important part of its subject matter is the system of transfer payments or grants by which a central government shares its revenues with lower levels of government.

a. 130-30 fund
b. 100-year flood
c. 1921 recession
d. Fiscal federalism

46. _____ in economic theory is the use of modern economic tools to study problems that are traditionally in the province of political science.

In particular, it studies the behavior of politicians and government officials as mostly self-interested agents and their interactions in the social system either as such or under alternative constitutional rules. These can be represented a number of ways, including standard constrained utility maximization, game theory, or decision theory.

a. Public choice
b. Rational ignorance
c. Public interest theory
d. Paradox of voting

47. _____ was a Scottish moral philosopher and a pioneer of political economy. One of the key figures of the Scottish Enlightenment, Smith is the author of The Theory of Moral Sentiments and An Inquiry into the Nature and Causes of the Wealth of Nations. The latter, usually abbreviated as The Wealth of Nations, is considered his magnum opus and the first modern work of economics.

a. Adolph Fischer
b. Adam Smith
c. Adolf Hitler
d. Alan Greenspan

48. _____ in political thought refers to economic theories of social organization advocating collective ownership and administration of the means of production and distribution of goods, and a society characterized by equality for all individuals, with an egalitarian method of compensation. Modern _____ originated in the late 19th-century intellectual and working class political movement that criticized the effects of industrialization and private ownership on society. Karl Marx posited that _____ would be achieved via class struggle and a proletarian revolution after a transitional stage from capitalism called the dictatorship of the proletariat.

a. Adam Smith
b. Socialism
c. Adolph Fischer
d. Adolf Hitler

49. The _____ is a situation noted by the Marquis de Condorcet in the late 18th century, in which collective preferences can be cyclic, even if the preferences of individual voters are not. This is paradoxical, because it means that majority wishes can be in conflict with each other. When this occurs, it is because the conflicting majorities are each made up of different groups of individuals.

a. 1921 recession
b. Voting paradox
c. 100-year flood
d. 130-30 fund

50. The _____ is the apparent contradiction that although water is on the whole more useful, in terms of survival, than diamonds, diamonds command a higher price in the market. The economist Adam Smith is often considered to be the classic presenter of this paradox. Nicolaus Copernicus, John Locke, John Law and others had previously tried to explain the disparity.

a. 100-year flood
b. St. Petersburg paradox
c. 130-30 fund
d. Paradox of value

Chapter 16. Government Taxation and Expenditure

51. A _____ is a period used for calculating annual financial statements in businesses and other organizations. In many jurisdictions, regulatory laws regarding accounting and taxation require such reports once per twelve months, but do not require that the period reported on constitutes a calendar year (i.e., January through December.) _____s vary between businesses and countries.
- a. 130-30 fund
- b. 100-year flood
- c. 1921 recession
- d. Fiscal year

52. _____ is a company's financial statement that indicates how the revenue is transformed into the net income The purpose of the _____ is to show managers and investors whether the company made or lost money during the period being reported.

The important thing to remember about an _____ is that it represents a period of time.

- a. ACCRA Cost of Living Index
- b. Income statement
- c. AD-IA Model
- d. ACEA agreement

53. The phrase _____, according to the Organization for Economic Co-operation and Development, refers to 'creative work undertaken on a systematic basis in order to increase the stock of knowledge, including knowledge of man, culture and society, and the use of this stock of knowledge to devise new applications [sic]'

New product design and development is more than often a crucial factor in the survival of a company. In an industry that is fast changing, firms must continually revise their design and range of products. This is necessary due to continuous technology change and development as well as other competitors and the changing preference of customers.

- a. 130-30 fund
- b. 1921 recession
- c. 100-year flood
- d. Research and development

54. _____ is used to assign the available resources in an economic way. It is part of resource management.

In strategic planning,is a plan for using available resources, for example human resources, especially in the near term, to achieve goals for the future.

- a. Resource allocation
- b. 1921 recession
- c. 100-year flood
- d. 130-30 fund

55. The principle that taxes should vary according to an individual's level of wealth or income is the _____ principle.
- a. AD-IA Model
- b. Ability-to-pay
- c. ACEA agreement
- d. ACCRA Cost of Living Index

56. _____ is the concept or idea of fairness in economics, particularly as to taxation or welfare economics.

In welfare economics, _____ may be distinguished from economic efficiency in overall evaluation of social welfare. Although '_____' has broader uses, it may be posed as a counterpart to economic inequality in yielding a 'good' distribution of welfare.

a. ACEA agreement
b. ACCRA Cost of Living Index
c. Equity
d. AD-IA Model

57. The term direct tax has more than one meaning: a colloquial meaning and, in the United States, a constitutional law meaning. Certain taxes may be _____ in the colloquial sense but indirect taxes in the constitutional sense.

In the UK, direct tax refers to tax levied directly off of an organisation or an individual person, like income tax.

a. National War Tax Resistance Coordinating Committee
b. Taxation as theft
c. Honorarium
d. Direct taxes

58. An _____ is a tax levied on the financial income of people, corporations, or other legal entities. Various _____ systems exist, with varying degrees of tax incidence. Income taxation can be progressive, proportional, or regressive.
   a. ACCRA Cost of Living Index
   b. ACEA agreement
   c. AD-IA Model
   d. Income tax

59. The term _____ has more than one meaning.

In the colloquial sense, an _____, or goods and services tax (GST)) is a tax collected by an intermediary (such as a retail store) from the person who bears the ultimate economic burden of the tax (such as the customer.) The intermediary later files a tax return and forwards the tax proceeds to government with the return.

a. Indirect tax
b. Optimal tax
c. User charge
d. Olivera-Tanzi effect

60. A _____ is a tax by which the tax rate increases as the taxable amount increases. 'Progressive' describes a distribution effect on income or expenditure, referring to the way the rate progresses from low to high, where the average tax rate is less than the marginal tax rate. It can be applied to individual taxes or to a tax system as a whole; a year, multi-year, or lifetime.
   a. Proportional tax
   b. 130-30 fund
   c. 100-year flood
   d. Progressive tax

61. A _____ is a tax imposed so that the tax rate is fixed as the amount subject to taxation increases. In simple terms, it imposes an equal burden (relative to resources) on the rich and poor. 'Proportional' describes a distribution effect on income or expenditure, referring to the way the rate remains consistent (does not progress from 'low to high' or 'high to low' as income or consumption changes), where the marginal tax rate is equal to the average tax rate.
   a. 100-year flood
   b. Regressive tax
   c. 130-30 fund
   d. Proportional tax

62. A _____ is a tax imposed in such a manner that the tax rate decreases as the amount subject to taxation increases. In simple terms, a _____ imposes a greater burden (relative to resources) on the poor than on the rich -- there is an inverse relationship between the tax rate and the taxpayer's ability to pay as measured by assets, consumption, or income. 'Regressive' describes a distribution effect on income or expenditure, referring to the way the rate progresses from high to low, where the average tax rate exceeds the marginal tax rate.

a. 130-30 fund	b. 100-year flood
c. Proportional tax	d. Regressive tax

63. Under the system of feudalism, a _____, fief, feud, feoff often consisted of inheritable lands or revenue-producing property granted by a liege lord, generally to a vassal, in return for a form of allegiance, originally to give him the means to fulfill his military duties when called upon. However anything of value could be held in fief, such as an office, a right of exploitation (e.g., hunting, fishing) or any other type of revenue, rather than the land it comes from.

Originally, the feudal institution of vassalage did not imply the giving or receiving of landholdings (which were granted only as a reward for loyalty), but by the eighth century the giving of a landholding was becoming standard.

a. 100-year flood	b. 130-30 fund
c. 1921 recession	d. Fiefdom

Chapter 16. Government Taxation and Expenditure

64. A _____ is:

- Rewrite _____, in generative grammar and computer science
- Standardization, a formal and widely-accepted statement, fact, definition, or qualification
- Operation, a determinate _____ for performing a mathematical operation and obtaining a certain result (Mathematics, Logic)
    - Unary operation
    - Binary operation
- _____ of inference, a function from sets of formulae to formulae (Mathematics, Logic)
- _____ of thumb, principle with broad application that is not intended to be strictly accurate or reliable for every situation. Also often simply referred to as a _____
- Moral, an atomic element of a moral code for guiding choices in human behavior
- Heuristic, a quantized '_____' which shows a tendency or probability for successful function
- A regulation, as in sports
- A Production _____, as in computer science
- Procedural law, a _____ set governing the application of laws to cases
    - A law, which may informally be called a '_____'
    - A court ruling, a decision by a court
- In the U.S. Government, a regulation mandated by Congress, but written or expanded upon by the Executive Branch.
- Norm (sociology), an informal but widely accepted _____, concept, truth, definition, or qualification (social norms, legal norms, coding norms)
- Norm (philosophy), a kind of sentence or a reason to act, feel or believe
- 'Rulership' is the concept of governance by a government:
    - Military _____, governance by a military body
    - Monastic _____, a collection of precepts that guides the life of monks or nuns in a religious order where the superior holds the place of Christ
- Slide _____

- '_____,' a song by Ayumi Hamasaki
- '_____,' a song by rapper Nas
- '_____s,' an album by the band The Whitest Boy Alive
- _____s: Pyaar Ka Superhit Formula, a 2003 Bollywood film
- ruler, an instrument for measuring lengths
- _____, a component of an astrolabe, circumferator or similar instrument
- The _____s, a bestselling self-help book
- _____ Project (Run Up-to-date Linux Everywhere), a project that aims to use up-to-date Linux software on old PCs
- _____ engine, a software system that helps managing business _____s
- Ja _____, a hip hop artist
    - R.U.L.E., a 2005 greatest hits album by rapper Ja _____
- '_____s,' a KMFDM song

a. Technocracy
b. Procter ' Gamble
c. Demand
d. Rule

Chapter 16. Government Taxation and Expenditure

65. To _____ is to impose a financial charge or other levy upon a taxpayer by a state or the functional equivalent of a state.

_____es are also imposed by many subnational entities. _____es consist of direct _____ or indirect _____, and may be paid in money or as its labour equivalent (often but not always unpaid.)

a. 1921 recession
c. Tax
b. 130-30 fund
d. 100-year flood

66. To tax is to impose a financial charge or other levy upon a taxpayer by a state or the functional equivalent of a state.

_____ are also imposed by many subnational entities. _____ consist of direct tax or indirect tax, and may be paid in money or as its labour equivalent (often but not always unpaid.)

a. 1921 recession
c. 100-year flood
b. 130-30 fund
d. Taxes

67. The _____ is 'the basic residential unit in which economic production, consumption, inheritance, child rearing, and shelter are organized and carried out'; [the _____] 'may or may not be synonymous with family'.

The _____ is the basic unit of analysis in many social, microeconomic and government models. The term refers to all individuals who live in the same dwelling.

a. 130-30 fund
c. Family economics
b. 100-year flood
d. Household

68. In business and accounting, _____ are everything of value that is owned by a person or company. It is a claim on the property your income of a borrower. The balance sheet of a firm records the monetary value of the _____ owned by the firm.

a. ACEA agreement
c. Amortization schedule
b. ACCRA Cost of Living Index
d. Assets

69. In statistics, the _____ problem occurs when one considers a set of statistical inferences simultaneously. Errors in inference, including confidence intervals that fail to include their corresponding population parameters are more likely to occur when one considers the family as a whole. Several statistical techniques have been developed to prevent this from happening, allowing significance levels for single and _____ to be directly compared.

a. False discovery rate
c. Hypotheses suggested by the data
b. Familywise error rate
d. Multiple comparisons

70. A _____ refers to any type debt instrument, such as a loan, bond, mortgage that does not have a fixed rate of interest over the life of the instrument. Such debt typically uses an index or other base rate for establishing the interest rate for each relevant period. One of the most common rates to use as the basis for applying interest rates is the London Inter-bank Offered Rate, or LIBOR

a. Moneylender
c. Money market
b. Disposal tax effect
d. Floating interest rate

Chapter 16. Government Taxation and Expenditure

71. The term _____ describes two different concepts:

- The first is a recognition of partial payment already made towards taxes due.
- The second is a state benefit paid to workers through the tax system, which has the effect of increasing (rather than reducing) net income.

Within the Australian, Canadian, United Kingdom, and United States tax systems, a _____ is a recognition of partial payment already made towards taxes due. A similar concept exists (fr:Avoir fiscal) in the French tax system. This situation arises, for example, when standard rate tax has been deducted at source, but the tax-payer is subject to further taxation at a higher rate. It also applies in dividend imputation systems.

a. 100-year flood
c. 130-30 fund
b. 1921 recession
d. Tax credit

72. A _____ product is a product designed for cheapness and short-term convenience rather than medium to long-term durability, with most products only intended for single use. The term is also sometimes used for products that may last several months (ex. _____ air filters) to distinguish from similar products that last indefinitely (ex.

a. 1921 recession
c. 130-30 fund
b. 100-year flood
d. Disposable

73. _____ is gross income minus income tax on that income.

Discretionary income is income after subtracting taxes and normal expenses (such as rent or mortgage, utilities, insurance, medical, transportation, property maintenance, child support, inflation, food and sundries, 'c.) to maintain a certain standard of living.

a. Stamp Act
c. Taxation as theft
b. Disposable income
d. Disposable personal income

74. A _____ is a tax system with a constant tax rate. Usually the term _____ would refer to household income (and sometimes corporate profits) being taxed at one marginal rate, in contrast with progressive taxes that may vary according to such parameters as income or usage levels. _____es generally offer simplicity in the tax code, which has been reported to increase compliance and decrease administration costs.

a. 130-30 fund
c. 1921 recession
b. 100-year flood
d. Flat tax

75. In a company, _____ is the sum of all financial records of salaries, wages, bonuses and deductions.

A paycheck, is traditionally a paper document issued by an employer to pay an employee for services rendered. While most commonly used in the United States, recently the physical paycheck has been increasingly replaced by electronic direct deposit to bank accounts.

a. Total Expense Ratio
c. 100-year flood
b. Tax expense
d. Payroll

Chapter 16. Government Taxation and Expenditure

76. A _____ is a tax on spending on goods and services. The term refers to a system with a tax base of consumption. It usually takes the form of an indirect tax, such as a sales tax or value added tax.
   a. 130-30 fund
   b. 1921 recession
   c. 100-year flood
   d. Consumption tax

77. _____, in law and economics, is a form of risk management primarily used to hedge against the risk of a contingent loss. _____ is defined as the equitable transfer of the risk of a loss, from one entity to another, in exchange for a premium, and can be thought of as a guaranteed small loss to prevent a large, possibly devastating loss. An insurer is a company selling the _____; an insured or policyholder is the person or entity buying the _____.
   a. ACEA agreement
   b. ACCRA Cost of Living Index
   c. AD-IA Model
   d. Insurance

78. _____s are payments made by a corporation to its shareholders. It is the portion of corporate profits paid out to stockholders. When a corporation earns a profit or surplus, that money can be put to two uses: it can either be re-invested in the business (called retained earnings), or it can be paid to the shareholders as a _____.
   a. Dividend
   b. Dividend yield
   c. Dividend cover
   d. Dividend puzzle

79. _____ is an ad valorem tax that an owner is required to pay on the value of the property being taxed. _____ can be defined as 'generally, tax imposed by municipalities upon owners of property within their jurisdiction based on the value of such property.' There are three species or types of property: Land, Improvements to Land (immovable manmade objects; i.e., buildings), and Personal (movable manmade objects.) Real estate, real property or realty are all terms for the combination of land and improvements.
   a. Community property
   b. Property tax
   c. Bank regulation
   d. Chief Financial Officers Act of 1990

80. A _____ is a consumption tax charged at the point of purchase for certain goods and services. The tax is usually set as a percentage by the government charging the tax. There is usually a list of exemptions.
   a. 130-30 fund
   b. 1921 recession
   c. Sales tax
   d. 100-year flood

81. The supply of labor is the number of total hours that workers wish to work at a given real wage rate.

_____ curves are derived from the 'labor-leisure' trade-off. More hours worked earn higher incomes but necessitate a cut in the amount of leisure that workers enjoy.

   a. Human trafficking
   b. Labor supply
   c. Creative capitalism
   d. Late capitalism

82. _____ is a school of macroeconomic thought that argues that economic growth can be most effectively created using incentives for people to produce (supply) goods and services, such as adjusting income tax and capital gains tax rates, and by allowing greater flexibility by reducing regulation. Consumers will then benefit from a greater supply of goods and services at lower prices.

The term _____ was coined by journalist Jude Wanniski in 1975, and popularized the ideas of economists Robert Mundell and Arthur Laffer.

a. Commodity trading advisors
b. Clap note
c. Fiscal stimulus plans
d. Supply-side economics

83. In economics and especially in the theory of competition, _____ are obstacles in the path of a firm that make it difficult to enter a given market.

_____ are the source of a firm's pricing power - the ability of a firm to raise prices without losing all its customers.

The term refers to hindrances that an individual may face while trying to gain entrance into a profession or trade.

a. Limit price
b. Group boycott
c. Barriers to entry
d. Social dumping

84. The _____ is the market for securities, where companies and governments can raise longterm funds. It is a market in which money is lent for periods longer than a year. The _____ includes the stock market and the bond market.

a. Financial instrument
b. Multi-family office
c. Performance attribution
d. Capital market

85. In law and economics, the _____, describes the economic efficiency of an economic allocation or outcome in the presence of externalities. The theorem states that when trade in an externality is possible and there are no transaction costs, bargaining will lead to an efficient outcome regardless of the initial allocation of property rights. In practice, obstacles to bargaining or poorly defined property rights can prevent Coasian bargaining.

a. General Mining Act of 1872
b. Means test
c. Prior appropriation water rights
d. Coase theorem

86. A _____ is a tax that is a fixed amount no matter what the change in circumstance of the taxed entity. (A lump-sum subsidy or lump-sum redistribution is defined similarly.) It is a regressive tax, such that the lower income is, the higher percentage of income applicable to the tax.

a. Budget deficit
b. Funding body
c. Lump-sum tax
d. Grant-in-aid

87. _____, short for Ecological taxation, can refer to:

A policy that introduces taxes intended to promote ecologically sustainable activities via economic incentives. Such a policy can complement or avert the need for regulatory approaches. Often, such a policy intends to maintain overall tax revenue by proportionately reducing other taxes, e.g. on human labor and renewable resources, in which case it is known as the green tax shift towards ecological taxation.

a. Ecotax
b. AD-IA Model
c. ACCRA Cost of Living Index
d. ACEA agreement

88. _____ is a concept within public finance, a sub-discipline within economics, that refers to the combined overall economic impact of both government taxation and expenditures on the real economic income of individuals. While taxation reduces the economic well-being of individuals, government expenditures raise their economic well-being. _____ is the term for the overall impact of government taxing and spending considered together.

Chapter 16. Government Taxation and Expenditure

a. Lump-sum tax
c. Tax increment financing
b. Funding body
d. Fiscal incidence

89. In economics, _____ is the analysis of the effect of a particular tax on the distribution of economic welfare. _____ is said to 'fall' upon the group that, at the end of the day, bears the burden of the tax. The key concept is that the _____ or tax burden does not depend on where the revenue is collected, but on the price elasticity of demand and price elasticity of supply.

a. Tax incidence
c. 1921 recession
b. 100-year flood
d. 130-30 fund

90. In economics, the _____ is used to illustrate the idea that increases in the rate of taxation do not necessarily increase tax revenue. (For instance, whereas a 0% income tax rate will generate no revenue, neither will a 100% rate, as citizens will have no incentive to make money.) Increasing taxes beyond the peak of the curve point will decrease tax revenue.

a. Laffer curve
c. 100-year flood
b. 1921 recession
d. 130-30 fund

Chapter 17. Promoting More Efficient Markets

1. _____ is a situation in which the limited resources of a firm are allocated in accordance with the wishes of consumers. An allocatively efficient economy produces an 'optimal mix' of commodities. A firm is allocatively efficient when its price is equal to its marginal costs (that is, P = MC) in a perfect market.

   a. ACCRA Cost of Living Index   b. ACEA agreement
   c. Allocative efficiency   d. Economic efficiency

2. Competition law, known in the United States as _____ law, has three main elements:

- prohibiting agreements or practices that restrict free trading and competition between business entities. This includes in particular the repression of cartels.
- banning abusive behaviour by a firm dominating a market, or anti-competitive practices that tend to lead to such a dominant position. Practices controlled in this way may include predatory pricing, tying, price gouging, refusal to deal, and many others.
- supervising the mergers and acquisitions of large corporations, including some joint ventures. Transactions that are considered to threaten the competitive process can be prohibited altogether, or approved subject to 'remedies' such as an obligation to divest part of the merged business or to offer licences or access to facilities to enable other businesses to continue competing.

The substance and practice of competition law varies from jurisdiction to jurisdiction. Protecting the interests of consumers (consumer welfare) and ensuring that entrepreneurs have an opportunity to compete in the market economy are often treated as important objectives. Competition law is closely connected with law on deregulation of access to markets, state aids and subsidies, the privatisation of state owned assets and the establishment of independent sector regulators. In recent decades, competition law has been viewed as a way to provide better public services.

   a. Antitrust   b. Intellectual property law
   c. United Kingdom competition law   d. Anti-Inflation Act

3. In economic theory, _____ is the competitive situation in any market where the conditions necessary for perfect competition are not satisfied. It is a market structure that does not meet the conditions of perfect competition.

Forms of _____ include:

- Monopoly, in which there is only one seller of a good.
- Oligopoly, in which there is a small number of sellers.
- Monopolistic competition, in which there are many sellers producing highly differentiated goods.
- Monopsony, in which there is only one buyer of a good.
- Oligopsony, in which there is a small number of buyers.

There may also be _____ in markets due to buyers or sellers lacking information about prices and the goods being traded.

There may also be _____ due to a time lag in a market.

a. AD-IA Model
b. ACCRA Cost of Living Index
c. ACEA agreement
d. Imperfect competition

4. The _____ was a regulatory body in the United States created by the Interstate Commerce Act of 1887, which was signed into law by President Grover Cleveland. The agency was abolished in 1995, and the agency's remaining functions were transferred to the Surface Transportation Board.

The Commission's five members were appointed by the President with the consent of the United States Senate.

a. Office of Thrift Supervision
b. ACEA agreement
c. Interstate Commerce Commission
d. ACCRA Cost of Living Index

5. In economics, the _____ is the term economists use to describe the self-regulating nature of the marketplace. The _____ is a metaphor coined by the economist Adam Smith in The Wealth of Nations.

Adam Smith mentions the metaphor in Book IV of The Wealth of Nations, arguing that people in any society will certainly employ their capital in foreign trading only if the profits available by that method far exceed those available locally, and that in such a case it is better for society as a whole if they so did.

a. AD-IA Model
b. ACEA agreement
c. ACCRA Cost of Living Index
d. Invisible hand

6. In economics, a _____ exists when the production or use of goods and services by the market is not efficient. That is, there exists another outcome where all involved can be made better off. _____s can be viewed as scenarios where individuals' pursuit of pure self-interest leads to results that are not efficient - that can be improved upon from the societal point-of-view.

a. Financial economics
b. Market failure
c. Fixed exchange rate
d. General equilibrium

7. In economics, _____ is the ability of a firm to alter the market price of a good or service. A firm with _____ can raise prices without losing all customers to competitors.

When a firm has _____ it faces a downward-sloping demand curve.

a. Market power
b. Revenue-cap regulation
c. Price makers
d. Pacman conjecture

8. In neoclassical economics and microeconomics, _____ describes the perfect being a market in which there are many small firms, all producing homogeneous goods. In the short term, such markets are productively inefficient as output will not occur where mc is equal to ac, but allocatively efficient, as output under _____ will always occur where mc is equal to mr, and therefore where mc equals ar. However, in the long term, such markets are both allocatively and productively efficient.

a. General equilibrium
b. Co-operative economics
c. Perfect competition
d. Law of supply

9. A _____ describes one of a number of pieces of legislation relating to the reduction of smog and air pollution in general. The use by governments to enforce clean air standards has contributed to an improvement in human health and longer life spans. Critics argue it has also sapped corporate profits and contributed to outsourcing, while defenders counter that improved environmental air quality has generated more jobs than it has eliminated.
   a. 130-30 fund
   b. Smog
   c. Clean Air Act
   d. 100-year flood

10. _____s is the social science that studies the production, distribution, and consumption of goods and services. The term _____s comes from the Ancient Greek oá¼°κονομῖα from oá¼¶κος (oikos, 'house') + vĺŒμος (nomos, 'custom' or 'law'), hence 'rules of the house(hold)'. Current _____ models developed out of the broader field of political economy in the late 19th century, owing to a desire to use an empirical approach more akin to the physical sciences.
    a. Opportunity cost
    b. Inflation
    c. Energy economics
    d. Economic

11. _____ are conceptually similar to economies of scale. Whereas economies of scale primarily refer to efficiencies associated with supply-side changes, such as increasing or decreasing the scale of production, of a single product type, _____ refer to efficiencies primarily associated with demand-side changes, such as increasing or decreasing the scope of marketing and distribution, of different types of products. _____ are one of the main reasons for such marketing strategies as product bundling, product lining, and family branding.
    a. Economies of scale
    b. Economic production quantity
    c. Economies of scope
    d. Isoquant

12. In economics, a _____ is a mechanism that allows people to easily buy and sell (trade) financial securities (such as stocks and bonds), commodities (such as precious metals or agricultural goods), and other fungible items of value at low transaction costs and at prices that reflect the efficient-market hypothesis.

_____s have evolved significantly over several hundred years and are undergoing constant innovation to improve liquidity.

Both general markets (where many commodities are traded) and specialized markets (where only one commodity is traded) exist.

   a. Market anomaly
   b. Convertible arbitrage
   c. Noise trader
   d. Financial market

13. In economics, a _____ occurs when, due to the economies of scale of a particular industry, the maximum efficiency of production and distribution is realized through a single supplier.

Natural monopolies arise where the largest supplier in an industry, often the first supplier in a market, has an overwhelming cost advantage over other actual or potential competitors. This tends to be the case in industries where capital costs predominate, creating economies of scale which are large in relation to the size of the market, and hence high barriers to entry; examples include water services and electricity.

   a. Collective goods
   b. Common-pool resource
   c. Privatizing profits and socializing losses
   d. Natural monopoly

14. The _____ refers to the 'common well-being' or 'general welfare.' The _____ is central to policy debates, politics, democracy and the nature of government itself. While nearly everyone claims that aiding the common well-being or general welfare is positive, there is little, if any, consensus on what exactly constitutes the _____.

There are different views on how many members of the public must benefit from an action before it can be declared to be in the _____: at one extreme, an action has to benefit every single member of society in order to be truly in the _____; at the other extreme, any action can be in the _____ as long as it benefits some of the population and harms none.

- a. Second-class citizen
- b. Stealth tax
- c. Power Elite
- d. Public interest

15. A public utility (usually just utility) is an organization that maintains the infrastructure for a public service (often also providing a service using that infrastructure.) _____ are subject to forms of public control and regulation ranging from local community-based groups to state-wide government monopolies. Common arguments in favor of regulation include the desire to control market power, facilitate competition, promote investment or system expansion, or stabilize markets.
- a. 100-year flood
- b. 130-30 fund
- c. 1921 recession
- d. Public utilities

16. _____ is the removal or simplification of government rules and regulations that constrain the operation of market forces. _____ does not mean elimination of laws against fraud, but eliminating or reducing government control of how business is done, thereby moving toward a more free market.

The stated rationale for '_____' is often that fewer and simpler regulations will lead to a raised level of competitiveness, therefore higher productivity, more efficiency and lower prices overall.

- a. Fundamental psychological law
- b. Macroeconomic policy instruments
- c. Deregulation
- d. Secular basis

17. In economics and sociology, an _____ is any factor (financial or non-financial) that enables or motivates a particular course of action, or counts as a reason for preferring one choice to the alternatives. It is an expectation that encourages people to behave in a certain way. Since human beings are purposeful creatures, the study of _____ structures is central to the study of all economic activity (both in terms of individual decision-making and in terms of co-operation and competition within a larger institutional structure.)
- a. Incentive
- b. Isocost
- c. Epstein-Zin preferences
- d. Economic reform

18. _____ is a fee paid on borrowed assets. It is the price paid for the use of borrowed money, or, money earned by deposited funds. Assets that are sometimes lent with _____ include money, shares, consumer goods through hire purchase, major assets such as aircraft, and even entire factories in finance lease arrangements.
- a. Internal debt
- b. Interest
- c. Asset protection
- d. Insolvency

Chapter 17. Promoting More Efficient Markets

19. In economics, a _____ exists when a specific individual or enterprise has sufficient control over a particular product or service to determine significantly the terms on which other individuals shall have access to it. Monopolies are thus characterized by a lack of economic competition for the good or service that they provide and a lack of viable substitute goods. The verb 'monopolize' refers to the process by which a firm gains persistently greater market share than what is expected under perfect competition.
   a. 1921 recession
   b. Monopoly
   c. 100-year flood
   d. 130-30 fund

20. In finance, a _____ is a debt security, in which the authorized issuer owes the holders a debt and, depending on the terms of the _____, is obliged to pay interest (the coupon) and/or to repay the principal at a later date, termed maturity. A _____ is a formal contract to repay borrowed money with interest at fixed intervals.

   Thus a _____ is like a loan: the issuer is the borrower (debtor), the holder is the lender (creditor), and the coupon is the interest.

   a. Bond
   b. Prize Bond
   c. Callable
   d. Zero-coupon

21. _____ is a broad label that refers to any individuals or households that use goods and services generated within the economy. The concept of a _____ is used in different contexts, so that the usage and significance of the term may vary.

   Typically when business people and economists talk of _____s they are talking about person as _____, an aggregated commodity item with little individuality other than that expressed in the buy/not-buy decision.

   a. 100-year flood
   b. 1921 recession
   c. 130-30 fund
   d. Consumer

22. _____ is an equity (stock) exchange located at 11 Wall Street in lower Manhattan, New York, USA. It is the largest stock exchange in the world by dollar value of its listed companies' securities. As of October 2008, the combined capitalization of all domestic _____ listed companies was US$10.1 trillion.
   a. 130-30 fund
   b. 100-year flood
   c. New York Stock Exchange
   d. 1921 recession

23. _____ in economics and business is the result of an exchange and from that trade we assign a numerical monetary value to a good, service or asset. If Alice trades Bob 4 apples for an orange, the _____ of an orange is 4 apples. Inversely, the _____ of an apple is 1/4 oranges.
   a. Price book
   b. Premium pricing
   c. Price war
   d. Price

24. In economics, _____ and economies of scale are related terms that describe what happens as the scale of production increases. They are different terms and should not be used interchangeably.

   _____ refers to a technical property of production that examines changes in output subsequent to a proportional change in all inputs (where all inputs increase by a constant factor.)

Chapter 17. Promoting More Efficient Markets 227

  a. Customer equity
  b. Necessity good
  c. Constant returns to scale
  d. Returns to scale

25. A security is a fungible, negotiable instrument representing financial value. _____ are broadly categorized into debt _____; equity _____, e.g., common stocks; and derivative (finance) contracts such as forwards, futures, options and swaps. The company or other entity issuing the security is called the issuer.
  a. Pass-Through Certificates
  b. Red herring prospectus
  c. Settlement risk
  d. Securities

26. The U.S. _____ is an independent agency of the United States government which holds primary responsibility for enforcing the federal securities laws and regulating the securities industry, the nation's stock and options exchanges, and other electronic securities markets. The SEC was created by section 4 of the Securities Exchange Act of 1934 (now codified as 15 U.S.C. § 78d and commonly referred to as the 1934 Act.)
  a. 130-30 fund
  b. 100-year flood
  c. 1921 recession
  d. Securities and Exchange Commission

27. A _____ is a corporation or mutual organization which provides trading facilities for stock brokers and traders, to trade stocks and other securities. It may be a physical trading room where the traders gather, or a formalised communications network. Creation of a _____ is a strategy of economic development.
  a. 100-year flood
  b. Primary shares
  c. SEAQ
  d. Stock Exchange

28. _____, in microeconomics, are the cost advantages that a business obtains due to expansion. They are factors that cause a producere;s average cost per unit to fall as scale is increased. _____ is a long run concept and refers to reductions in unit cost as the size of a facility, or scale, increases.
  a. Economies of scale
  b. Isoquant
  c. Underinvestment employment relationship
  d. Economic production quantity

29. In economics, an _____ or spillover of an economic transaction is an impact on a party that is not directly involved in the transaction. In such a case, prices do not reflect the full costs or benefits in production or consumption of a product or service. A positive impact is called an external benefit, while a negative impact is called an external cost.
  a. Environmental impact assessment
  b. Existence value
  c. Environmental tariff
  d. Externality

30. _____ is an economic concept with commonplace familiarity. It is the price that a good or service is offered at, or will fetch, in the marketplace. It is of interest mainly in the study of microeconomics.
  a. Noisy market hypothesis
  b. Paper trading
  c. Market anomaly
  d. Market price

31. A _____ association is a financial institution that specializes in accepting savings deposits and making mortgage and other loans. The S'L or thrift term is mainly used in the United States; similar institutions in the United Kingdom, Ireland and some Commonwealth countries include building societies and trustee savings banks.

They are often mutually held, meaning that the depositors and borrowers are members with voting rights, and have the ability to direct the financial and managerial goals of the organization, similar to the policyholders of a mutual insurance company.

a. Collective investment scheme
b. Participating policy
c. Fonds commun de placement
d. Savings and loan

32. In economics, _____ is equal to total cost divided by the number of goods produced (the output quantity, Q.) It is also equal to the sum of average variable costs (total variable costs divided by Q) plus average fixed costs (total fixed costs divided by Q.) _____ s may be dependent on the time period considered (increasing production may be expensive or impossible in the short term, for example.)
   a. Average cost
   b. Average fixed cost
   c. Explicit cost
   d. Average variable cost

33. _____ is one of the ways government regulate a monopoly market. Monopolists tend to produce less than the optimal quantity pushing the prices up. Government may use _____ as a tool to regulate prices monopolists may charge.
   a. ACCRA Cost of Living Index
   b. Average cost pricing
   c. ACEA agreement
   d. AD-IA Model

34. _____ is one of the four Ps of the marketing mix. The other three aspects are product, promotion, and place. It is also a key variable in microeconomic price allocation theory.
   a. Premium pricing
   b. Point of total assumption
   c. Guaranteed Maximum Price
   d. Pricing

35. A _____ is a price discrimination technique in which the price of a product or service is composed of two parts - a lump-sum fee as well as a per-unit charge. In general, price discrimination techniques only occur in partially or fully monopolistic markets. It is designed to enable the firm to capture more consumer surplus than it otherwise would in a non-discriminating pricing environment.
   a. Price floor
   b. Two-part tariff
   c. Penetration pricing
   d. Big ticket item

36. In economics, a _____ is a graph of the costs of production as a function of total quantity produced. In a free market economy, productively efficient firms use these curves to find the optimal point of production, where they make the most profits. There are a few different types of _____ s, each relevant to a different area of economics.
   a. Phillips curve
   b. Cost curve
   c. Demand curve
   d. Kuznets curve

37. A _____ is a duty imposed on goods when they are moved across a political boundary. They are usually associated with protectionism, the economic policy of restraining trade between nations. For political reasons, _____ s are usually imposed on imported goods, although they may also be imposed on exported goods.
   a. 100-year flood
   b. 130-30 fund
   c. Tariff
   d. 1921 recession

38. The _____ consists of a number of economic theories which describe the nature of the firm, company including its existence, its behaviour, and its relationship with the market.

In simplified terms, the _____ aims to answer these questions:

1. Existence - why do firms emerge, why are not all transactions in the economy mediated over the market?
2. Boundaries - why the boundary between firms and the market is located exactly there? Which transactions are performed internally and which are negotiated on the market?
3. Organization - why are firms structured in such specific way? What is the interplay of formal and informal relationships?

Despite looking simple, these questions are not answered by the established economic theory, which usually views firms as given, and treats them as black boxes without any internal structure.

The First World War period saw a change of emphasis in economic theory away from industry-level analysis which mainly included analysing markets to analysis at the level of the firm, as it became increasingly clear that perfect competition was no longer an adequate model of how firms behaved. Economic theory till then had focussed on trying to understand markets alone and there had been little study on understanding why firms or organisations exist.

a. Technology gap
b. Theory of the firm
c. Policy Ineffectiveness Proposition
d. Khazzoom-Brookes postulate

39. Monopoly power is an example of market failure which occurs when one or more of the participants has the ability to influence the price or other outcomes in some general or specialized market. The most commonly discussed form of market power is that of a monopoly, but other forms such as monopsony, and more moderate versions of these two extremes, exist. Market participants that have market power are sometimes referred to as 'price makers', while those without are sometimes called '_____'.

a. Market concentration
b. Monopolization
c. Price takers
d. Market power

40. _____ is a term used in national accounts statistics and macroeconomics. It basically refers to the net additions to the (physical) capital stock in an accounting period, or, to the value of the increase of the capital stock; though it may occasionally also refer to the (growth of the) total stock of capital formed.

Thus, in UNSNA, _____ equals fixed capital investment, the increase in the value of inventories held, plus (net) lending to foreign countries, during an accounting period.

a. Capital flight
b. Capital intensity
c. Consumption of fixed capital
d. Capital formation

41. In economics, _____ is a measure of the relative satisfaction from consumption of various goods and services. Given this measure, one may speak meaningfully of increasing or decreasing _____, and thereby explain economic behavior in terms of attempts to increase one's _____. For illustrative purposes, changes in _____ are sometimes expressed in units called utils.

a. Expected utility hypothesis
b. Ordinal utility
c. Utility
d. Utility function

42. _____ is exchange of capital, goods, and services across international borders or territories. In most countries, it represents a significant share of gross domestic product (GDP.) While _____ has been present throughout much of history, its economic, social, and political importance has been on the rise in recent centuries.
   a. International trade
   b. Incoterms
   c. Import license
   d. Intra-industry trade

43. _____ is used to refer to a number of related concepts. It is the using resources in such a way as to maximize the production of goods and services. A system can be called economically efficient if:

   - No one can be made better off without making someone else worse off.
   - More output cannot be obtained without increasing the amount of inputs.
   - Production proceeds at the lowest possible per-unit cost.

   These definitions of efficiency are not equivalent, but they are all encompassed by the idea that nothing more can be achieved given the resources available.

   An economic system is more efficient if it can provide more goods and services for society without using more resources.

   a. ACCRA Cost of Living Index
   b. ACEA agreement
   c. Efficient contract theory
   d. Economic efficiency

44. In 1940, President Franklin Roosevelt split the authority into two agencies, the Civil Aeronautics Administration (CAA) and the _____ The CAA was responsible for air traffic control, safety programs, and airway development. The _____ was entrusted with safety rulemaking, accident investigation, and economic regulation of the airlines.
   a. 1921 recession
   b. 130-30 fund
   c. 100-year flood
   d. Civil Aeronautics Board

45. _____ is the incidence or process of transferring ownership of a business, enterprise, agency or public service from the public sector (government) to the private sector (business.) In a broader sense, _____ refers to transfer of any government function to the private sector including governmental functions like revenue collection and law enforcement.

   The term '_____' also has been used to describe two unrelated transactions.

   a. Privatization
   b. Ricardian equivalence
   c. Compound empowerment
   d. Performance reports

46. The _____ or cash market is a commodities or securities market in which goods are sold for cash and delivered immediately. Contracts bought and sold on these markets are immediately effective. _____s can operate wherever the infrastructure exists to conduct the transaction.
   a. Currency band
   b. Foreign exchange trading
   c. Triangular arbitrage
   d. Spot market

Chapter 17. Promoting More Efficient Markets 231

47. _____, or corporate _____ are political and business scandals which arise with the disclosure of misdeeds by trusted executives of large public corporations. Such misdeeds typically involve complex methods for misusing or misdirecting funds, overstating revenues, understating expenses, overstating the value of corporate assets or underreporting the existence of liabilities, sometimes with the cooperation of officials in other corporations or affiliates.

In public companies, this type of 'creative accounting' can amount to fraud and investigations are typically launched by government oversight agencies, such as the Securities and Exchange Commission (SEC) in the United States.

- a. Accounting scandals
- b. ACCRA Cost of Living Index
- c. AD-IA Model
- d. ACEA agreement

48.

The _____ was the first United States Federal statute to limit cartels and monopolies. It falls under antitrust law.

The Act provides: 'Every contract, combination in the form of trust or otherwise, or conspiracy, in restraint of trade or commerce among the several States, or with foreign nations, is declared to be illegal'. The Act also provides: 'Every person who shall monopolize, or attempt to monopolize, or combine or conspire with any other person or persons, to monopolize any part of the trade or commerce among the several States, or with foreign nations, shall be deemed guilty of a felony [. . .]' The Act put responsibility upon government attorneys and district courts to pursue and investigate trusts, companies and organizations suspected of violating the Act. The Clayton Act extended the right to sue under the antitrust laws to 'any person who shall be injured in his business or property by reason of anything forbidden in the antitrust laws.' Under the Clayton Act, private parties may sue in U.S. district court and should they prevail, they may be awarded treble damages and the cost of suit, including reasonable attorney's fees.

- a. Sherman Antitrust Act
- b. 100-year flood
- c. 1921 recession
- d. 130-30 fund

49. _____ refers to when a retailer or wholesaler is e;tiede; to purchase from a supplier on the understanding that no other distributor will be appointed or receive supplies in a given area. When the sales outlets are owned by the supplier, _____ is because of vertical integration, where the outlets are independent _____ is illegal due to the Restrictive Trade Practices Act, however, if it is registered and approved it is allowed.

_____ can be a barrier to entry.

- a. Exclusive dealing
- b. ACEA agreement
- c. ACCRA Cost of Living Index
- d. AD-IA Model

50.

Chapter 17. Promoting More Efficient Markets

The _____ is an independent agency of the United States government, created, directed, and empowered by Congressional statute , and with the majority of its commissioners appointed by the current President. The _____ works towards six strategic goals in the areas of broadband, competition, the spectrum, the media, public safety and homeland security, and modernizing the _____.

a. 1921 recession
c. 100-year flood
b. Federal Communications Commission
d. 130-30 fund

51. The phrase _____ and acquisitions refers to the aspect of corporate strategy, corporate finance and management dealing with the buying, selling and combining of different companies that can aid, finance, or help a growing company in a given industry grow rapidly without having to create another business entity.

An acquisition, also known as a takeover or a buyout, is the buying of one company (the 'target') by another. An acquisition may be friendly or hostile.

a. Differential accumulation
c. Political economy
b. Mergers
d. Peace dividend

52. _____ exists when sales of identical goods or services are transacted at different prices from the same provider. In a theoretical market with perfect information, no transaction costs or prohibition on secondary exchange (or re-selling) to prevent arbitrage, _____ can only be a feature of monopoly and oligopoly markets, where market power can be exercised. Otherwise, the moment the seller tries to sell the same good at different prices, the buyer at the lower price can arbitrage by selling to the consumer buying at the higher price but with a tiny discount.

a. Lerner Index
c. Loss leader
b. Transfer pricing
d. Price discrimination

53. _____ is the practice of selling a product or service at a very low price, intending to drive competitors out of the market, or create barriers to entry for potential new competitors. If competitors or potential competitors cannot sustain equal or lower prices without losing money, they go out of business or choose not to enter the business. The predatory merchant then has fewer competitors or is even a de facto monopoly, and can then raise prices above what the market would otherwise bear.

a. Group boycott
c. Restraint of trade
b. Third line forcing
d. Predatory pricing

54. _____ is an agreement between business competitors to sell the same product or service at the same price. In general, it is an agreement intended to ultimately push the price of a product as high as possible, leading to profits for all the sellers. Price-fixing can also involve any agreement to fix, peg, discount or stabilize prices.

a. Non-price competition
c. Moral victory
b. Price fixing
d. Cut-throat competition

55. _____ is an agreement between business competitors to sell the same product or service at the same price. In general, it is an agreement intended to ultimately push the price of a product as high as possible, leading to profits for all the sellers. _____ can also involve any agreement to fix, peg, discount or stabilize prices.

a. Moral victory
b. Non-price competition
c. Cut-throat competition
d. Price-fixing

56. _____ is a common law doctrine relating to the enforceability of contractual restrictions on freedom to conduct business. In an old leading case of Mitchell v. Reynolds (1711) Lord Smith L.C. said,

'it is the privilege of a trader in a free country, in all matters not contrary to law, to regulate his own mode of carrying it on according to his own discretion and choice.

a. Third line forcing
b. Group boycott
c. Conscious parallelism
d. Restraint of trade

57. _____ was a predominant American integrated oil producing, transporting, refining, and marketing company. Established in 1870 as an Ohio Corporation, it was the largest oil refiner in the world and operated as a major company trust and was one of the world's first and largest multinational corporations until it was broken up by the United States Supreme Court in 1911. John D. Rockefeller was a founder, chairman and major shareholder, and the company made him a billionaire and eventually the richest man in history.

a. 1921 recession
b. 100-year flood
c. 130-30 fund
d. Standard Oil

58. In economics, the _____ of an industry is used as an indicator of the relative size of firms in relation to the industry as a whole. It is calculated as the sum of the percent market share of the top n industries. This may also assist in determining the market structure of the industry.

a. Monopolization
b. Pacman conjecture
c. Concentration ratio
d. Quasi-rent

59. In economics, a _____ is the combination of two or more firms competing in the same market with the same good or service. See Horizontal integration.

a. Federal Reserve districts
b. Financial system
c. Market dominance
d. Horizontal merger

60. A _____ is an expression that compares quantities relative to each other. The most common examples involve two quantities, but any number of quantities can be compared. _____s are represented mathematically by separating each quantity with a colon, for example the _____ 2:3, which is read as the _____ 'two to three'.

a. Y-intercept
b. 100-year flood
c. 130-30 fund
d. Ratio

61. A _____ is officially defined as being 'any merger that is not horizontal or vertical; in general, it is the combination of firms in different industries or firms operating in different geographic areas'. _____s can serve various purposes, including extending corporate territories and extending a product range. One example of a _____ was the merger between the Walt Disney Company and the American Broadcasting Company.

a. Borrowing base
b. Conglomerate merger
c. Factor cost
d. Cost-effectiveness analysis

62. In economics, a firm is said to reap _____s when a lack of viable market competition allows it to set its prices above the equilibrium price for a good or service without losing profits to competitors. _____ is a type of economic profit, that is, it is a profit greater than the normal profit that is typical in a perfectly competitive industry. The resulting price is known as the monopoly price.
   a. First-price sealed-bid auction
   b. Borrowing base
   c. Monopoly profit
   d. Cleanup clause

63. _____, known in the United States as antitrust law, has three main elements:

   - prohibiting agreements or practices that restrict free trading and competition between business entities. This includes in particular the repression of cartels.
   - banning abusive behaviour by a firm dominating a market, or anti-competitive practices that tend to lead to such a dominant position. Practices controlled in this way may include predatory pricing, tying, price gouging, refusal to deal, and many others.
   - supervising the mergers and acquisitions of large corporations, including some joint ventures. Transactions that are considered to threaten the competitive process can be prohibited altogether, or approved subject to 'remedies' such as an obligation to divest part of the merged business or to offer licences or access to facilities to enable other businesses to continue competing.

   The substance and practice of _____ varies from jurisdiction to jurisdiction. Protecting the interests of consumers (consumer welfare) and ensuring that entrepreneurs have an opportunity to compete in the market economy are often treated as important objectives. _____ is closely connected with law on deregulation of access to markets, state aids and subsidies, the privatisation of state owned assets and the establishment of independent sector regulators. In recent decades, _____ has been viewed as a way to provide better public services.

   a. Due diligence
   b. Hostile work environment
   c. Fee simple
   d. Competition law

64. In economics, an _____ is any good (e.g. a commodity) or service brought into one country from another country in a legitimate fashion, typically for use in trade. It is a good that is brought in from another country for sale. _____ goods or services are provided to domestic consumers by foreign producers. An _____ in the receiving country is an export to the sending country.
   a. Incoterms
   b. Economic integration
   c. Import quota
   d. Import

65. _____, in strategic management and marketing is, according to Carlton O'Neal, the percentage or proportion of the total available market or market segment that is being serviced by a company. It can be expressed as a company's sales revenue (from that market) divided by the total sales revenue available in that market. It can also be expressed as a company's unit sales volume (in a market) divided by the total volume of units sold in that market.
   a. Product differentiation
   b. Customer to customer
   c. Market share
   d. Pricing science

Chapter 18. Protecting the Environment

1. The _____ is a protocol to the United Nations Framework Convention on Climate Change (UNFCCC or FCCC), an international environmental treaty produced at the United Nations Conference on treaty is intended to achieve 'stabilization of greenhouse gas concentrations in the atmosphere at a level that would prevent dangerous anthropogenic interference with the climate system.' The _____ establishes legally binding commitments for the reduction of four greenhouse gases (carbon dioxide, methane, nitrous oxide, sulphur hexafluoride), and two groups of gases (hydrofluorocarbons and perfluorocarbons) produced by 'Annex I' (industrialized) nations, as well as general commitments for all member countries. As of January 14 2009, 183 parties have ratified the protocol, which was initially adopted for use on 11 December 1997 in Kyoto, Japan and which entered into force on 16 February 2005. Under Kyoto, industrialized countries agreed to reduce their collective GHG emissions by 5.2% compared to the year 1990.
   a. Carbon offset
   b. Kyoto Protocol
   c. Green New Deal
   d. Greenhouse gases

2. _____s is the social science that studies the production, distribution, and consumption of goods and services. The term _____s comes from the Ancient Greek οἰκονομία from οἶκος (oikos, 'house') + νόμος (nomos, 'custom' or 'law'), hence 'rules of the house(hold)'. Current _____ models developed out of the broader field of political economy in the late 19th century, owing to a desire to use an empirical approach more akin to the physical sciences.
   a. Inflation
   b. Opportunity cost
   c. Energy economics
   d. Economic

3. _____ is the increase in the amount of the goods and services produced by an economy over time. It is conventionally measured as the percent rate of increase in real gross domestic product, or real GDP. Growth is usually calculated in real terms, i.e. inflation-adjusted terms, in order to net out the effect of inflation on the price of the goods and services produced.
   a. AD-IA Model
   b. ACEA agreement
   c. ACCRA Cost of Living Index
   d. Economic growth

4. _____ is the concept of adding accumulated interest back to the principal, so that interest is earned on interest from that moment on. The act of declaring interest to be principal is called compounding (i.e., interest is compounded.) A loan, for example, may have its interest compounded every month: in this case, a loan with $100 principal and 1% interest per month would have a balance of $101 at the end of the first month.
   a. Fama-French three factor model
   b. General purpose technologies
   c. Compound interest
   d. Foreclosure data providers

5. In economics, _____ refers to how the marginal contribution of a factor of production usually decreases as more of the factor is used. According to this relationship, in a production system with fixed and variable inputs, beyond some point, each additional unit of the variable input yields smaller and smaller increases in output. Conversely, producing one more unit of output costs more and more in variable inputs.
   a. Diminishing returns
   b. Patent troll
   c. Derivatives law
   d. Community property

6. _____ is a fee paid on borrowed assets. It is the price paid for the use of borrowed money, or, money earned by deposited funds. Assets that are sometimes lent with _____ include money, shares, consumer goods through hire purchase, major assets such as aircraft, and even entire factories in finance lease arrangements.
   a. Interest
   b. Insolvency
   c. Asset protection
   d. Internal debt

7. A _____ is:

- Rewrite _____, in generative grammar and computer science
- Standardization, a formal and widely-accepted statement, fact, definition, or qualification
- Operation, a determinate _____ for performing a mathematical operation and obtaining a certain result (Mathematics, Logic)
    - Unary operation
    - Binary operation
- _____ of inference, a function from sets of formulae to formulae (Mathematics, Logic)
- _____ of thumb, principle with broad application that is not intended to be strictly accurate or reliable for every situation. Also often simply referred to as a _____
- Moral, an atomic element of a moral code for guiding choices in human behavior
- Heuristic, a quantized '_____' which shows a tendency or probability for successful function
- A regulation, as in sports
- A Production _____, as in computer science
- Procedural law, a _____ set governing the application of laws to cases
    - A law, which may informally be called a '_____'
    - A court ruling, a decision by a court
- In the U.S. Government, a regulation mandated by Congress, but written or expanded upon by the Executive Branch.
- Norm (sociology), an informal but widely accepted _____, concept, truth, definition, or qualification (social norms, legal norms, coding norms)
- Norm (philosophy), a kind of sentence or a reason to act, feel or believe
- 'Rulership' is the concept of governance by a government:
    - Military _____, governance by a military body
    - Monastic _____, a collection of precepts that guides the life of monks or nuns in a religious order where the superior holds the place of Christ
- Slide _____

- '_____,' a song by Ayumi Hamasaki
- '_____,' a song by rapper Nas
- '_____s,' an album by the band The Whitest Boy Alive
- _____s: Pyaar Ka Superhit Formula, a 2003 Bollywood film
- ruler, an instrument for measuring lengths
- _____, a component of an astrolabe, circumferator or similar instrument
- The _____s, a bestselling self-help book
- _____ Project (Run Up-to-date Linux Everywhere), a project that aims to use up-to-date Linux software on old PCs
- _____ engine, a software system that helps managing business _____s
- Ja _____, a hip hop artist
    - R.U.L.E., a 2005 greatest hits album by rapper Ja _____
- '_____s,' a KMFDM song

a. Technocracy
b. Rule
c. Procter ' Gamble
d. Demand

8. _____ was a survey conducted by the U.S. Department of Justice to gauge the prevalence of alcohol and illegal drug use among prior arrestees. It was a reformulation of the prior Drug Use Forecasting (DUF) program, focused on five drugs in particular: cocaine, marijuana, methamphetamine, opiates, and PCP.

Participants were randomly selected from arrest records in major metropolitan areas; because no personally identifying information is taken from each record chosen, the resulting data can be correlated to arrest rates, but not to the total population of persons charged.

a. AD-IA Model
b. ACEA agreement
c. ACCRA Cost of Living Index
d. Arrestee Drug Abuse Monitoring

9. _____ was a Scottish moral philosopher and a pioneer of political economy. One of the key figures of the Scottish Enlightenment, Smith is the author of The Theory of Moral Sentiments and An Inquiry into the Nature and Causes of the Wealth of Nations. The latter, usually abbreviated as The Wealth of Nations, is considered his magnum opus and the first modern work of economics.

a. Alan Greenspan
b. Adolph Fischer
c. Adolf Hitler
d. Adam Smith

10. The _____ was a period in the late 18th and early 19th centuries when major changes in agriculture, manufacturing, mining, and transportation had a profound effect on the socioeconomic and cultural conditions in Britain. The changes subsequently spread throughout Europe, North America, and eventually the world. The onset of the _____ marked a major turning point in human society; almost every aspect of daily life was eventually influenced in some way.

a. Adam Smith
b. Adolph Fischer
c. Adolf Hitler
d. Industrial Revolution

11. The _____ is a 1972 book modeling the consequences of a rapidly growing world population and finite resource supplies, commissioned by the Club of Rome. Its authors were Donella H. Meadows, Dennis L. Meadows, Jørgen Randers, and William W. Behrens III. The book used the World3 model to simulate the consequence of interactions between the Earth's and human systems.

a. The Wealth of Nations
b. Limits to Growth
c. Principles of Political Economy and Taxation
d. Fail-Safe Investing

12. _____ is any long-term change in the patterns of average weather of a specific region or the Earth as a whole. _____ reflects abnormal variations to the Earth's climate and subsequent effects on other parts of the Earth, such as in the ice caps over durations ranging from decades to millions of years.

In recent usage, especially in the context of environmental policy, _____ usually refers to changes in modern climate

a. 1921 recession
b. 130-30 fund
c. 100-year flood
d. Climate change

13. _____ is the development of economic wealth of countries or regions for the well-being of their inhabitants. It is the process by which a nation improves the economic, political, and social well being of its people. From a policy perspective, _____ can be defined as efforts that seek to improve the economic well-being and quality of life for a community by creating and/or retaining jobs and supporting or growing incomes and the tax base.

a. Experimental economics
b. Economic development
c. Economic methodology
d. Inflation

14. The term '_____' refers to the concept of collecting information and attempting to spot a pattern in the information. In some fields of study, the term '_____' has more formally-defined meanings.

In project management _____ is a mathematical technique that uses historical results to predict future outcome.

a. Coefficient of determination
b. Probit model
c. Quantile regression
d. Trend analysis

15. _____s (economically referred to as land or raw materials) occur naturally within environments that exist relatively undisturbed by mankind, in a natural form. A _____'s is often characterized by amounts of biodiversity existent in various ecosystems.

Mining, petroleum extraction, fishing, hunting, and forestry are generally considered natural-resource industries.

a. 100-year flood
b. 1921 recession
c. 130-30 fund
d. Natural resource

16. A natural resource is a _____ resource if it is replaced by natural processes at a rate comparable or faster than its rate of consumption by humans. Solar radiation, tides, winds and hydroelectricity are perpetual resources that are in no danger of long-term availability. _____ resources may also mean commodities such as wood, paper, and leather, if harvesting is performed in a sustainable manner.

a. 1921 recession
b. Renewable
c. 100-year flood
d. 130-30 fund

17. A natural resource is a _____ if it is replaced by natural processes at a rate comparable or faster than its rate of consumption by humans. Solar radiation, tides, winds and hydroelectricity are perpetual resources that are in no danger of long-term availability. _____s may also mean commodities such as wood, paper, and leather, if harvesting is performed in a sustainable manner.

a. 100-year flood
b. 1921 recession
c. 130-30 fund
d. Renewable resource

18. In microeconomics, _____ is quite simply the conversion of inputs into outputs. It is an economic process that uses resources to create a good or service that is suitable for exchange. This can include manufacturing, storing, shipping, and packaging.

a. Production
b. Solved
c. MET
d. Red Guards

19. In law and economics, the _____, describes the economic efficiency of an economic allocation or outcome in the presence of externalities. The theorem states that when trade in an externality is possible and there are no transaction costs, bargaining will lead to an efficient outcome regardless of the initial allocation of property rights. In practice, obstacles to bargaining or poorly defined property rights can prevent Coasian bargaining.

a. Coase theorem
c. General Mining Act of 1872
b. Prior appropriation water rights
d. Means test

20. _____ refers to the stock of skills and knowledge embodied in the ability to perform labor so as to produce economic value. It is the skills and knowledge gained by a worker through education and experience. Many early economic theories refer to it simply as labor, one of three factors of production, and consider it to be a fungible resource -- homogeneous and easily interchangeable. Other conceptions of labor dispense with these assumptions.
   a. Price theory
   b. Law of increasing costs
   c. General equilibrium
   d. Human capital

21. In microeconomic theory, an _____ is a graph showing different bundles of goods, each measured as to quantity, between which a consumer is indifferent. That is, at each point on the curve, the consumer has no preference for one bundle over another. In other words, they are all equally preferred.
   a. Engel curve
   b. Indifference map
   c. Expenditure minimization problem
   d. Indifference curve

22. In economics, an _____ is a contour line drawn through the set of points at which the same quantity of output is produced while changing the quantities of two or more inputs. While an indifference curve helps to answer the utility-maximizing problem of consumers, the _____ deals with the cost-minimization problem of producers. _____s are typically drawn on capital-labor graphs, showing the tradeoff between capital and labor in the production function, and the decreasing marginal returns of both inputs.
   a. Economic production quantity
   b. Isoquant
   c. Underinvestment employment relationship
   d. Economies of scale

23. _____ is the extension of the economic notion of capital (manufactured means of production) to environmental goods and services. _____ is thus the stock of natural ecosystems that yields a flow of valuable ecosystem goods or services into the future. For example, a stock of trees or fish provides a flow of new trees or fish, a flow which can be sustainable indefinitely.
   a. Non-conventional oil
   b. Hubbert peak theory
   c. Natural capital
   d. Hydrogen economy

24. In business and accounting, _____ are everything of value that is owned by a person or company. It is a claim on the property your income of a borrower. The balance sheet of a firm records the monetary value of the _____ owned by the firm.
   a. ACCRA Cost of Living Index
   b. Amortization schedule
   c. ACEA agreement
   d. Assets

25. _____ is a common concept in economics, and gives rise to derived concepts such as consumer debt. Generally _____ is defined by opposition to production. But the precise definition can vary because different schools of economists define production quite differently.
   a. Cash or share options
   b. Consumption
   c. Federal Reserve Bank Notes
   d. Foreclosure data providers

26. _____ is an economic concept with commonplace familiarity. It is the price that a good or service is offered at, or will fetch, in the marketplace. It is of interest mainly in the study of microeconomics.

a. Paper trading
c. Market price
b. Noisy market hypothesis
d. Market anomaly

27. Competition law, known in the United States as _____ law, has three main elements:

- prohibiting agreements or practices that restrict free trading and competition between business entities. This includes in particular the repression of cartels.
- banning abusive behaviour by a firm dominating a market, or anti-competitive practices that tend to lead to such a dominant position. Practices controlled in this way may include predatory pricing, tying, price gouging, refusal to deal, and many others.
- supervising the mergers and acquisitions of large corporations, including some joint ventures. Transactions that are considered to threaten the competitive process can be prohibited altogether, or approved subject to 'remedies' such as an obligation to divest part of the merged business or to offer licences or access to facilities to enable other businesses to continue competing.

The substance and practice of competition law varies from jurisdiction to jurisdiction. Protecting the interests of consumers (consumer welfare) and ensuring that entrepreneurs have an opportunity to compete in the market economy are often treated as important objectives. Competition law is closely connected with law on deregulation of access to markets, state aids and subsidies, the privatisation of state owned assets and the establishment of independent sector regulators. In recent decades, competition law has been viewed as a way to provide better public services.

a. Intellectual property law
c. United Kingdom competition law
b. Anti-Inflation Act
d. Antitrust

28. _____ in economics and business is the result of an exchange and from that trade we assign a numerical monetary value to a good, service or asset. If Alice trades Bob 4 apples for an orange, the _____ of an orange is 4 apples. Inversely, the _____ of an apple is 1/4 oranges.
   a. Price book
   c. Price war
   b. Price
   d. Premium pricing

29. The _____ is a heterodox school of economics that emphasizes the spontaneous organizing power of the price mechanism. It holds that the complexity of subjective human choices makes mathematical modelling of the evolving market extremely difficult and advocates a laissez faire approach to the economy. _____ economists advocate the enforcement of voluntary contractual agreements between economic agents, but otherwise the smallest imposition of coercive force on commercial transactions.
   a. ACCRA Cost of Living Index
   c. ACEA agreement
   b. Economic calculation problem
   d. Austrian School

30. A _____ is a good that has the three following properties :

- It is non-rivalrous. Consumption of this good by anyone does not reduce the quantity available to other agents.
- It is non-excludable. It is impossible to prevent anyone from consuming that good.
- It is available worldwide.

This concept is an extension of Samuelson's notion of public goods to the economics of globalisation.

Chapter 18. Protecting the Environment 241

The theoretical concept of public goods does not distinguish with regard to the geographical region in which a good may be produced or consumed. However some theorists (such as Inge Kaul) use the term _____ to mean a public good which is non-rival and non-excludable throughout the whole world, as opposed to a public good which exists in just one national area. Knowledge is a canonical example of a _____.[Joseph E. Stiglitz, Knowledge as a _____ in _____s, ISBN 978-0-19-513052-2</ref>.]

a. Monopoly price
b. Black-Litterman model
c. Community indifference curve
d. Global public good

31. A _____ is an object whose consumption increases the utility of the consumer, for which the quantity demanded exceeds the quantity supplied at zero price. _____s are usually modeled as having diminishing marginal utility. The first individual purchase has high utility; the second has less.

a. Good
b. Composite good
c. Merit good
d. Pie method

32. In economics, economic output is divided into physical goods and intangible services. Consumption of _____ is assumed to produce utility. It is often used when referring to a _____ Tax.

a. Manufactured goods
b. Composite good
c. Goods and services
d. Private good

33. In economics, a _____ exists when the production or use of goods and services by the market is not efficient. That is, there exists another outcome where all involved can be made better off. _____s can be viewed as scenarios where individuals' pursuit of pure self-interest leads to results that are not efficient - that can be improved upon from the societal point-of-view.

a. Financial economics
b. General equilibrium
c. Market failure
d. Fixed exchange rate

34. In economics, a _____ is a good that is non-rivaled and non-excludable. This means, respectively, that consumption of the good by one individual does not reduce availability of the good for consumption by others; and that no one can be effectively excluded from using the good. In the real world, there may be no such thing as an absolutely non-rivaled and non-excludable good; but economists think that some goods approximate the concept closely enough for the analysis to be economically useful.

a. Happiness economics
b. Public good
c. Demand-pull theory
d. Neoclassical synthesis

35. A _____ is defined in economics as a good that exhibits these properties:

- Excludable - it is reasonably possible to prevent a class of consumers (e.g. those who have not paid for it) from consuming the good.
- Rivalrous - consumptions by one consumer prevents simultaneous consumption by other consumers. _____s satisfies an individual want while public good satisfies a collective want of the society.

A _____ is the opposite of a public good, as they are almost exclusively made for profit.

Chapter 18. Protecting the Environment

An example of the _____ is bread: bread eaten by a given person cannot be consumed by another (rivalry), and it is easy for a baker to refuse to trade a loaf (excludable

a. Positional goods
c. Private Good

b. Demerit good
d. Pie method

36. _____ is a situation in which the limited resources of a firm are allocated in accordance with the wishes of consumers. An allocatively efficient economy produces an 'optimal mix' of commodities. A firm is allocatively efficient when its price is equal to its marginal costs (that is, P = MC) in a perfect market.

a. ACEA agreement
c. Allocative efficiency

b. Economic efficiency
d. ACCRA Cost of Living Index

37. _____ is a term that refers both to:

- a formal discipline used to help appraise, or assess, the case for a project or proposal, which itself is a process known as project appraisal; and
- an informal approach to making decisions of any kind.

Under both definitions the process involves, whether explicitly or implicitly, weighing the total expected costs against the total expected benefits of one or more actions in order to choose the best or most profitable option. The formal process is often referred to as either CBA (_____) or BCost-benefit analysis

A hallmark of CBA is that all benefits and all costs are expressed in money terms, and are adjusted for the time value of money, so that all flows of benefits and flows of project costs over time (which tend to occur at different points in time) are expressed on a common basis in terms of their e;present value.e; Closely related, but slightly different, formal techniques include Cost-effectiveness analysis, Economic impact analysis, Fiscal impact analysis and Social Return on Investment(SROI) analysis. The latter builds upon the logic of _____, but differs in that it is explicitly designed to inform the practical decision-making of enterprise managers and investors focused on optimising their social and environmental impacts.

a. Cost-benefit analysis
c. 130-30 fund

b. Decision theory
d. 100-year flood

38. _____ is a broad label that refers to any individuals or households that use goods and services generated within the economy. The concept of a _____ is used in different contexts, so that the usage and significance of the term may vary.

Typically when business people and economists talk of _____s they are talking about person as _____, an aggregated commodity item with little individuality other than that expressed in the buy/not-buy decision.

a. 100-year flood
c. Consumer

b. 1921 recession
d. 130-30 fund

Chapter 18. Protecting the Environment

39. The term surplus is used in economics for several related quantities. The _____ is the amount that consumers benefit by being able to purchase a product for a price that is less than they would be willing to pay. The producer surplus is the amount that producers benefit by selling at a market price mechanism that is higher than they would be willing to sell for.
   a. Consumer surplus
   b. Microeconomic reform
   c. Necessity good
   d. Marginal rate of technical substitution

40. _____ is a survey-based economic technique for the valuation of non-market resources, such as environmental preservation or the impact of contamination. While these resources do give people utility, certain aspects of them do not have a market price as they are not directly sold--for example, people receive benefit from a beautiful view of a mountain, but it would be tough to value using price-based models. _____ surveys are one technique which is used to measure these aspects.
   a. Habitat destruction
   b. Positive externalities
   c. Total Economic Value
   d. Contingent valuation

41. A _____ describes one of a number of pieces of legislation relating to the reduction of smog and air pollution in general. The use by governments to enforce clean air standards has contributed to an improvement in human health and longer life spans. Critics argue it has also sapped corporate profits and contributed to outsourcing, while defenders counter that improved environmental air quality has generated more jobs than it has eliminated.
   a. Clean Air Act
   b. 130-30 fund
   c. Smog
   d. 100-year flood

42. Under the system of feudalism, a _____, fief, feud, feoff often consisted of inheritable lands or revenue-producing property granted by a liege lord, generally to a vassal, in return for a form of allegiance, originally to give him the means to fulfill his military duties when called upon. However anything of value could be held in fief, such as an office, a right of exploitation (e.g., hunting, fishing) or any other type of revenue, rather than the land it comes from.

Originally, the feudal institution of vassalage did not imply the giving or receiving of landholdings (which were granted only as a reward for loyalty), but by the eighth century the giving of a landholding was becoming standard.

   a. 100-year flood
   b. 130-30 fund
   c. 1921 recession
   d. Fiefdom

43. _____ describes a deliberate attempt to interfere with the free and fair operation of the market and create artificial, false or misleading appearances with respect to the price of a security, commodity or currency. _____ is prohibited under Section 9(a)(2) of the Securities Exchange Act of 1934, and in Australia under Section s 1041A of the Corporations Act 2001. The Act defines _____ as transactions which create an artificial price or maintain an artificial price for a tradable security.
   a. Net domestic product
   b. Managerial economics
   c. Legal monopoly
   d. Market manipulation

44. A public utility (usually just utility) is an organization that maintains the infrastructure for a public service (often also providing a service using that infrastructure.) _____ are subject to forms of public control and regulation ranging from local community-based groups to state-wide government monopolies. Common arguments in favor of regulation include the desire to control market power, facilitate competition, promote investment or system expansion, or stabilize markets.

a. 1921 recession
c. 100-year flood
b. 130-30 fund
d. Public utilities

45. _____ is the removal or simplification of government rules and regulations that constrain the operation of market forces. _____ does not mean elimination of laws against fraud, but eliminating or reducing government control of how business is done, thereby moving toward a more free market.

The stated rationale for '_____' is often that fewer and simpler regulations will lead to a raised level of competitiveness, therefore higher productivity, more efficiency and lower prices overall.

a. Fundamental psychological law
c. Macroeconomic policy instruments
b. Secular basis
d. Deregulation

46. _____ is the increase in the average temperature of the Earth's near-surface air and oceans since the mid-twentieth century and its projected continuation. Global surface temperature increased 0.74 ± 0.18 °C (1.33 ± 0.32 °F) during the last century. The Intergovernmental Panel on Climate Change (IPCC) concludes that anthropogenic greenhouse gases are responsible for most of the observed temperature increase since the middle of the twentieth century, and that natural phenomena such as solar variation and volcanoes probably had a small warming effect from pre-industrial times to 1950 and a small cooling effect afterward.

a. Controlled Foreign Corporations
c. Consumer goods
b. Dividend unit
d. Global warming

47. A _____ is the exclusive authority to determine how a resource is used, whether that resource is owned by government or by individuals. All economic goods have a _____s attribute. This attribute has three broad components

1. The right to use the good
2. The right to earn income from the good
3. The right to transfer the good to others

The concept of _____s as used by economists and legal scholars are related but distinct. The distinction is largely seen in the economists' focus on the ability of an individual or collective to control the use of the good.

a. Holder in due course
c. Post-sale restraint
b. High-reeve
d. Property right

48. To _____ is to impose a financial charge or other levy upon a taxpayer by a state or the functional equivalent of a state.

_____es are also imposed by many subnational entities. _____es consist of direct _____ or indirect _____, and may be paid in money or as its labour equivalent (often but not always unpaid.)

a. 100-year flood
c. 1921 recession
b. 130-30 fund
d. Tax

49. _____ is a practice of protecting the environment, on individual, organisational or governmental level, for the benefit of the natural environment and (or) humans.

Chapter 18. Protecting the Environment

Due to the pressures of population and technology the biophysical environment is being degraded, sometimes permanently. This has been recognised and governments began placing restraints on activities that caused environmental degradation.

a. ACEA agreement
c. AD-IA Model
b. ACCRA Cost of Living Index
d. Environmental Protection

Chapter 19. Efficiency vs. Equality: The Big Tradeoff

1. _____ is a situation in which the limited resources of a firm are allocated in accordance with the wishes of consumers. An allocatively efficient economy produces an 'optimal mix' of commodities. A firm is allocatively efficient when its price is equal to its marginal costs (that is, P = MC) in a perfect market.
   a. Economic efficiency
   b. ACCRA Cost of Living Index
   c. ACEA agreement
   d. Allocative efficiency

2. In mathematics, an _____ is a statement about the relative size or order of two objects, or about whether they are the same or not

   - The notation a < b means that a is less than b.
   - The notation a > b means that a is greater than b.
   - The notation a ≠ b means that a is not equal to b, but does not say that one is greater than the other or even that they can be compared in size.

   In each statement above, a is not equal to b. These relations are known as strict inequalities. The notation a < b may also be read as 'a is strictly less than b'.

   a. ACEA agreement
   b. ACCRA Cost of Living Index
   c. AD-IA Model
   d. Inequality

3. In economics, the _____ is a graphical representation of the cumulative distribution function of a probability distribution; it is a graph showing the proportion of the distribution assumed by the bottom y% of the values. It is a curve that illustrates income distribution. It is often used to represent income distribution, where it shows for the bottom x% of households, what percentage y% of the total income they have.
   a. Demand curve
   b. Kuznets curve
   c. Phillips curve
   d. Lorenz curve

4. A variety of measures of _____ and output are used in economics to estimate total economic activity in a country or region, including gross domestic product (GDP), gross national product (GNP), and net _____

   There are three main ways of calculating these numbers; the output approach, the income approach and the expenditure approach. In theory, the three must yield the same, because total expenditures on goods and services must equal the total income paid to the producers (Gnational income), and that must also equal the total value of the output of goods and services (GNP.)

   a. Gross world product
   b. Volume index
   c. GNI per capita
   d. National income

5. Total _____ is defined by the United States' Bureau of Economic Analysis as

   income received by persons from all sources. It includes income received from participation in production as well as from government and business transfer payments. It is the sum of compensation of employees (received), supplements to wages and salaries, proprietors' income with inventory valuation adjustment (IVA) and capital consumption adjustment (CCAdj), rental income of persons with CCAdj, _____ receipts on assets, and personal current transfer receipts, less contributions for government social insurance.

a. Dividend Discount Model
b. Greater fool theory
c. Bidding
d. Personal income

6. _____ is the shortage of common things such as food, clothing, shelter and safe drinking water, all of which determine the quality of life. It may also include the lack of access to opportunities such as education and employment which aid the escape from _____ and/or allow one to enjoy the respect of fellow citizens. According to Mollie Orshansky who developed the _____ measurements used by the U.S. government, 'to be poor is to be deprived of those goods and services and pleasures which others around us take for granted.' Ongoing debates over causes, effects and best ways to measure _____, directly influence the design and implementation of _____-reduction programs and are therefore relevant to the fields of public administration and international development.
   a. Poverty map
   b. Growth Elasticity of Poverty
   c. Liberal welfare reforms
   d. Poverty

7. _____ in political thought refers to economic theories of social organization advocating collective ownership and administration of the means of production and distribution of goods, and a society characterized by equality for all individuals, with an egalitarian method of compensation. Modern _____ originated in the late 19th-century intellectual and working class political movement that criticized the effects of industrialization and private ownership on society. Karl Marx posited that _____ would be achieved via class struggle and a proletarian revolution after a transitional stage from capitalism called the dictatorship of the proletariat.
   a. Adolph Fischer
   b. Adolf Hitler
   c. Adam Smith
   d. Socialism

8. To _____ is to impose a financial charge or other levy upon a taxpayer by a state or the functional equivalent of a state.

_____es are also imposed by many subnational entities. _____es consist of direct _____ or indirect _____, and may be paid in money or as its labour equivalent (often but not always unpaid.)

   a. 1921 recession
   b. 100-year flood
   c. 130-30 fund
   d. Tax

9. A _____ is a political struggle to repeal, limit, or roll back a government-imposed tax.

In the United States, it is often used to refer to a series of anti-tax state initiative campaigns. The first significant wave of these campaigns was during the 1930s.

   a. Taxable wage
   b. Tax revolt
   c. Religious Freedom Peace Tax Fund Act
   d. Tax farming

Chapter 19. Efficiency vs. Equality: The Big Tradeoff

10. There are two main interpretations of the idea of a _____:

    - A model in which the state assumes primary responsibility for the welfare of its citizens. This responsibility in theory ought to be comprehensive, because all aspects of welfare are considered and universally applied to citizens as a 'right'. _____ can also mean the creation of a 'social safety net' of minimum standards of varying forms of welfare. Here is found some confusion between a '_____' and a 'welfare society' in common debate about the definition of the term.
    - The provision of welfare in society. In many '_____s', especially in continental Europe, welfare is not actually provided by the state, but by a combination of independent, voluntary, mutualist and government services. The functional provider of benefits and services may be a central or state government, a state-sponsored company or agency, a private corporation, a charity or another form of non-profit organization. However, this phenomenon has been more appropriately termed a 'welfare society,' and the term 'welfare system' has been used to describe the range of _____ and welfare society mixes that are found.

    The English term '_____' is believed by Asa Briggs to have been coined by Archbishop William Temple during the Second World War, contrasting wartime Britain with the 'warfare state' of Nazi Germany. Friedrich Hayek contends that the term derived from the older German word Wohlfahrtsstaat, which itself was used by nineteenth century historians to describe a variant of the ideal of Polizeistaat . It was fully developed by the German academic Sozialpolitiker--'socialists of the chair'--from 1870 and first implemented through Bismarck's 'state socialism'. Bismarck's policies have also been seen as the creation of a _____.

    a. 100-year flood
    b. 130-30 fund
    c. 1921 recession
    d. Welfare state

11. A _____ represents the combinations of goods and services that a consumer can purchase given current prices and his income. Consumer theory uses the concepts of a _____ and a preference map to analyze consumer choices. Both concepts have a ready graphical representation in the two-good case.
    a. Joint demand
    b. Budget constraint
    c. Quality bias
    d. Revealed preference

12. _____s is the social science that studies the production, distribution, and consumption of goods and services. The term _____s comes from the Ancient Greek οἰκονομία from οἶκος (oikos, 'house') + νόμος (nomos, 'custom' or 'law'), hence 'rules of the house(hold)'. Current _____ models developed out of the broader field of political economy in the late 19th century, owing to a desire to use an empirical approach more akin to the physical sciences.
    a. Inflation
    b. Opportunity cost
    c. Energy economics
    d. Economic

13. A _____ product is a product designed for cheapness and short-term convenience rather than medium to long-term durability, with most products only intended for single use. The term is also sometimes used for products that may last several months (ex. _____ air filters) to distinguish from similar products that last indefinitely (ex.
    a. 100-year flood
    b. Disposable
    c. 1921 recession
    d. 130-30 fund

14. _____ is gross income minus income tax on that income.

Discretionary income is income after subtracting taxes and normal expenses (such as rent or mortgage, utilities, insurance, medical, transportation, property maintenance, child support, inflation, food and sundries, 'c.) to maintain a certain standard of living.

   a. Taxation as theft
   b. Stamp Act
   c. Disposable personal income
   d. Disposable income

15. The _____ is 'the basic residential unit in which economic production, consumption, inheritance, child rearing, and shelter are organized and carried out'; [the _____] 'may or may not be synonomous with family'.

The _____ is the basic unit of analysis in many social, microeconomic and government models. The term refers to all individuals who live in the same dwelling.

   a. 100-year flood
   b. 130-30 fund
   c. Family economics
   d. Household

16. In economics, _____ is how a natione;s total economy is distributed among its population. ._____ has always been a central concern of economic theory and economic policy. Classical economists such as Adam Smith, Thomas Malthus and David Ricardo were mainly concerned with factor _____, that is, the distribution of income between the main factors of production, land, labour and capital.

   a. Equipment trust certificate
   b. Eco commerce
   c. Authorised capital
   d. Income distribution

17. In probability theory and statistics, a _____ is described as the number separating the higher half of a sample, a population from the lower half. The _____ of a finite list of numbers can be found by arranging all the observations from lowest value to highest value and picking the middle one. If there is an even number of observations, the _____ is not unique, so one often takes the mean of the two middle values.

   a. Labour vouchers
   b. Fiscal stimulus plans
   c. First player wins
   d. Median

18. In business and accounting, _____ are everything of value that is owned by a person or company. It is a claim on the property your income of a borrower. The balance sheet of a firm records the monetary value of the _____ owned by the firm.

   a. ACCRA Cost of Living Index
   b. ACEA agreement
   c. Assets
   d. Amortization schedule

19. The _____ is a measure of statistical dispersion, commonly used as a measure of inequality of income distribution or inequality of wealth distribution. It is defined as a ratio with values between 0 and 1: A low _____ indicates more equal income or wealth distribution, while a high _____ indicates more unequal distribution. 0 corresponds to perfect equality (everyone having exactly the same income) and 1 corresponds to perfect inequality (where one person has all the income, while everyone else has zero income.)

   a. Suits index
   b. Compensating variation
   c. Leapfrogging
   d. Gini coefficient

20. In mathematics, a _____ is a constant multiplicative factor of a certain object. For example, in the expression $9x^2$, the _____ of x^2 is 9.

The object can be such things as a variable, a vector, a function, etc.

a. 1921 recession
b. 130-30 fund
c. 100-year flood
d. Coefficient

21. _____ is a comparison of the wealth of various members or groups in a society. It differs from the distribution of income in a manner analogous to the difference between position and speed.

Wealth is a person's net worth, expressed as:

    wealth = assets - liabilities

The word 'wealth' is often confused with 'income'.

a. 100-year flood
b. Wealth condensation
c. 130-30 fund
d. Distribution of wealth

22. In economics, a _____ is the tax on money or property that one living person gives to another. See Gift (law) #Taxation or _____ in the United States.
a. Taxation as slavery
b. Succession duty
c. Fiscal drag
d. Gift tax

23. Inheritance tax, _____ and death duty are the names given to various taxes which arise on the death of an individual. It is a tax on the estate, or total value of the money and property, of a person who has died. In international tax law, there is a distinction between an _____ and an inheritance tax: the former taxes the personal representatives of the deceased, while the latter taxes the beneficiaries of the estate.
a. ACCRA Cost of Living Index
b. AD-IA Model
c. ACEA agreement
d. Estate tax

24. _____, often referred to by his initials _____, was the 32nd President of the United States. He was a central figure of the 20th century during a time of worldwide economic crisis and world war. Elected to four terms in office, he served from 1933 to 1945 and is the only U.S. president to have served more than two terms.
a. Adolph Fischer
b. Franklin Delano Roosevelt
c. Adam Smith
d. Adolf Hitler

25. _____ is a term used to describe how different aspects between economies are integrated. The basics of this theory were written by the Hungarian Economist Béla Balassa in the 1960s. As _____ increases, the barriers of trade between markets diminishes.
a. Import
b. Import license
c. Inward investment
d. Economic integration

26. To tax is to impose a financial charge or other levy upon a taxpayer by a state or the functional equivalent of a state.

Chapter 19. Efficiency vs. Equality: The Big Tradeoff 251

_____ are also imposed by many subnational entities. _____ consist of direct tax or indirect tax, and may be paid in money or as its labour equivalent (often but not always unpaid.)

a. 1921 recession
c. 130-30 fund
b. 100-year flood
d. Taxes

27. _____ is the returns received on factors of production: rent is return on land, wages on labor, interest on capital, and profit on entrepreneurship. It is also known as Net Factor Payments (NFP.)

Part of current account with balance of trade (exports minus imports of goods and services) and net transfer payments (such as foreign aid.)

a. Redistributive justice
c. 130-30 fund
b. 100-year flood
d. Factor income

28. A _____ is a place of residence or refuge and comfort. It is usually a place in which an individual or a family can rest and be able to store personal property. Most modern-day households contain sanitary facilities and a means of preparing food.

a. 130-30 fund
c. 100-year flood
b. Home
d. 1921 recession

29. _____ is the period of time that an individual spends at paid occupational labor. Unpaid labors such as housework are not considered part of the working week. Many countries regulate the work week by law, such as stipulating minimum daily rest periods, annual holidays and a maximum number of working hours per week.

a. 130-30 fund
c. 1921 recession
b. 100-year flood
d. Working time

30. _____ refers to the stock of skills and knowledge embodied in the ability to perform labor so as to produce economic value. It is the skills and knowledge gained by a worker through education and experience. Many early economic theories refer to it simply as labor, one of three factors of production, and consider it to be a fungible resource -- homogeneous and easily interchangeable. Other conceptions of labor dispense with these assumptions.

a. Price theory
c. Law of increasing costs
b. General equilibrium
d. Human capital

31. In economics, the people in the _____ are the suppliers of labor. The _____ is all the nonmilitary people who are employed or unemployed. In 2005, the worldwide _____ was over 3 billion people.

a. Distributed workforce
c. Departmentalization
b. Labor force
d. Grenelle agreements

32. The _____ consists of a number of economic theories which describe the nature of the firm, company including its existence, its behaviour, and its relationship with the market.

252   *Chapter 19. Efficiency vs. Equality: The Big Tradeoff*

In simplified terms, the _____ aims to answer these questions:

1. Existence - why do firms emerge, why are not all transactions in the economy mediated over the market?
2. Boundaries - why the boundary between firms and the market is located exactly there? Which transactions are performed internally and which are negotiated on the market?
3. Organization - why are firms structured in such specific way? What is the interplay of formal and informal relationships?

Despite looking simple, these questions are not answered by the established economic theory, which usually views firms as given, and treats them as black boxes without any internal structure.

The First World War period saw a change of emphasis in economic theory away from industry-level analysis which mainly included analysing markets to analysis at the level of the firm, as it became increasingly clear that perfect competition was no longer an adequate model of how firms behaved. Economic theory till then had focussed on trying to understand markets alone and there had been little study on understanding why firms or organisations exist.

- a. Theory of the firm
- b. Policy Ineffectiveness Proposition
- c. Technology gap
- d. Khazzoom-Brookes postulate

33. The _____ is the market for securities, where companies and governments can raise longterm funds. It is a market in which money is lent for periods longer than a year. The _____ includes the stock market and the bond market.
- a. Financial instrument
- b. Multi-family office
- c. Performance attribution
- d. Capital market

34. _____ according to Onuoha (2007) is the practice of starting new organizations or revitalizing mature organizations, particularly new businesses generally in response to identified opportunities. _____ is often a difficult undertaking, as a vast majority of new businesses fail. Entrepreneurial activities are substantially different depending on the type of organization that is being started.
- a. ACEA agreement
- b. ACCRA Cost of Living Index
- c. Intrapreneurship
- d. Entrepreneurship

35. In statistics, the _____ problem occurs when one considers a set of statistical inferences simultaneously. Errors in inference, including confidence intervals that fail to include their corresponding population parameters are more likely to occur when one considers the family as a whole. Several statistical techniques have been developed to prevent this from happening, allowing significance levels for single and _____ to be directly compared.
- a. Familywise error rate
- b. False discovery rate
- c. Hypotheses suggested by the data
- d. Multiple comparisons

36. _____ is a broad label that refers to any individuals or households that use goods and services generated within the economy. The concept of a _____ is used in different contexts, so that the usage and significance of the term may vary.

Typically when business people and economists talk of _____s they are talking about person as _____, an aggregated commodity item with little individuality other than that expressed in the buy/not-buy decision.

   a. 1921 recession
   b. 130-30 fund
   c. 100-year flood
   d. Consumer

37. A _____ is a measure of the average price of consumer goods and services purchased by households. A _____ measures a price change for a constant market basket of goods and services from one period to the next within the same area (city, region, or nation.) It is a price index determined by measuring the price of a standard group of goods meant to represent the typical market basket of a typical urban consumer.
   a. CPI
   b. Cost-of-living index
   c. Consumer price index
   d. Lipstick index

38. _____ is a common concept in economics, and gives rise to derived concepts such as consumer debt. Generally _____ is defined by opposition to production. But the precise definition can vary because different schools of economists define production quite differently.
   a. Foreclosure data providers
   b. Federal Reserve Bank Notes
   c. Cash or share options
   d. Consumption

39. _____ is the cost of maintaining a certain standard of living. Changes in the _____ over time are often operationalized in a _____ index. _____ calculations are also used to compare the cost of maintaining a certain standard of living in different geographic areas.
   a. Decision process tool
   b. Bear raid
   c. Restructuring
   d. Cost of living

40. The _____ is the minimum level of income deemed necessary to achieve an adequate standard of living in a given country. In practice, like the definition of poverty, the official or common understanding of the poverty line is significantly higher in developed countries than in developing countries.

The common international poverty line has been roughly $1 a day, or more precisely $1.08 at 1993 purchasing-power parity (PPP.)

   a. Poverty map
   b. Poverty
   c. Poverty reduction
   d. Poverty threshold

41. The _____ is the name for legislation first introduced by United States President Lyndon B. Johnson during his State of the Union address on January 8, 1964. This legislation was proposed by Johnson in response to a national poverty rate of around nineteen percent. The speech led the United States Congress to pass the Economic Opportunity Act, which established the Office of Economic Opportunity (OEO) to administer the local application of federal funds targeted against poverty.
   a. 100-year flood
   b. 130-30 fund
   c. Supplemental Nutrition Assistance Program
   d. War on poverty

42. _____ in economics and business is the result of an exchange and from that trade we assign a numerical monetary value to a good, service or asset. If Alice trades Bob 4 apples for an orange, the _____ of an orange is 4 apples. Inversely, the _____ of an apple is 1/4 oranges.

a. Price
b. Price war
c. Price book
d. Premium pricing

43. A _____ is a normalized average (typically a weighted average) of prices for a given class of goods or services in a given region, during a given interval of time. It is a statistic designed to help to compare how these prices, taken as a whole, differ between time periods or geographical locations.

Price indices have several potential uses.

a. Product sabotage
b. Transactional Net Margin Method
c. Two-part tariff
d. Price index

44. _____ is the income of individuals or nations after adjusting for inflation. It is calculated by subtracting inflation from the nominal income. Real variables, such as _____, real GDP, and real interest rate are variables that are measured in physical units, while nominal variables such as nominal income, nominal GDP, and nominal interest rate are measured in monetary units.

a. Windfall gain
b. Family income
c. Net national income
d. Real income

45. A _____ is any worker who has some special skill, knowledge, or (usually acquired) ability in his work. A _____ may have attended a college, university or technical school. Or, a _____ may have learned his skills on the job.

a. Time and attendance
b. Timebar scheduling
c. Global Career Development Facilitator
d. Skilled worker

46. The term '_____' refers to the concept of collecting information and attempting to spot a pattern in the information. In some fields of study, the term '_____' has more formally-defined meanings.

In project management _____ is a mathematical technique that uses historical results to predict future outcome.

a. Trend analysis
b. Quantile regression
c. Coefficient of determination
d. Probit model

47. _____ to the arrival of new individuals into a habitat or population. It is a biological concept and is important in population ecology, differentiated from emigration and migration.

_____ is a modern phenomenon.

a. ACEA agreement
b. ACCRA Cost of Living Index
c. AD-IA Model
d. Immigration

Chapter 19. Efficiency vs. Equality: The Big Tradeoff

48. _____ is widely regarded as the first modern school of economic thought. It is the idea that free markets can regulate themselves. Its major developers include Adam Smith, David Ricardo, Thomas Malthus and John Stuart Mill. Sometimes the definition of _____ is expanded to include William Petty, Johann Heinrich von Thünen.
   a. Tendency of the rate of profit to fall
   b. Schools of economic thought
   c. Classical economics
   d. Marginalism

49. In economics, _____ is the transfer of income, wealth or property from some individuals to others.

One premise of _____ is that money should be distributed to benefit the poorer members of society, and that the rich have an obligation to assist the poor, thus creating a more financially egalitarian society. Another argument is that the rich exploit the poor or otherwise gain unfair benefits.

   a. 1921 recession
   b. 130-30 fund
   c. 100-year flood
   d. Redistribution

50. In economics, _____ refers to the ability of a person or a country to produce a particular good at a lower marginal cost and opportunity cost than another person or country. It is the ability to produce a product most efficiently given all the other products that could be produced. It can be contrasted with absolute advantage which refers to the ability of a person or a country to produce a particular good at a lower absolute cost than another.
   a. Hot money
   b. Comparative advantage
   c. Triffin dilemma
   d. Gravity model of trade

51. _____ is a term that refers both to:

   - a formal discipline used to help appraise, or assess, the case for a project or proposal, which itself is a process known as project appraisal; and
   - an informal approach to making decisions of any kind.

Under both definitions the process involves, whether explicitly or implicitly, weighing the total expected costs against the total expected benefits of one or more actions in order to choose the best or most profitable option. The formal process is often referred to as either CBA (_____) or BCost-benefit analysis

A hallmark of CBA is that all benefits and all costs are expressed in money terms, and are adjusted for the time value of money, so that all flows of benefits and flows of project costs over time (which tend to occur at different points in time) are expressed on a common basis in terms of their e;present value.e; Closely related, but slightly different, formal techniques include Cost-effectiveness analysis, Economic impact analysis, Fiscal impact analysis and Social Return on Investment(SROI) analysis. The latter builds upon the logic of _____, but differs in that it is explicitly designed to inform the practical decision-making of enterprise managers and investors focused on optimising their social and environmental impacts.

   a. 130-30 fund
   b. Decision theory
   c. Cost-benefit analysis
   d. 100-year flood

52. In microeconomics, _____ is quite simply the conversion of inputs into outputs. It is an economic process that uses resources to create a good or service that is suitable for exchange. This can include manufacturing, storing, shipping, and packaging.

a. Solved
b. Red Guards
c. MET
d. Production

53. _____ or equality of condition is a form of egalitarianism which seeks to reduce or eliminate differences in material condition between individuals or households in a society. This usually means equalizing income and/or total wealth to a certain degree.

In theory, _____ can be distinguished from equal opportunity.

a. Equality of outcome
b. AD-IA Model
c. ACCRA Cost of Living Index
d. ACEA agreement

54.

_____ was a German philosopher, political economist, historian, political theorist, sociologist, communist and revolutionary credited as the founder of communism.

Marx summarized his approach to history and politics in the opening line of the first chapter of The Communist Manifesto : e;The history of all hitherto existing society is the history of class struggles.e; Marx argued that capitalism, like previous socioeconomic systems, will produce internal tensions which will lead to its destruction. Just as capitalism replaced feudalism, socialism will in its turn replace capitalism and lead to a stateless, classless society which will emerge after a transitional period, the 'dictatorship of the proletariat'.

a. Marxism
b. Adam Smith
c. Karl Heinrich Marx
d. Neo-Gramscianism

55. _____ is used to refer to a number of related concepts. It is the using resources in such a way as to maximize the production of goods and services. A system can be called economically efficient if:

- No one can be made better off without making someone else worse off.
- More output cannot be obtained without increasing the amount of inputs.
- Production proceeds at the lowest possible per-unit cost.

These definitions of efficiency are not equivalent, but they are all encompassed by the idea that nothing more can be achieved given the resources available.

An economic system is more efficient if it can provide more goods and services for society without using more resources.

a. ACEA agreement
b. ACCRA Cost of Living Index
c. Efficient contract theory
d. Economic efficiency

56. The _____ is the largest national economy in the world. Its gross domestic product (GDP) was estimated as $14.2 trillion in 2008. The U.S. economy maintains a high level of output per person (GDP per capita, $46,800 in 2008, ranked at around number ten in the world.)

a. ACEA agreement
b. AD-IA Model
c. ACCRA Cost of Living Index
d. Economy of the United States

57. In economics, a _____ is a redistribution of income in the market system. These payments are considered to be nonexhaustive because they do not directly absorb resources or create output. Examples of certain _____s include welfare (financial aid), social security, and government subsidies for certain businesses (firms.)
   a. 130-30 fund
   b. 1921 recession
   c. 100-year flood
   d. Transfer payment

58. A _____ is the transfer of wealth from one party (such as a person or company) to another. A _____ is usually made in exchange for the provision of goods, services or both, or to fulfill a legal obligation.

The simplest and oldest form of _____ is barter, the exchange of one good or service for another.

   a. Soft count
   b. Going concern
   c. Payment
   d. Social gravity

59. _____ is a voluntary transfer of resources from one country to another, given at least partly with the objective of benefiting the recipient country. It may have other functions as well: it may be given as a signal of diplomatic approval, or to strengthen a military ally, to reward a government for behaviour desired by the donor, to extend the donor's cultural influence, to provide infrastructure needed by the donor for resource extraction from the recipient country, or to gain other kinds of commercial access. Humanitarianism and altruism are, nevertheless, significant motivations for the giving of _____.
   a. ACEA agreement
   b. ACCRA Cost of Living Index
   c. AD-IA Model
   d. Aid

60. _____ was a federal assistance program in effect from 1935 to 1997, which was administered by the United States Department of Health and Human Services. This program provided financial assistance to children whose families had low or no income.

The program was created under the name Aid to Dependent Children (ADC) by the Social Security Act of 1935 as part of the New Deal; the words 'families with' were added to the name in 1960, partly due to concern that the program's rules discouraged marriage.

   a. ACCRA Cost of Living Index
   b. ACEA agreement
   c. Aid to Families with Dependent Children
   d. AD-IA Model

61. In economics and sociology, an _____ is any factor (financial or non-financial) that enables or motivates a particular course of action, or counts as a reason for preferring one choice to the alternatives. It is an expectation that encourages people to behave in a certain way. Since human beings are purposeful creatures, the study of _____ structures is central to the study of all economic activity (both in terms of individual decision-making and in terms of co-operation and competition within a larger institutional structure.)
   a. Isocost
   b. Economic reform
   c. Incentive
   d. Epstein-Zin preferences

Chapter 19. Efficiency vs. Equality: The Big Tradeoff

62. In the United States, _____ federal benefits is defined as any federal program, project, service, and activity provided by the federal government that directly assists or benefits the American public in the areas of education, health, public safety, public welfare, and public works, among others. The assistance, which can reach to over $400 billion dollars annually, is provided and administered by federal government agencies, such as the U.S. Department of Housing and Urban Development and the U.S. Department of Health and Human Services, through special programs to recipients.

The term assistance is defined by the federal government as:

In order to provide _____ in an organized manner, the federal government provides assistance through federal agencies.

   a. State Revolving Fund
   c. Federal assistance
   b. General Assistance
   d. Federal Medical Assistance Percentages

63. A _____ refers to any type debt instrument, such as a loan, bond, mortgage that does not have a fixed rate of interest over the life of the instrument. Such debt typically uses an index or other base rate for establishing the interest rate for each relevant period. One of the most common rates to use as the basis for applying interest rates is the London Inter-bank Offered Rate, or LIBOR
   a. Disposal tax effect
   c. Moneylender
   b. Money market
   d. Floating interest rate

64. The term _____ describes two different concepts:

   - The first is a recognition of partial payment already made towards taxes due.
   - The second is a state benefit paid to workers through the tax system, which has the effect of increasing (rather than reducing) net income.

Within the Australian, Canadian, United Kingdom, and United States tax systems, a _____ is a recognition of partial payment already made towards taxes due. A similar concept exists (fr:Avoir fiscal) in the French tax system. This situation arises, for example, when standard rate tax has been deducted at source , but the tax-payer is subject to further taxation at a higher rate. It also applies in dividend imputation systems.

   a. Tax credit
   c. 100-year flood
   b. 1921 recession
   d. 130-30 fund

65. In a federal system of government, a _____ is a large sum of money granted by the national government to a regional government with only general provisions as to the way it is to be spent. This can be contrasted with a categorical grant which has more strict and specific provisions on the way it is to be spent.

An advantage of _____s is that they allow regional governments to experiment with different ways of spending money with the same goal in mind, though it is very difficult to compare the results of such spending and reach a conclusion.

   a. Transactions deposit
   c. 100-year flood
   b. Block grant
   d. Financial Industry Regulatory Authority

Chapter 19. Efficiency vs. Equality: The Big Tradeoff   259

66. A _____ usually refers to an individual entity seeking a more favorable outcome at the expense of other entities by upsetting an equilibrium to their own favor, only to cause an inevitable retaliation by the other individuals to rebalance the equilibrium, resulting in all participants having an overall less favorable outcome. For example, people may have a tendency to buy increasingly larger, heavier, and often more expensive cars because the additional weight can help make the car safer in a collision with a smaller, lighter car. Thus to keep up with the average vehicle weight for safety's sake, drivers must buy heavier, more expensive, less efficient cars, while safety on the whole does not improve compared to when the average vehicle was lighter.
   a. Fear factor
   b. Stylized fact
   c. Race to the bottom
   d. Trailing twelve months

67. _____ is the United States of America's federal assistance program, formerly known as 'welfare'. It began on July 1, 1997, and succeeded the Aid to Families with Dependent Children program, providing cash assistance to indigent American families with dependent children through the United States Department of Health and Human Services. Prior to 1997, the federal government designed the overall program requirements and guidelines, while states administered the program and determined eligibility for benefits.
   a. 100-year flood
   b. Temporary Assistance for Needy Families
   c. 130-30 fund
   d. 1921 recession

68. _____ is a company's financial statement that indicates how the revenue is transformed into the net income The purpose of the _____ is to show managers and investors whether the company made or lost money during the period being reported.

The important thing to remember about an _____ is that it represents a period of time.

   a. ACEA agreement
   b. Income statement
   c. ACCRA Cost of Living Index
   d. AD-IA Model

69. _____ refers to the actions that governments take in the economic field. It covers the systems for setting interest rates and government deficit as well as the labour market, national ownership, and many other areas of government.

Such policies are often influenced by international institutions like the International Monetary Fund or World Bank as well as political beliefs and the consequent policies of parties.

   a. AD-IA Model
   b. Economic policy
   c. ACCRA Cost of Living Index
   d. ACEA agreement

70. _____ is the branch of economics that incorporates value judgments (that is, normative judgements) about what the economy ought to be like or what particular policy actions ought to be recommended to achieve a desirable goal. _____ looks at the desirability of certain aspects of the economy. It underlies expressions of support for particular economic policies.
   a. Normative economics
   b. Double bottom line
   c. Nanoeconomics
   d. Broad money

71. _____ is the branch of economics that concerns the description and explanation of economic phenomena (Wong, 1987, p. 920.) It focuses on facts and cause-and-effect relationships and includes the development and testing of economics theories.

a. Regulatory economics
b. 100-year flood
c. 130-30 fund
d. Positive economics

72. A _____ is the procedure of systematically acquiring and recording information about the members of a given population. It is a regularly occurring and official count of a particular population. The term is used mostly in connection with national 'population and door to door _____es' (to be taken every 10 years according to United Nations recommendations), agriculture, and business _____es.
   a. 130-30 fund
   b. Census
   c. 1921 recession
   d. 100-year flood

73. The _____, asbl is a non-profit project which produces a cross-national database of micro-economic income data for social science research. The project started in 1983 and is headquartered in Luxembourg. In 2006 the database included data from 30 countries on four continents, with some countries represented for over 30 years.
   a. Deutsche Bank
   b. Luxembourg Income Study
   c. Leading stock
   d. Bankruptcy of Lehman Brothers

ANSWER KEY

Chapter 1
1. b	2. d	3. a	4. b	5. a	6. d	7. d	8. d	9. a	10. b
11. d	12. b	13. d	14. d	15. a	16. d	17. d	18. d	19. d	20. d
21. a	22. c	23. d	24. d	25. b	26. d	27. c	28. d	29. b	30. d
31. a	32. c	33. b	34. c	35. d	36. d	37. d	38. c	39. d	40. d
41. d	42. c	43. d	44. a	45. d	46. d	47. c	48. c	49. a	50. a
51. a	52. c	53. a	54. d	55. b	56. c	57. c			

Chapter 2
1. a	2. d	3. d	4. b	5. c	6. d	7. d	8. d	9. a	10. b
11. d	12. b	13. d	14. a	15. d	16. d	17. a	18. c	19. c	20. d
21. d	22. b	23. d	24. a	25. d	26. b	27. d	28. d	29. d	30. b
31. d	32. d	33. d	34. d	35. d	36. d	37. c	38. a	39. b	40. d
41. c	42. c	43. b	44. d	45. c	46. c	47. a	48. d	49. b	50. d
51. b	52. d	53. a	54. b	55. d	56. a	57. b	58. d	59. d	60. c
61. c	62. b	63. b	64. d	65. d	66. a	67. c	68. d	69. d	70. b
71. d	72. d	73. c	74. d	75. d	76. a	77. d	78. d	79. d	80. a
81. d	82. d	83. d	84. b	85. b	86. d	87. c	88. d	89. d	90. a
91. c	92. a	93. d	94. a	95. b	96. a	97. d	98. c	99. a	100. d
101. d	102. d	103. b	104. a						

Chapter 3
1. d	2. c	3. d	4. a	5. d	6. d	7. d	8. b	9. a	10. d
11. c	12. d	13. d	14. c	15. c	16. d	17. d	18. d	19. c	20. c
21. c	22. d	23. a	24. c	25. b	26. d	27. d	28. d	29. b	30. b
31. a	32. a	33. b							

Chapter 4
1. b	2. d	3. c	4. d	5. d	6. c	7. d	8. c	9. d	10. b
11. a	12. d	13. a	14. d	15. b	16. c	17. a	18. d	19. a	20. b
21. c	22. d	23. a	24. d	25. d	26. d	27. b	28. d	29. d	30. a
31. a	32. d	33. a	34. d	35. d	36. d	37. d	38. d	39. d	40. d
41. a	42. b	43. c	44. d	45. c	46. d	47. a	48. d	49. d	

Chapter 5
1. b	2. d	3. d	4. d	5. d	6. c	7. c	8. d	9. b	10. d
11. d	12. b	13. c	14. c	15. c	16. c	17. d	18. a	19. c	20. d
21. d	22. d	23. b	24. d	25. c	26. d	27. c	28. a	29. d	30. c
31. d	32. d	33. b	34. d	35. b	36. d	37. d	38. d	39. a	40. b
41. b	42. d	43. c	44. a	45. d	46. d	47. c	48. c	49. c	50. d

Chapter 6

1. b	2. b	3. a	4. c	5. d	6. d	7. a	8. b	9. d	10. d
11. d	12. d	13. d	14. d	15. d	16. d	17. d	18. d	19. b	20. c
21. a	22. d	23. d	24. a	25. a	26. b	27. c	28. d	29. a	30. d
31. d	32. b	33. d	34. b	35. b	36. d	37. d	38. b	39. d	40. a
41. d	42. d	43. d	44. a	45. b	46. c	47. d	48. b	49. d	50. d
51. c	52. d	53. b	54. a	55. b	56. d	57. c			

Chapter 7

1. a	2. c	3. d	4. d	5. c	6. b	7. d	8. d	9. d	10. d
11. d	12. b	13. d	14. d	15. d	16. d	17. d	18. d	19. a	20. a
21. d	22. a	23. b	24. c	25. d	26. d	27. c	28. c	29. c	30. c
31. d	32. d	33. c	34. d	35. d	36. b	37. a	38. d	39. a	40. a
41. d	42. b	43. d	44. d	45. d	46. d	47. d	48. b	49. b	50. d
51. b	52. a								

Chapter 8

1. d	2. d	3. a	4. d	5. b	6. b	7. d	8. d	9. a	10. b
11. b	12. d	13. d	14. c	15. c	16. d	17. a	18. d	19. b	20. d
21. c	22. d	23. a	24. d	25. b	26. d	27. a	28. b	29. b	30. d
31. d	32. c	33. d	34. d	35. b	36. b	37. a	38. d	39. d	40. d
41. a	42. a	43. c	44. b	45. b	46. d	47. c	48. a	49. d	50. a
51. c	52. d	53. a	54. c						

Chapter 9

1. d	2. d	3. d	4. b	5. d	6. d	7. c	8. d	9. a	10. d
11. d	12. d	13. b	14. d	15. d	16. b	17. d	18. a	19. d	20. d
21. d	22. b	23. d	24. c	25. d	26. d	27. a	28. b	29. c	30. d
31. a	32. d	33. a	34. c	35. c	36. d	37. a	38. d	39. c	40. a
41. d	42. a	43. d	44. a	45. a	46. d	47. b	48. d	49. a	50. a
51. c	52. b	53. d	54. d	55. d					

Chapter 10

1. d	2. d	3. a	4. a	5. a	6. c	7. d	8. c	9. b	10. d
11. d	12. d	13. b	14. d	15. d	16. d	17. a	18. d	19. d	20. d
21. d	22. d	23. d	24. d	25. b	26. d	27. d	28. b	29. d	30. d
31. d	32. a	33. b	34. d	35. a	36. b	37. d	38. a	39. b	40. c
41. a	42. a	43. d	44. b	45. c	46. d	47. a	48. a	49. a	50. d
51. d	52. d	53. a	54. a	55. b	56. c	57. c	58. b	59. d	60. d
61. a	62. d	63. a	64. a	65. b	66. a	67. a	68. b	69. d	70. d
71. c	72. d	73. a	74. a	75. d					

ANSWER KEY

Chapter 11

1. b	2. d	3. d	4. c	5. d	6. d	7. b	8. c	9. d	10. d
11. d	12. c	13. a	14. a	15. a	16. c	17. d	18. d	19. d	20. b
21. d	22. a	23. d	24. b	25. b	26. a	27. d	28. c	29. d	30. c
31. b	32. a	33. d	34. d	35. d	36. d	37. b	38. d	39. d	40. d
41. d	42. d	43. b	44. d	45. b	46. a	47. d	48. a	49. a	50. d
51. c	52. d	53. d	54. a	55. d	56. d	57. d	58. d		

Chapter 12

1. d	2. d	3. d	4. a	5. d	6. b	7. d	8. c	9. d	10. d
11. d	12. d	13. d	14. b	15. b	16. b	17. b	18. b	19. d	20. c
21. d	22. d	23. a	24. a	25. d	26. c	27. c	28. c	29. d	30. c
31. b	32. d	33. d	34. b	35. b	36. a	37. c	38. a	39. d	40. c
41. d	42. c	43. c	44. d	45. d	46. d	47. d	48. d	49. d	50. b
51. d	52. c	53. d	54. d	55. d	56. c	57. a	58. d		

Chapter 13

1. b	2. d	3. d	4. d	5. c	6. a	7. b	8. a	9. b	10. d
11. a	12. a	13. c	14. d	15. b	16. b	17. d	18. b	19. d	20. a
21. d	22. d	23. d	24. c	25. d	26. d	27. b	28. a	29. b	30. d
31. b	32. a	33. d	34. d	35. c	36. d	37. b	38. b	39. b	40. b
41. c	42. c	43. a	44. d	45. c	46. d	47. a	48. c	49. a	50. c
51. b	52. c	53. b	54. c						

Chapter 14

1. d	2. a	3. b	4. c	5. b	6. b	7. d	8. d	9. d	10. b
11. d	12. c	13. c	14. d	15. b	16. d	17. d	18. c	19. d	20. a
21. d	22. d	23. c	24. d	25. d	26. c	27. b	28. d	29. b	30. c
31. b	32. d	33. d	34. a	35. d	36. c	37. a	38. a	39. c	40. a
41. a	42. a	43. d	44. b	45. d	46. d	47. d	48. d	49. a	50. c
51. d	52. d	53. b	54. a	55. c	56. c	57. a	58. b	59. d	60. d
61. c	62. d	63. d	64. b	65. b	66. d	67. c	68. a	69. b	70. b
71. b	72. d	73. c	74. d	75. c	76. a	77. d	78. d	79. c	80. a
81. c	82. d	83. d	84. d	85. a	86. b	87. d	88. d	89. a	90. a
91. d									

Chapter 15

1. d	2. c	3. d	4. c	5. d	6. d	7. b	8. d	9. d	10. a
11. d	12. c	13. d	14. d	15. d	16. d	17. b	18. d	19. d	20. c
21. d	22. c	23. c	24. d	25. d	26. d	27. b	28. b	29. d	30. c
31. a	32. d	33. d	34. d	35. d	36. d	37. d	38. a	39. a	40. d
41. d	42. b	43. c	44. d	45. d	46. b	47. d	48. d	49. b	50. b
51. d	52. a	53. c	54. b	55. b	56. d	57. d	58. d	59. d	60. d
61. c	62. b	63. c	64. d	65. c	66. d	67. a	68. c	69. c	70. c
71. d									

Chapter 16

1. d	2. c	3. a	4. b	5. d	6. b	7. b	8. a	9. c	10. a
11. b	12. d	13. d	14. b	15. a	16. c	17. d	18. a	19. d	20. d
21. d	22. d	23. a	24. b	25. b	26. a	27. d	28. d	29. b	30. a
31. c	32. b	33. b	34. d	35. d	36. d	37. a	38. d	39. b	40. b
41. a	42. d	43. b	44. d	45. d	46. a	47. b	48. b	49. b	50. d
51. d	52. b	53. d	54. a	55. b	56. c	57. d	58. d	59. a	60. d
61. d	62. d	63. d	64. d	65. c	66. d	67. d	68. d	69. d	70. d
71. d	72. d	73. b	74. d	75. d	76. d	77. d	78. a	79. b	80. c
81. b	82. d	83. c	84. d	85. d	86. c	87. a	88. d	89. a	90. a

Chapter 17

1. c	2. a	3. d	4. c	5. d	6. b	7. a	8. c	9. c	10. d
11. c	12. d	13. d	14. d	15. d	16. c	17. a	18. b	19. b	20. a
21. d	22. c	23. d	24. d	25. d	26. d	27. d	28. a	29. d	30. d
31. d	32. a	33. b	34. d	35. b	36. b	37. c	38. b	39. c	40. d
41. c	42. a	43. d	44. d	45. a	46. d	47. a	48. a	49. a	50. b
51. b	52. d	53. d	54. b	55. d	56. d	57. d	58. c	59. d	60. d
61. b	62. c	63. d	64. d	65. c					

Chapter 18

1. b	2. d	3. d	4. c	5. a	6. a	7. b	8. d	9. d	10. d
11. b	12. d	13. b	14. d	15. d	16. b	17. d	18. a	19. a	20. d
21. d	22. b	23. c	24. d	25. b	26. c	27. d	28. b	29. d	30. d
31. a	32. c	33. c	34. b	35. c	36. c	37. a	38. c	39. a	40. d
41. a	42. d	43. d	44. d	45. d	46. d	47. d	48. d	49. d	

ANSWER KEY

Chapter 19

1. d	2. d	3. d	4. d	5. d	6. d	7. d	8. d	9. b	10. d
11. b	12. d	13. b	14. d	15. d	16. d	17. d	18. c	19. d	20. d
21. d	22. d	23. d	24. b	25. d	26. d	27. d	28. b	29. d	30. d
31. b	32. a	33. d	34. d	35. d	36. d	37. c	38. d	39. d	40. d
41. d	42. a	43. d	44. d	45. d	46. a	47. d	48. c	49. d	50. b
51. c	52. d	53. a	54. c	55. d	56. d	57. d	58. c	59. d	60. c
61. c	62. c	63. d	64. a	65. b	66. c	67. b	68. b	69. b	70. a
71. d	72. b	73. b							

www.ingramcontent.com/pod-product-compliance
Lightning Source LLC
Chambersburg PA
CBHW080728230426
43665CB00020B/2657